DATE			

A
CHAUCER HANDBOOK

COMPANION VOLUMES

A MILTON HANDBOOK

By James Holly Hanford
University of Michigan

A SHAKESPEARE HANDBOOK

By Raymond M. Alden
Late of Leland Stanford University

A
CHAUCER HANDBOOK

BY

ROBERT DUDLEY FRENCH , 1888-

Second Edition

APPLETON-CENTURY-CROFTS

EDUCATIONAL DIVISION

New York   MEREDITH CORPORATION

PREFACE

There are few poets who owe so much to scholarship as Geoffrey Chaucer. The labors of many men, extending over nearly two centuries and including the work of some of the best minds that have been dedicated to the study of English literature, have rescued the text of his poetry from the corruption into which it had been allowed to fall. The forgotten facts of his career have been brought together, out of the obscurity of scattered documents; and fantastic legends, which had gathered about his name, have been laid to rest. The sources from which he may have drawn materials have been explored, and we have been put in a position to know what books influenced his thinking and upon what foundations he built his works. If we are able, more than five hundred years after his death, to form something like a just estimate of the singular power of his genius, it is because scholarship has made clear the way.

The serious student of Chaucer, even though he make no especial pretense to learning, will naturally wish to derive as much benefit as possible from all this labor on the part of the learned. The teacher of Chaucer, moreover, will hardly feel that his duty has been done, if he has not been able to set before his students the material which scholarship has made available, for a truer estimation of the great poet whose works it is his privilege to interpret.

His problem, however, is not altogether an easy one. The material which he wishes to utilize is widely scattered and not everywhere accessible. Much of it he has usually been obliged to present himself, in the classroom, at the expense of precious time, which he would greatly prefer to spend upon discussion and interpretation. Some of it is of such a nature that it is of very little use to his students, unless it can be placed under their very eyes, for the closest study; and too much of it, most unfortunately, has been presented in such a form that it is either incomprehensible or quite unpalatable to anyone who is not a sturdy specialist, well inured to controversial literature and little daunted by the singular *patois* which certain scholars have sometimes felt obliged to use. Foreign languages, moreover, living, moribund, or dead, obstruct the study of certain phases of Chaucer's work with difficulties which it is impossible to require the modern undergraduate to surmount.

This volume has been prepared in the hope that it may be of service, in making readily available some of the material which scholarship has contributed to an understanding of the poetry of Chaucer. It is no part of its purpose to offer æsthetic criticism, either at first or second hand, since it may be assumed that no one will read these pages who is not interested in forming judgments of his own upon the value of Chaucer's works. To present information which may be of use in the formation of such judgments is the sole purpose of this book. It is designed to give the mature student of Chaucer and his poetry some knowledge of the world in which the poet lived, of the way his life shaped itself in that world, of the language which he spoke and wrote, of the dates, the sources, and the special significance of his works, so far as these things have been determined.

It has seemed best, in such a work as this, to adopt a somewhat conservative position on disputed matters, and to deal as impartially as possible with unsettled controversies; but the work which has been done within the more recent years has not, I believe, been overlooked, and in the bibliography, especial attention has been given to works which have put forth interesting theories and conjectures. A secondary purpose, in the bibliography and throughout the book, has been to suggest to the student the wide and fascinating range of interests which open out before the man who embarks upon the serious study of Chaucer and his century.

With so large a "feeld to ere," an editor can hardly hope to deal adequately with the material at his disposal. Something, doubtless, has been omitted from these pages through ignorance or oversight; and much has been deliberately excluded. My selection has been governed, in the last analysis, by my own practices as a teacher. I have endeavored to include in this volume the material which seems most likely to be of service to me, in my task of guiding the men who study Chaucer with me into a fuller appreciation of the poet's extraordinary genius.

My obligation to Chaucerian scholars, living and dead, is so manifold that it cannot be reckoned in all its particulars, but I have tried to indicate, in the footnotes, the specific sources from which I have drawn material. My particular thanks are due to Professor G. L. Hendrickson, for his courtesy in assisting me with my translation of Petrarch's tale of Griseldis, and to Professor Karl Young, who first suggested that I undertake the preparation of this volume and who has given me encouragement and advice along the way. I have had much valuable advice and criticism from a number of my former pupils. Their diffidence forbids my making more specific acknowledgment of my great obligation to them, but they know that they have my gratitude.

PREFACE TO THE SECOND EDITION

The second edition of this handbook represents a revision rather than a rewriting. Much of the material presented in the original edition, based on foundations laid by the mighty figures of the Golden Age of Chaucerian scholarship, remains valid after twenty years of continuous exploration of the field. My revision has attempted to take note, so far as limitations of space permit, of studies that have appeared during that score of years. In sifting some hundreds of notes on books and articles, I am sure to have overlooked or to have excluded material that will seem important to other teachers of Chaucer. To them and to the scholars whose studies I have not recorded, though I may have read them with much interest, I must plead once more the largeness of the "feeld to ere." I could not hope to do more than indicate, in the body of the text or in the bibliography, the unfailing stream of learning which has its source in a poet who has never failed to quicken and broaden every mind that has devoted itself to the study of his works.

I would record my especial gratitude to Professor Robert Armstrong Pratt for invaluable suggestions and to my secretary, Miss Margaret Sturgeon, and to Mr. Ignatius Mattingly, Bursary Aide to the Department of English at Yale, for their assistance in the preparation of my manuscript.

CONTENTS

Contents

A CHAUCER HANDBOOK

CHAPTER I

ENGLAND IN THE AGE OF CHAUCER

DURING the age of Chaucer, England passed through the first stages of her long journey out of mediævalism and came to the foothills of the modern world. Many of the events which took place during the poet's lifetime foreshadow so impressively the changes which were eventually to reshape the life of the nation, that historians have sometimes been at a loss to explain why those changes proceeded so slowly in the succeeding centuries. The tumultuous days of 1381, when the peasantry of England rose in revolt, seized the capital, and forced from a terrified government a show of compliance with their demands, are much more suggestive of the era of democratic revolutions than of the Middle Ages. A refractory parliament, stubbornly refusing to grant subsidies to the Crown until public grievances had been redressed, and forcing a reluctant monarch to accept ministers nominated by the House of Commons, hardly seems to belong to feudal times. The heresies of Wycliffe bear so close a resemblance to the protestantism of a later era that it is hard to realize that the great reformer lived so many years before Luther;

and the poor priests, his followers, upon whom the conservatives of the age fastened the contemptuous name of "Lollers," were not to find their true counterpart until the followers of John Wesley went about England preaching another reformation, four centuries nearer to the modern age.

These are but the most striking manifestations of a new spirit and of new ideas at work upon English society in this remarkable age. In less conspicuous ways, as well, the same tendencies toward change are made evident. The literature of the times is so pervaded with a questioning spirit as to make this a great age of satire. Of the four greatest English writers of the century, one was a religious reformer, whose writings attacked nearly every institution of the mediæval church, from the corrupt priesthood to the papacy itself. Another gave himself so completely to the exposure of the corruption of mediæval institutions that the most radical agitators of the age used his Peter the Ploughman as symbol of their revolutionary ideals. A third, though his spirit was clearly made for the most tranquil waters of literature, was so stirred by his disgust at things which he had witnessed that he, too, wrote many pages of vituperative satire. As for Chaucer himself, his work contains satirical passages so startling in their approach to our own point of view toward the decaying institutions of the Middle Ages that they have won him the doubtful compliment of being called "modern."

This satirical spirit in the poets seems to have been but a reflection of a way of thinking by no means limited to men of letters. That men and women were thinking for themselves at all, and that their thoughts so frequently called old truths in question, was certainly an indication of an altered temper of mind. The Age of Faith was passing into an age of scepticism, and authority of every sort was losing its grip upon the English public. The institutions of the feudal age, both in church and state, were so manifestly corrupt that even those whose duty it was to give them full support were little better than half-hearted in their devotion to the old ideals.

In such an age of transition between old and new, when a familiar world seems suddenly to totter under the impact of forces which no one can yet understand, men will always look back regretfully to a time that was untroubled by these novel phenomena of thought and action, which disturb them so violently. It was all the easier for Chaucer's contemporaries to cherish the illusion of an earlier and purer age because fortune had appeared to smile upon the England of their infancy. They had been born into a land which seemed destined for extraordinary prosperity and many years of orderly development. Violent and disastrous events, however, had separated the latter years of the fourteenth century from the period that came before, in a way that was too dramatic for the simplest mind to overlook; and it was natural enough that poets, prophets, and common men, who had to shape their lives amid the raw, new forces which had been let loose upon the world, should feel that the nation had seen its best days. Stern moralists found in the disasters that had fallen upon England the hand of an avenging God, venting His anger upon a sinful people. The less devout saw the order of cause and effect in the opposite way, tracing abuses to direct causes in the tragic events which they had witnessed. All alike manifested a tendency to date the corruption of so-

ciety from the reversal of fortune which had come so un
expectedly upon England in the middle of the century.

VICTORIES AND DISASTERS

From the pages of Froissart, we can still gain some
impression of the pride of victory which Englishmen had
known in the middle years of the fourteenth century. In
1346, on the field of Crécy, the English yeoman, standing
firm under assault, had put to rout the chivalry of France.
"There is no man," says Froissart, "unless he had been
present on that day, who can imagine or describe the confusion that took place, especially on the side of the French,
so bad was their order and array . . . The great lords
were so torn with desire to advance and attack the foe
that their battles did not wait, one upon the other, for
ordinance or array; but they charged all in disorder and
confusion, until they cut off the Genoese between themselves and the English, so that they could not flee. . . .
Those who were behind took no heed of the press, so that
they were thrown down among those who had fallen and
were unable to rise. On the other side, the archers shot
so cruelly and so continuously at those in front and on
the flanks that the horses, stung by the barbed arrows, did
strange things: some refused to advance, some reared,
some kicked, and some, mauger their riders, dashed back
toward the enemy under the sting of the arrows; and
those that felt death upon them fell in their tracks. The
English men-at-arms, who were drawn up on foot, advanced and launched themselves against these seigneurs
and their men, who found no succor in their horses or
themselves. The English were armed with daggers, axes,

and staves, and they killed at their ease, without resistance and with little fighting or defense, for the French could not aid or extricate each other. Never was seen such misadventure or the loss of so many good men with so little fighting." [1]

The victory of Crécy was followed almost immediately by the crushing defeat of the Scotch at Neville's Cross; and ten years later, on September 19, 1356, the Black Prince won another brilliant victory over the French near Poitiers. "All who were at this well-omened battle with the Prince of Wales," says Froissart, "were made rich with honor and with goods, what with the ransoms of the prisoners and with the winning of gold and of silver which was found there, the gold and silver plate, the rich jewels, and the trunks crammed full of rich and heavy belts and goodly mantles. Of arms and of harness and of casques, they took no count; for the French had come thither very richly equipped and with as much pomp as well might be, like men who well believed the day was theirs." [2] A part of this rich booty was the person of the French king himself, who was taken prisoner in the field; and before the year was out, the citizens of London had their patriotism stimulated by the sight of the King of France, a captive in England.

In those years of amazing good fortune, English supremacy had been as certain on the sea as upon land. In June, 1340, news was brought into England of a great victory over the enemy in the harbor of Sluys. "On the Saturday, St. John's Day," King Edward wrote to his

---

[1] Froissart: *Chroniques*, ed. Luce and Raynaud, III. 174, 417. Most of the passage quoted above occurs only in the *Ms. d'Amiens.*
[2] *Chroniques*, V. 61.

son, "soon after the hour of noune, with the tide, in the name of God, and in the confidence of our just quarrel, we entered into the said port against our enemies, who had placed their ships in very strong array, and made a right noble defence all that day, and the night after. But God, by his power and miracle granted us the victory over our enemies, for which we thank him as devoutly as we can. And we have you to know that the number of our enemies' ships, galleys, and great barges, amounted to nine score, which were all taken, save 24 in all, which made their escape; and of these some are since taken at sea. And the number of men-at-arms and other armed people amounted to 35,000, of which number it is estimated some 5,000 escaped; and the rest, as we are given to understand by some persons who are taken alive, lie dead in many places on the coast of Flanders." [3]

Such victories as these, with the slaughter which accompanied them, made the name of England terrible by land and sea. They also quickened the national consciousness at home and brought to birth that new thing which we now call "patriotism." The fact that the common citizenry of England had played so large a part in the military and naval achievements of those glorious decades, brought the sense of national power to classes in society which had taken little share in these things in earlier days; and the yeomen of fourteenth-century England must have shared with knights, esquires, and men-at-arms in the arrogance that comes to a people through military victories.

The military glory, which fostered this new nationalistic

[3] Dorothy Hughes: *Illustrations of Chaucer's England*, 122. From the Archives of the City of London, Register F.

spirit, departed as suddenly as it had come. Although the peace of Bretigny, concluded in 1360, made King Edward the master of a third of France, England hardly possessed the power to maintain her position of supremacy. Her conquests could be held only by maintaining large forces under arms upon the continent, and the wealth of the land was not great enough to bear such an expense. During the third quarter of the century, parliament after parliament grudgingly voted huge sums of money for the prosecution of the war; but for all the money that the country furnished, the return in military success constantly diminished. In 1367, the Black Prince won the last and most brilliant of his victories, at Nájera, in Spain; but the victory was entirely fruitless, and the Spanish war dragged on unprofitably for many years, wasting English lives and English money. In 1372, the Earl of Pembroke, leading a great army and bearing a rich treasure, set sail for France to carry on the war from the base of the English province of Aquitaine; but he was encountered upon the sea, off Rochelle, and his force was captured to a man. In 1373, the luckless John of Gaunt, who was vainly trying to carry on the military traditions of his brother, the Black Prince, led a magnificent army into France, only to have it decimated by disease and exhaustion without a battle with the enemy. French commanders, taught discretion by the experience of Crécy and Poitiers, had learned to avoid pitched battles with English armies; and more than one expensive expedition into France wasted the money that had been wrung from the English public and brought back no further tales of glorious victories. Poitou, Aquitaine, and other English possessions on the continent gradually passed into the hands of the French, and England was left with little to show for her glorious victories at Crécy and Poitiers save a foothold on the French coast at Calais.

France, in the meantime, had formed an alliance with Spain, and French and Spanish fleets combined to dispute with England her doubtful supremacy in the Channel. Since the English navy in the fourteenth century was composed of private vessels, commandeered in an emergency by the royal government, the maintenance of naval supremacy depended upon a flourishing merchant marine. Unfortunately, the methods adopted for securing ships for military purposes were not likely to encourage the growth of such a marine. In 1371, the Commons set before the king the causes of the decline of "la Navie," stating that "the arrests of ships . . . have often been made before our lord the King had occasion to make use of them; during which time those who owned them have always borne all the expense connected with them at their own cost, as well of the mariners as of all other appurtenances, without making any profit in the meantime; whereby many of them have been so impoverished that by insufficiency they have abandoned this calling, and allowed their ships to rot and be ruined." [4] In the following year, the Commons complained "that whereas 20 years ago, and always before that time, the shipping of the realm was so noble and plentiful, in every port and goodly town along the sea and on the rivers, that all countries used to consider and to call our lord the King of the Sea, and feared him and the realm the more, by sea and land, by reason of the said navy, it is now so diminished and reduced by various

[4] *Rolls of Parliament,* II. 307.

causes that there remains barely sufficient to defend the country." [5]

This statement was hardly exaggerated. For the first time in centuries, England knew the bitterness of invasion. Rye, Dartmouth, Plymouth, and other towns along the coast were sacked by landing parties; and one such invading force settled for a time in Sussex, occupying castles and other strongholds, and moving out only when winter storms threatened their communications with the continent. In 1385, invasion on a larger scale was threatened, and panic spread through England, as tales were passed about of the magnitude of the forces gathering across the Channel.

"When it was known for truth," says Walsingham, "that the King of France had collected his fleet, had made ready his army, and had fully determined to invade England, the Londoners, as timid as hares and as scared as mice, sought divers counsels on all sides, and peered about for hiding places. As if the city were already on the verge of capture, they began to mistrust their own strength and to despair of resistance. Men who proudly boasted, in times of peace, that they would blow all the Frenchmen out of England, on hearing the rumor of the advent of the foe, though it was but an empty rumor, thought that all England was hardly sufficient to protect them. Therefore, as if drunk with wine, they rushed to the city walls, tore down and destroyed the houses that abutted on the fortifications, and timorously did all the things which they were wont to do when placed in the direst extremity. As yet not one Frenchman had set foot aboard

[5] *Rolls of Parliament*, II. 311.

a ship, not one of the foe had put to sea; yet the Londoners were as frightened as if the whole land, all round about, had been conquered and overrun, as perturbed as if they saw the enemy at their very gates." [6]

Doubtless the monkish chronicler, writing in the security of the scriptorium at St. Albans, exaggerated the fears of the burgesses of London; but the danger had been real enough. The preparations were made in dead earnest, and the forces gathered for the purpose were formidable enough to cause alarm. The blow was averted by events in Flanders, which occupied the attention of the French; but the threat had brought home to the English public, in a very vivid way, the change which had taken place so suddenly in the military situation.

THE BLACK DEATH

During these years of disillusionment, when the fortunes of war were proving themselves so unstable, England was repeatedly visited by pestilence. The Black Death, which spread over all Europe in the middle of the fourteenth century, came at last to England. "It began in England," says Robert of Avesbury, "in the neighborhood of Dorchester, about the Feast of St. Peter ad Vinculas, in the year of our Lord, 1348, and immediately spread rapidly from place to place. Many persons who were in sound health in the early morning were snatched, before midday, from mortal affairs; none whom it marked down to die did it permit to live beyond three or four days, without choice of persons, save only in the case of a few rich people. . . . Coming to London about the Feast of All Saints,

[6] Walsingham: *Historia Anglicana*, ed. Riley, II. 145.

it slew many persons daily and increased so greatly that from the Feast of the Purification until just after Easter, in a newly-made cemetery at Smithfield, the bodies of more than 200 dead, besides those that were buried in other cemeteries in the same city, were buried every day. But through the intervention of the Holy Ghost, it withdrew from London at the Feast of Pentecost, proceeding toward the North, where it ceased also about the Feast of St. Michael." [7]

The loss of life in this first visitation of the Black Death was appalling, and the same mysterious pestilence returned three times in the course of the century. It has been estimated that one half the population of England was swept away in these epidemics. The effect upon the minds of men and women, confronted with such a calamity, we can only imagine; the practical effects of the pestilence are a matter of record. At first, prices fell sharply, "since there were very few people who set any store by riches or any sort of property" in the midst of such a disaster; but this natural phenomenon was followed by a steady advance in prices, and money did not again recover its former purchasing power. The loss in human life had produced an inevitable loss in wealth as well. "Sheep and oxen strayed at large through the fields and among the standing crops, and there was none to drive them away or to herd them; but they perished in countless numbers in remote ditches and fields throughout all districts, for lack of herdsmen. . . . Necessities became so dear that what had formerly been worth $1d$. was now worth $4d$. or $5d$." [8]

[7] Robert of Avesbury: *De Gestis Mirabilis, etc.,* ed. E. M. Thompson, 406, 407.

[8] Henry Knighton: *Chronicon,* ed. Lumby, II. 62, 65.

This decline in the value of money bore hardest upon
the laboring population, who lived close to the margin
of sustenance. For a century or more, a gradual process
of emancipation had been going on in England, by which
the serf of an earlier era had been transformed into a free
laborer, performing services on the demesne-lands in return for money wages, and holding his land in return for
a money rent, paid to the lord of the manor in lieu of
personal service. This process, though far from complete
by the middle of the century, was at work in practically
every section of England, and free or semi-free laborers
were working farm-land in every county. The scale of
wages for agricultural labor was pitifully low, but it had
been accepted without much complaint. After 1348, however, with money fallen to one quarter or one fifth of its
former value, the worker knew that he must receive more
for his labor or perish of starvation. The decrease in
population had placed him in a favorable position to en-
force his demands. Labor was scarce and at a premium,
and bailiffs on the manors throughout England found
themselves obliged to pay double or even treble the wages
they had paid before the first visitation of the Black Death,
in order to secure hands to work the demesne-lands.

THE STATUTES OF LABORERS

To the landed proprietors of the realm, such a state of
affairs seemed to threaten ruin. They took what steps they
could to bring these unreasonable peasants to terms by
force of the law. In the Autumn of 1349, the king had
issued a proclamation forbidding the payment of a higher
wage than had been given before; and the next parlia-

ment made this royal ordinance the law of the realm, by passing the famous Statute of Laborers. Under the terms of this statute, which was reaffirmed by successive parliaments, it was ordained, "That every man or woman of our realm of England, of what condition he be, free or bond, able in body, and within the age of threescore years, not living in merchandise, nor exercising any craft, nor having of his own whereof he may live, nor proper land, about whose tillage he may himself occupy, and not serving any other, if he in convenient service, his estate considered, be required to serve, he shall be bounden to serve him which so shall him require; and take only the wages, livery, meed, or salary, which were accustomed to be given in the places where he oweth to serve, in the xx. year of our reign (i. e., 1347), or five or six other common years next before." [9] The same ordinance endeavored to fix prices of necessary commodities, requiring "butchers, fishmongers, hostelers, brewers, bakers, pulters, and all other sellers of all manner of victual" to set a reasonable price upon their wares, so that they "shall have moderate gains and not excessive."

It is hardly necessary to record the failure of these attempts to escape the operation of economic laws. The "riche and sellers of vitaille" continued to regulate their prices according to the law of supply and demand, in defiance of the penalties decreed by parliament, and it is to be feared that they often took more than a moderate profit. Land-owners, who found themselves threatened with the loss of their crops, unless they could secure workers to harvest them, continued to break the law and to

[9] *Statutes of the Realm,* I. 307, 308 (23 Edw. III. 1349). I reproduce the eighteenth-century translation.

pay the higher wages that had been forbidden. The laborer, who was not slow to recognize his favorable position, continued to demand a living wage; and if he could not get it in one section of the country, he moved on to another, where employers were not so scrupulous in observing the law. "In the same year the statute of servants was declared," says the chronicler Knighton, "and from that time they served their masters worse from day to day than they had done before." [10]

The total effect of the dearth of laborers and of the repressive measures taken to meet the situation, was to foster a spirit of independence in the English peasant and to create a large floating population in the realm. The feudal loyalty to the lord of the manor was vanishing rapidly, and the stronger tie, which binds men to the land on which they have always lived, was breaking down. The natural results of the unfortunate Statutes of Laborers are well set forth in a petition to the king presented in parliament in 1376. The Commons, describing the contumacious nature of "laborers and artificers and other servants" complained that "as soon as their masters accuse them of mal-service, or wish to pay them for their services according to the form of the Statutes, they take flight and depart suddenly out of their employment, and out of their own district, from county to county, hundred to hundred, and town to town, in strange places unknown to their masters; so that they know not where to find them to have remedy or suit against them by virtue of the aforesaid Statutes." [11]

The Commons had to complain of even more serious

[10] Knighton: *Chronicon,* ed. Lumby, II. 74.
[11] *Rolls of Parliament,* II. 340.

consequences of the Statutes of Laborers. With remarkable shortsightedness, parliament had decreed that a workman who had been condemned under the statutes and whom the sheriff failed to arrest, should be declared an outlaw, whom any man might slay at sight. Such measures hardly fostered a law-abiding spirit in the peasantry. "Be it known to our Lord, the King, and to his Parliament," says the petition of 1376, "that many of these wandering laborers have become mendicant beggars, to lead an idle life, and they generally go out of their own district into cities, boroughs, and other good towns to beg, though they are able-bodied, and might well ease the community by living by their labor and service, if they were willing to serve. Many of them become staff-strikers, and lead an idle life, and commonly they rob poor people in simple villages, by two, three, or four together and are evilly suffered in their malice. The greater part generally become strong thieves, increasing their robberies and felonies every day on all sides, in destruction of the realm." [12]

Such laborers as the Ploughman of the *Canterbury Tales* would doubtless have been considered the exception by the Knights of the Shire who sat with Chaucer in the Parliament of 1386. Among his own fellows, the Ploughman's honesty, fidelity, and charity might have won him a reputation for simple-mindedness. Life upon the land was no easy existence in the fourteenth century, and few of the peasants were giving their labor away. Langland gives us a picture of the lean fare upon which the farm laborer must subsist between harvests, when the crops have been bad:

[12] *Rolls of Parliament*, II. 340.

"I haue no peny," quod peres "poletes forto bigge,
Ne neyther gees ne grys but two grene cheses,
A fewe cruddes and creem and an hauer cake,
And two loues of benes and bran y-bake for my fautis." [13]

It is hardly surprising that men who had lived most of
their lives fighting at close grips with hunger should attempt to profit by any opportunity to improve their situation; that they should relax their efforts, as they found
the conditions of their life unexpectedly improved by the
economic consequences of the pestilence; and that many
a ditcher and delver, instead of working with dumb patience through the weary hours, should "drive forth the
long day singing 'Dieu vous save, Dame Emma.'"

THE PEASANTS' REVOLT

In a society thus shaken loose from its moorings, restlessness and discontent spread rapidly. An improved situation and a growing spirit of independence contributed as
much to the outbreak of 1381 as the bitter conditions
which the laboring classes had previously known.

Laboreres that haue no lande to lyue on but her handes,
Deyned nought to dyne a-day nyght-olde wortes.
May no peny-ale hem paye ne no pece of bakoun,
But if it be fresch flesch other fische fryed other bake,
And that *chaude* or *plus chaud* for chillyng of here mawe. [14]

So Langland, keen-eyed observer of the changes taking
place around him, records the altered spirit of the fourteenth-century workman. Organization, of a rudimentary

[13] *Piers the Plowman,* B-text, VI. 282-5.
[14] *Piers the Plowman,* B-text, VI. 309-13.

sort, supported the laborer in his demands for higher pay, furnishing him with a foretaste of the greater power that was to come with trade-unionism. In short, the labor movement of a later era appeared to be well under way in England, in the latter half of the fourteenth century.

Radical agitators were not wanting, to give the movement a very sinister appearance, and to lend some show of verity to the charges, brought forward by the wealthier and more conservative elements in society, that the refractory peasants wished to overturn the established social order. There is no evidence at all that the rising of 1381 had communistic objects. The revolted peasantry contented themselves with a demand for personal freedom and the commutation of all services for a rent of 4d. an acre. When these demands had been met by the king, most of the rebels dispersed to their homes. Among the leaders and fomenters of the revolt, however, were some who seem to have preached communism as the only remedy for the ills of society. John Ball, the "mad priest" of Kent, had been going through England for some twenty years, doing what he could to fill the minds of the poorer people with a sense of the injustice of the existing order of things.

"On Sundays after Mass," says Froissart, "when all the people came out of the minster, this John Ball was accustomed to betake himself to the market-place and preach to them, saying 'Good people, matters cannot go well in England and never will until all things shall be in common, and there shall be neither villeins nor gentlemen, but we shall all be equal. By what right are they whom we call lords greater folk than we, and on what grounds have they merited such honor? why do they hold us in bondage? If we are all descended from the same parents, Adam and Eve, what can they show, or what reason can they give, why they should be more masters than ourselves, save that they make us earn with our toil what they dispend? They are clothed in velvet and rich stuffs, trimmed with ermine and gray fur, while we are clothed in rags. They have wines, spices, and fine breads, while we have only rye and the refuse of the straw, and for our drink, water. They have handsome seats and manors, and we have pain and labor, the rain and wind in the fields. And from us and from our toil must come the means by which they keep their state! We are called slaves, and if we do not readily perform their commands, we are beaten; and we have no sovereign to whom we can complain or who would be willing to hear us and to right our wrongs. Let us go to the king—for he is young—and remonstrate with him about our servitude. Let us tell him that we wish matters to be altered, or we shall seek the remedy ourselves. If we go to him at once and all together, all manner of folk who are called slaves and held in servitude will follow us, to gain their freedom; and when the king sees us and hears us, he will provide the remedy, either by fair means or foul.' " [15]

How accurately the courtly chronicler has reported the sentiments of the radical agitator, we do not know; nor can we tell how far such ideas as these gained a foothold in the minds of the fourteenth-century peasants. At any rate, the men who rose in 1381 acted upon the advice with which John Ball's sermon, as reported by Froissart, was concluded. They marched upon London, determined to lay their demands before the king and pathetically sure

[15] *Chroniques,* ed. Luce and Raynaud, X. 96.

of winning his sympathy, if they could separate him from the malevolent influences which they conceived to be surrounding him.

On Wednesday, June 12, the Kentish rebels, who had seized Canterbury two days before and had marched up along the old pilgrims' way—"like a tempest, destroying all the houses belonging to attorneys, king's proctors, and the archbishop, which came in their way" [16]—encamped upon Blackheath, a few miles outside of London. Some sort of organization seems to have directed the outbreak, for rebellion had flared out in many quarters of the land simultaneously, and bodies of men from all directions were marching upon London. The mob was but poorly armed and not in the least disciplined; but with no armed forces available to deal with the outbreak, the government of the realm was powerless. The king, the queen mother, Archbishop Sudbury, and other members of the royal council were in the Tower, practically in a state of siege.

On the following day, the rebels gained admittance to the city, over London Bridge, and made themselves masters of the place. Joined by sympathizers within the metropolis, they proceeded instantly and systematically to take vengeance upon persons and classes for whom they cherished a particular hatred. John of Gaunt's town house, the Savoy—"cui nullum usquam in regno in pulchritudine et nobilitate potuit comparari" [17]—was burned to the ground. Their motive was not a desire for plunder, but a blind hatred for the Duke of Lancaster, who was popularly supposed to be the principal cause of half the ills of England, as he was undoubtedly the wealthiest and most con-

[16] *Chroniques,* ed. Luce and Raynaud, X. 101.
[17] Walsingham: *Historia Anglicana,* ed. Riley, I. 457.

spicuous representative of the system of things against which the peasants had rebelled. Rich furniture, gold and silver vases, and other articles of priceless value were hurled out of the palace—and scrupulously hacked to pieces with axes, thrown into the Thames, or hurled into sewers. There were some thieves, of course, among the rioters, and some of the plunder found its way into their hands; but most of the rebels were bent upon the destruction of the duke's property, not upon its appropriation to their own use.

The Inns of Court were next attacked, for the peasantry felt a particular hatred for the oppressive class of lawyers; and the rolls and records of the Temple were carried "to the great chimney" and burned. A proclamation declared that all lawyers should be beheaded, and as the rebels, on their march up to London, had hanged more than one member of the profession, it was evident that they were in earnest. The manor-house of Robert Hales, treasurer of the realm, was destroyed; and because Hales was Master of the Order of St. John of Jerusalem, the buildings of that society were given over to pillage and destruction.

For three days the reign of terror in London continued. There were bold spirits among those besieged in the Tower who advised a sally in force, sure of assistance from the more conservative of the burgesses and from Sir Robert Knolles, who was holding his own house in the city with his band of retainers,—a hard-handed company of warriors, who had won a reputation abroad for callous cruelty. More prudent counsels prevailed. It was the Earl of Salisbury, according to Froissart, who advised the king to appease his revolted subjects by fair words; "for should we begin what we cannot go through," he said, "it will be all over with us and our heirs, and England will be a desert." [18]

Following Salisbury's suggestion, the young king rode forth at dawn on Friday, moving to meet the rebels at Mile End, whither they had been summoned by royal proclamation. In the meadows where the meeting took place, Richard listened to the complaints of his subjects and met all their demands with immediate and full concession. All the serfs in England should be freed; all feudal services should straightway be commuted for a money rent at 4d. a day; a general pardon should be extended to all concerned in the rebellion. " 'Now, therefore,' said the King, 'return to your homes . . . and let two or three from each village be left behind, and I will order letters to be given with my seal, which they can take back with them, fully and freely granting every demand you have made. And in order that you may be the better comforted and assured, I will direct that my banners be sent to every stewardship, castlewick, and corporation.' " [19]

These were "fair words," indeed, and, to give them show of substance, the king set thirty secretaries to work, drawing up the letters he had promised. The clerks worked rapidly, and as the letters of the king were distributed, many of the rebels quietly took their departure and returned home, armed with these new instruments of freedom. "The principal mischief, however," declares Froissart, "remained behind: I mean Wat Tyler, Jack Straw, and John Ball, who declared, that though these people were satisfied, they would not take their departure on such terms; and with them were more than 30,000, all of the

---

[18] *Chroniques,* ed. Luce and Raynaud, X. 110.
[19] *Ibid.,* X. 112, 113.

same mind. These all continued in London and made no great ado to receive the letters or the king's seals, but did all they could to throw the town into such confusion, that the lords and rich citizens might be murdered and their houses pillaged and destroyed." [20]

The leaders of the rebels probably had no such bloodthirsty intentions, but enough had happened to lend some color of justice to the accusation. While the king was at Mile End, conferring with such of the rebels as had been induced to meet him there, some four or five hundred of them had gained admittance to the Tower. They dragged out Archbishop Sudbury and the treasurer, Robert Hales, from the chapel, and butchered them on Tower Hill. Sudbury was the gentlest and most inoffensive of men; but as chancellor of the realm, he was regarded as the chief instrument of an oppressive government. He probably knew, when the king rode forth that morning to Mile End, that he was to be made a sacrifice, and he had been celebrating the Mass when the mob came upon him.

The rebels speedily found other victims. The most wanton of their outrages was the massacre of the Flemings, to which Chaucer refers in the *Nonne Preestes Tale*.[21] These foreigners, who lived in a colony of their own along the banks of the Thames, appear to have been peaceful settlers, who had come to England for purposes of trade and industry; and the motives which led the rioters to fall upon them probably had their roots in race hatreds and commercial jealousies, which had no part among the feelings that had caused the general uprising. The worst ele-

[20] *Chroniques,* ed. Luce and Raynaud, X. 113, 114.
[21] *Cant. Tales,* B. 4584-86.

ments in the mob were clearly gaining the upper hand. Looting, murder, and arson were going on in the city; and the departure of some of the rebellious peasants, so far from alleviating the situation, merely made matters worse, by removing the very men whose purposes were least vindictive, and who were most likely to keep their riotous comrades within bounds.

It was the young king, as every one knows, who saved the situation. Meeting the rebels again on Saturday morning, at Smithfield, he showed the most admirable courage when one of his impulsive followers struck down Wat Tyler, the leader of the insurgents. Riding straight toward the threatening crowd of rebels, before they could be quite certain that Tyler had been murdered, he offered himself as their leader, and contrived to persuade them to follow him out of the city into the meadows near the ruins of the St. John's Hospital, which they had so recently destroyed. Thither they were speedily followed by armed men, who could now be rallied within the city; and by this display of force, they were easily persuaded to lay down such arms as they possessed and to disperse. Some of them were escorted through the city and dismissed upon their homeward road. Others made off into the countryside, to continue the rebellion, if possible, in other parts of the realm. The three-days' reign of terror was over. The young king rode back to join his mother in the Garde Robe, in Counter Lane, whither she had fled from the Tower on the previous day. "When she saw her son the king," says Froissart, "she was much rejoiced, and said, 'Ah, fair son, what pain and anguish have I not suffered for you this day!' Then said the king, in answer, 'Certes, Madame,

I know it well. But now rejoice, for all is well; and thank God, for I have this day regained my inheritance and the realm of England, which I had lost.' " [22]

Richard had, indeed, shown himself master of the situation, and he has been sufficiently praised for the coolness and fearlessness which he displayed in his dealings with the mob. Perhaps it is ungenerous to point out that the boy's gallant part was acted against a background of duplicity. From his own point of view, and from that of the classes in whose interests England was governed in the fourteenth century, Richard was doubtless justified in fooling his people; and the fact that he risked his life, to accomplish his purposes, may make his actions in 1381 appear admirable. The plain fact of the deceit which he practised on his rebellious subjects cannot be obscured. Only the simple peasants could have believed that he meant to keep his word with them and to put substance and reality behind the promises which he made so readily. The more intelligent leaders of the revolt apparently saw through the deception, and it seems to have been their purpose to maintain their position in command of the capital, where they could overawe the king and his government, until the reforms which they had demanded rested on a firmer foundation than the parchments prepared by Richard's thirty secretaries.

As soon as the mob had been dislodged from the city, the emptiness of the king's promises began to be apparent. He had promised general pardon, but the heads of Wat Tyler, John Ball, and Jack Straw were soon decorating London Bridge. Armed forces were speedily brought together and sent out from the capital to put down the rebel-

[22] *Chroniques,* ed. Luce and Raynaud, X. 123, 124.

lion through the neighboring counties. They had little difficulty in subduing the half-armed and badly-disciplined bands which they encountered, and the massacre of the rebels frequently followed their defeat. The Chief Justice, Robert Tressilian, accompanied by the king, moved in the wake of the conquering forces, holding his "bloody assizes." Even conservative-minded men, who had little sympathy with the revolted peasants, were somewhat horrified by Tressilian's severity, for he spared scarcely any of those who were brought before him. The king, by his presence, lent his sanction to these severities, on the part of the army and of the court, and showed how little in earnest he had been when he promised a general amnesty.

He was soon to give evidence that he had been no more serious in promising manumission. "Serfs you are, and serfs you will remain," he is said to have declared to a deputation of peasants who waited upon him at Waltham; and on July 2, he revoked the charters he had given. The same deliberate process by which the serfs of England had been gaining freedom, over a space of many years, went on; but the rising of 1381 had certainly not completed its work.

John Gower, in his *Vox Clamantis,* gives us a picture of the horrors of 1381, under an allegory, in which the peasants are represented as domestic beasts who suddenly abandon their serviceable way of life and overrun the countryside, demanding outrageous privileges, unsuited to their humble place in the world. It is clear that the poet had little sympathy with the peasants; and a picture which he draws of the terror and suffering of a seigneur, forced by the advance of the mob to abandon his manor-house and take refuge in the woods, quickens one's own sympathies with the victims of the uprising.[23] Nevertheless, with the passage of the cooling years, the wisdom of the simple peasants shines above the wisdom of the poet, as above the shrewdness of Richard and his councillors. What the peasants demanded of their king, and what he granted them at Mile End, would have established, at one stroke, a free peasantry upon the farm-land of England, as a firm basis for a more prosperous and stable society.

EXTRAVAGANCE AND DISHONESTY

The instability of society in fourteenth-century England was dramatically demonstrated by the events of 1381; it was manifested less strikingly in many other ways. The growth of commerce and of manufacture, together with the large booty captured in the wars abroad, had brought increased wealth to England; but it was so unevenly distributed that it deepened class distinctions and became an increasing cause of class jealousy and strife. The simple scale of living which had characterized an earlier age yielded place to a desire for sumptuous fare and costly dress and furniture. The signs of personal extravagance which Chaucer quietly records, in his descriptions of many of the Canterbury Pilgrims, were not only tokens of increasing national wealth, but evidence, also, of a worldly spirit which gave the gravest concern to the moralists of the age. The literature of the period is full of references to the expensive tastes which were to be found in every class of society, and the satirists return again and again to their attack upon the person whom Langland and other poets call "Waster."

[23] *Vox Clamantis,* Book I. cap. xvi.

It was in matters of dress and of food that this new spirit of extravagance most moved the disgust of conservative folk, who lamented the passing of simpler habits. "The Commons were besotted in excess of apparel," says an account written about 1362, "in wide surcoats reaching to their loins, some in a garment reaching to their heels, close before and strowting out on the side, so that on the back they make men seem women. . . . Their hoods are little, tied under the chin, and buttoned like the women's but set with gold, silver, and precious stones. Their lirripippes reach to their heels all jagged. They have another weed of silk which they call a Paltok. Their hose are of two colours, or pied with more, which with lachets, which they called Herlots, they tie to their Paltoks, without any breeches. Their girdles are of gold and silver, some worth 20 marks. . . . Their shoes and pattens are snowted and piked more than a finger long, crooking upwards, which they call 'crackows,' resembling the Divel's claws, which were fastened to the knees with chains of gold and silver." [24]

To combat this extravagance in dress, Parliament issued sumptuary ordinances, regulating the apparel of all ranks in society. Trades-people were forbidden to use silver for the trimming of their knives; servants and their families were required to limit the cost of their apparel to two marks; and husbandmen of all sorts were directed to "wear no cloth save blanket and russet, 12d. the yard." [25] Needless to say, these statutes were not observed, and they were withdrawn, on petition, in 1365.

The same ordinances had endeavored to regulate the

[24] William Camden: *Remains Concerning Britain* (London, 1870) 211, 212.
[25] *Statutes of the Realm*, I. 378 (37 Edw. III, 1363).

diet of certain classes in society. A description of a feast, from a poem of the middle of the century, gives us what is probably no very highly exaggerated account of the sort of entertainment provided at the tables of the very rich in Chaucer's day:

> The boar's head shall be brought with bays aloft,
> Bucktails full broad in broths therewithal,
> Venison with the fruments, and pheasants full rich,
> Baked meats near by, on the board well set,
> Chewets of chopped flesh, and chickens grilled;
> Each several guest has six men's share.
> Were this not enough, another course follows,—
> Roast with rich sauces and royal spice,
> Kids cleft in the back, quartered swans,
> Tarts of ten inches. It tortures my heart
> To see the board o'er-spread with blazing dishes,
> As a rood arrayed with rings and with stones.
> The third mess to me were a marvel to tell,
> For all is Martinmass meat that I mostly know of,
> Nought but worts with flesh-meat, without wild fowl,
> Save a hen unto him that the house owneth;
> And ye will have basted birds broach'd on a spit,
> Barnacle-geese and bitterns, and many billed snipes,
> Larks and linnets, lapp'd all in sugar,
> Woodcocks and woodpeckers, full warm and hot,
> Teals and titmice, to take what you please;
> Caudels of conies, and custards sweet,
> Dariols and dishmeats, that dearly cost,
> Maumeny, as men call it, your maws to fill;
> Twelve dishes at a time between two men.[26]

[26] *Winner and Waster*, ed. by Sir Israel Gollancz (London, 1920), modernized version, lines 332–56.

Even though we were to make allowance for some poetic exaggeration in such poems as this, or in the passages in which Langland turns his scorn upon the extravagance of Waster, it should be remembered that such poems were probably very widely known and carried, to the poorer people of the realm, a conception of the wealth that ran to waste in classes which seemed to be winning their riotous pleasures at the expense of the toiling multitude.

> Some putten hem to the plow pleyed ful selde,
> In settyng and in sowyng swonken ful harde,
> And wonnen that wastours with glotonye destruyeth.[27]

These lines from the Prologue of *Piers the Plowman* are a poignant expression, typical of the poet, of the sense of the injustice of life, as the peasant of the fourteenth century saw it.

Discrepancies in fortune could have been borne more patiently if they had not often been founded upon palpable fraud. Dishonesty among merchants of the age is as often the target of Langland's satire as the extravagance of Waster. Selling by short weight, adulteration of their wares, unscrupulous suppression of competition, and outrageous overcharging are among the practices attributed by the satirist to the tradesmen of the age. The power of the victualling trades in the government of the city of London was notorious, and that it was used to maintain the high price of food-stuffs was the general belief. John of Northampton, during his two years as mayor of the city, had reduced the prices of food; but when he stood

[27] *Piers the Plowman,* B-text, Prol. 20–23.

for reëlection in 1383, the king himself interfered to carry by force the election of Nicholas Brembre, chief of the grocers.

Abuse of the powers of public office for private ends was no uncommon thing, particularly in the latter years of the reign of Edward III. At the time when John of Gaunt was maintaining an undisputed influence over the king, some of the duke's henchmen profited by positions which he had given them upon the council board, to buy up the public debt at a reduced figure, and then to pay themselves out of a depleted treasury at the full value of the debt. One of these high-placed scoundrels, Richard Lyons, a wealthy London merchant, when appointed farmer of the customs of Calais, levied a higher duty than had been authorized by parliament, pocketing the difference himself. He secured permission from his colleagues in the government to export his own wool, duty free, and secured the same privilege for other merchants, probably in return for considerable bribes.

Such shameless peculations as these were not so common after the time of the Good Parliament of 1376. The specific reforms introduced by that memorable body came to nothing, as Langland points out in his fable of the cat and the rats;[28] but from that time forward, the Commons exercised more power over the choice of royal ministers. Although the succeeding governments were usually inefficient, the public service did not again reach the depths of dishonesty which it reached in the days of Latimer and Lyons.

Even under an honest government, however, the people of England could hardly expect an administration of affairs

[28] *Piers the Plowman*, B-text, Prol. 146–207.

that brought prosperity, or even justice, to all alike. The nobles of the land, with their armed and liveried retainers, held the real power in their hands, and no central government was strong enough to prevent abuses. In accordance with a custom known as "maintenance," any criminal who wore the livery of a nobleman could be sure that an armed force, all wearing the same livery, would gather at the assizes to overawe the king's court by their presence and the threat which it implied. That a poor or obscure citizen could secure justice under such circumstances was out of the question. The effect of such a system upon the retainers themselves can be imagined. Many of them were soldiers returned from wars abroad, with memories of pillage in foreign territory fresh in their minds. It is not surprising to hear of gentlemen robbers raiding the peaceful midland counties at the head of their own little armies, of powerful noblemen dispossessing their neighbors of their property, under threat of death, of heiresses carried off and married by force. In an earlier age, when the sheriffs under the Norman kings or under Henry II were among the most powerful barons and prelates of the realm, such depredations were unheard of, unless it were along the Scotch and Welsh marches, where the unstable conditions of "border law" prevailed. That such high-handed crimes could go unpunished in the heart of England was one more indication of the breaking down of ancient institutions.

Another abuse of power, which bore more directly on the peasantry, was the "purveyance" of supplies for the royal household. The purveyors were supposed to give payment for value received, but they seem to have been more than careless in the exercise of their office. A tract.

addressed to Edward III in 1333 and written by Simon Islip, later Archbishop of Canterbury, informs the king that "The purveyors of your court . . . and divers grooms of your household . . . violently seize many goods from their owners . . . for which practically nothing is paid; and on account of extortion of this sort, many poor people have not wherewith to sow their land. . . . Likewise, those of your household, in the forest of Windsor and thereabouts, seize men and carts, and horses of the poor and compell them to withdraw from their own farm-lands . . . not only for three or four days, but for more: and although it is agreed that they shall be paid for their labor, they are paid nothing. And on account of diabolical deeds of this sort, the lands of the poor are neither ploughed nor sown, nor have the poor any property by which they can sustain such burdens." [29] A statute, passed by parliament in 1363, speaks of "the grievous complaint which hath been made of purveyors of victuals of the Houses of the King, the Queen, and their eldest son, and of other lords and ladies of the realm." [30] As the years wore on, this particular form of abuse was brought under some sort of regulation, but the purveyor remained an unpopular figure throughout the age of Langland and Chaucer.

The twin evils of purveyance and maintenance had brought the feudal aristocracy into general opprobrium among the very classes which were coming into a new position of prominence and importance in fourteenth-century England. The knights of the shire, who represented the small land-holding gentry in the parliament of

[29] *De Speculo Regis,* ed. Moisant, 94, 100.
[30] *Statutes of the Realm,* I. 371.

1381, were not men who were likely to have much sympathy with the peasantry that had just turned the realm upside down, nor a very clear understanding of the motives which governed the uprising; but instead of attributing the rebellion to the general depravity of the poor and ignorant, as one might have expected, they sturdily pointed out to the king the abuses of power which oppressed the countryside, attributing the ills which had so lately fallen on the land to grievances that had plenty of justification. They spoke of the men who lived in the king's household off the royal bounty and at the expense of the realm, of the corrupt officials of the king's courts and of the exchequer, of the "embracers of quarrels and maintainers who behave like kings in the countryside;" and they endeavored to make it clear that the nation could not long endure the "oppressions done to them by divers servants of the King and of the seigneurs of the Realm." [31]

The machinery of feudal society, in short, was breaking down. With fierce earnestness and stern simplicity, Langland sets forth his picture of a land governed by the old ideals under the old system: of a king supported by the will of his common people; of learned councillors governing according to the dictates of reason and trained in the ideals of the Church; of a knighthood whose sole business was to protect their tenantry from wild beasts and evil doers; of a peasantry left in possession of the products of their toil and contented with their lot. The passage is a cry of despair: the poet knows that this is not a picture of the England which he has seen.

With more subtlety, but no less earnestly, Chaucer puts before us his picture of a society in which mediæval ideals

[31] *Rolls of Parliament*, III. 10°

had become so old-fashioned that only a few quixotic persons any longer allowed them to interfere with their materialistic purposes. His keenest satire, perhaps, is to be found in his pictures of those out-of-date persons, so far from representative of their kind: the professional man-at-arms who held true to the old ideals of truth and honor, generosity and courtesy; the village priest who performed the difficult tasks of his unremunerative position in the sacrificial spirit which had once been held to belong particularly to his calling; the college undergraduate who cared most for books and study; the peasant who could be called "a trewe swinker," and who actually was such a fool as to give his labor away, "withouten hyre"! Modern readers, with an idea that Chaucer is describing life in "merrie England," in the palmiest days of the Middle Ages, sometimes miss the point in these particular passages in the Prologue to the *Canterbury Tales*. Fourteenth-century readers can hardly have failed to perceive that a poet with a very keen sense of the decay of old institutions was setting before them, in these old-world figures, the exceptional survivors of a passing order. Other persons among the Canterbury pilgrims could be recognized as less exceptional, as men who let

> olde thinges pace,
> And held after the newe world the space.

The thieving miller, the piratical shipman, the worldly monk, the manciple, who, by the grace of God, was able to cheat more than thirty lawyers,—all these were the children of the new age.

Corruption in the Church

Most conspicuous among these easy-going worldlings, who are described so genially that it is easy to overlook the satirical purpose of Chaucer's pictures of them, are the churchmen. No institution in fourteenth-century England was so often the object of satire as the Church. The great organization, with its wealth, its power, and its conservative traditions, might have been expected to offer a safeguard against social decay; but the Church itself was a fruitful breeding-ground for the very things which were disorganizing feudal society. A spirit of sacrifice, a respect for authority, an acceptance of discipline, and at least a modicum of otherworldliness were the characteristics which the Church must foster, if it was to retain its position and discharge its function in society. Anyone acquainted with Chaucer's monk, friar, pardoner, and summoner hardly needs to be told that such characteristics were often wanting in the very servants of the Church. The principal characteristics of these churchmen are greedy self-seeking, contempt for authority, evasion of discipline self-imposed in the vows of monks and friars, and a thorough-going worldliness, which not only sought the good things of life, but sought them at the expense of the needy.

> "What? trowe ye, the whyles I may preche,
> And winne gold and silver for I teche,
> That I wol live in povert wilfully?
> Nay, nay, I thoghte it never trewely!
> For I wol preche and begge in sondry londes;
> I wol not do no labour with myn hondes,
> Ne make baskettes, and live thereby,

Because I wol nat beggen ydelly.
I wol non of the apostles counterfete;
I wol have money, wolle, chese, and whete,
Al were it yeven of the povrest page,
Or of the povrest widwe in a village,
Al sholde hir children sterve for famyne.
Nay! I wol drinke licour of the vyne,
And have a Ioly wenche in every toun."

No one would pretend that every fourteenth-century churchman was so thoroughly depraved as Chaucer's Pardoner, or that the poet's other pictures of servants of the Church were entirely without exaggeration. If we make some allowance, however, for the license which must be permitted every satirist, we can accept his portraits as a just representation of the corruption of the Church of Christ in fourteenth-century England. Every point which he makes is amply supported by evidence from other sources. Other writers of the age, both obscure and famous, have the same story to tell, the same departures from ancient ideals to lament. Official documents record the attempts made, from time to time, to curb the abuses which were bringing the Church into contempt and weakening the influence of religion upon men's lives. The high dignitaries of the Church itself have left us their testimony to the encroaching spirit of worldliness, which some of them resisted manfully,—while others made it the guiding force of their own careers. No age in the history of the Church has been without its greed and worldliness; but there is abundant evidence that the late fourteenth century furnished a spectacle of general corruption, from top to bottom of the institution, which has seldom been equalled.

The "captivity" of the Pope at Avignon, which began in 1309, was a conspicuous proof of the weakening of the strength of the Church in its struggle with the secular powers of the world. This situation was followed by the Great Schism and the edifying spectacle of two rival popes, both claiming divine authority and each calling down the curse of God upon all who supported his rival. In 1382, a bishop of the English Church, encouraged by his easy successes at the head of a force against the un-organized rebels of 1381, undertook to lead a crusade against the followers of Pope Clement upon the con-tinent. He secured from Pope Urban the most liberal in-dulgences for all who fought in this holy cause, and large numbers flocked to his standard, induced by such promises of the remission of their sins. The crusaders made a dis-graceful exhibition of themselves in Europe, pillaging the fields and seizing the towns of England's allies in Flan-ders, and retreating in something like a panic before the first threat of formidable opposition.

"And now in oure dayes," says Wycliffe, writing of this crusade and of the methods used to win recruits, "out of the nest of Antecrist is come an hard maundement, and seith to men in sentence, that hoso confermeth Ante-cristis ordeynaunce in dowynge of the Chirche, and let-tith Cristis ordynaunce, he is fully soylled, and wendith stright to hevene, withouten ony peyne her or in pur-gatorie. . . . And sithe Crist was maad man I herde nevere more blasfemye." [32]

This widely advertised crusade was a particularly con-spicuous example of the use which the Church made of its power over men, in order to serve its own worldly ends.

[32] *Select English Works of John Wyclif*, ed. Arnold, III. 246.

It was certainly not the only "blasfemye" of which Wycliffe held his fellow churchmen guilty. At the outset of his career, he attacked the Church solely on the grounds of its worldliness, deploring the fact that it held so much wealth and that its possessions had turned the minds of its priests and prelates from their spiritual duties. "For nowe," he says, "prelatis and grete religious possessioners ben so occupied aboute worldly lordischipis and plea and bysinesse in herte, that thei may not be in devocion of preiynge, and thought of hevenely thingis, and of here owene synnys and othere mennys, and studie and prechynge of the gospel, and visitynge and confortynge of pore men in here diocisis and lordischipis. . . . And for drede of losse of thes temporaltees, thei doren not reprove synne of lordis and myghtty men, ne frely dampne coveitise in worldly men." [33]

Whatever one may think of Wycliffe and of the work he undertook to do, there is no denying the justice of his criticism in this fundamental matter. At the root of all the evils in the fourteenth-century church, lay this spirit of worldly self-seeking. It was this which drew the parish priest away from his ill-paid and toilsome duties in the country, to seek easy employment singing masses in a chantry established by some wealthy person's bequest; it was this which increased the swarms of secular "clerks," who sought their living in government posts or in the households of the rich; it was this which produced the "heap of hermits" whom Langland saw making their way toward the shrine of Walsingham,—"great lanky lubbers who are loth to work."

While these obscure persons brought the profession of

[33] *Select English Works of John Wyclif,* III. 215.

churchmen into contempt, more conspicuous members of the church body, by shameful extortion and dishonesty, gave the poor people of England reason to entertain a stronger feeling than contempt for the representatives of the institution which was supposed to exist for their comfort and consolation. The begging friars were spread upon the country districts like a plague of locusts. Though they might sometimes win popularity by their easy manners and superficial cultivation, and might exercise some hold upon the superstitious by promising the particular favor of Heaven to all who gave money to the "povre freres," their assiduous wheedling frequently became an insupportable burden. The pardoner, sent out under the sanction of Rome, not only "blered the eyes" of the poor by accepting money for his authorized wares, but carried on a thriving business of his own in fraudulent relics, whose potency few purchasers could put to the test with any satisfaction to themselves. The monks, although they adhered scrupulously to the tradition which made them the dispensers of an indiscriminate charity to all who applied at their gates, proved to be harsh landlords on their own estates and were less ready than the nobles themselves to accept social and economic reforms. In the meanwhile, tithes and other ecclesiastical dues were rigorously collected, although, in the same community, every other function of the Church might be frankly neglected. By the system of "appropriation" of the tithes, the money thus collected went frequently to absentees, who might even be foreigners, living in a land at war with England and ready enough to use English money to damage the interests of the land from which they drew their revenue. Failure to pay the tithe made a man liable to prosecution in the ecclesiastical courts, where a case of this sort was not likely to go in favor of the defendant.

Under the theory of divided authority between Church and State, the ecclesiastical courts had jurisdiction over certain types of cases, which could not be tried in the civil courts. The probate of wills, cases concerning marriage and divorce, clerical suits for arrears of tithes and other church dues, and prosecution for sins punishable by the Church, were all within the jurisdiction of the Courts Christian. In the discharge of some of these functions, they were probably no more corrupt than the king's courts; but in the use of their power over private morals, they had a field of corruption all to themselves. Any person who had not confessed to his priest and performed the penance laid upon him, could be summoned before the church courts and punished for his omission. Councils of the Church had repeatedly forbidden the acceptance of a fine, in lieu of penance, in such cases; but there is plenty of evidence that money fines were accepted, and it even appears that some persons actually paid annual bribes to the courts to forestall inquiry into their habits. No reader of Chaucer needs to be told how the corruption in the ecclesiastical courts spread to the under-officers of those courts, the summoners, who carried on a thriving business in blackmail, with the authority of the archdeacon's curse to give them the power of terror to support their unholy demands.

Conditions in the Church cried aloud for reform, and it is not surprising that the first great reformer should be found in Chaucer's century. Wycliffe, of course, was a dangerous heretic, and perhaps one should not give too much attention to the charges of blasphemy which he so frequently brought against the servants of the Church. He was forced out of his position as a teacher at Oxford, his writings were proscribed, he himself was excommunicated. Such a person's opinions of church officials, one might say, were likely to be colored by an unreasoning radicalism. Yet they will be found, upon examination, to agree amazingly with those presented by good churchmen, who remained within the fold. Wycliffe pointed out what was all too obvious to any candid observer, and his criticism of the Church was so well founded that he won partial support from many conservative citizens, who were very far from sharing his heretical opinions on church doctrines. It was true that the Church had absorbed too large a share of the wealth of England, that too many churchmen employed their time and energy in secular pursuits, that many of them were corrupt and dishonest, and that the hold which the Church had once held over the consciences of men was being weakened by these conditions. Much of what Wycliffe had to say was founded so clearly on the truth, that his outspoken utterances were not at first found very shocking.

The fact is that Wycliffe's heresy was a natural phenomenon in an age when men and women were beginning to exercise their private judgment upon all sorts of matters which they had once accepted without question. The existence of this new spirit of intellectual freedom is the all-important thing about these interesting times which we have been considering; and the most significant events of the age are those in which this spirit is made manifest. In the next century, reaction was to gain the upper hand for a season. The grandson of John of Gaunt was to bring back a brief era of such military glory as had been known in the days of the Black Prince. The Wars of the Roses were to check the growth of social and economic reform and to annihilate the progress which had been made toward parliamentary government in the reign of Richard II. The Church was to rouse itself to a sense of its danger and to conduct a vigorous persecution of the Lollards, who propagated the heresies of Wycliffe. Neither persecution nor reaction, however, could altogether subdue the new influences that had begun their work in the fourteenth century. It is not strictly true to say that the Renaissance began in England in the age of Chaucer and Wycliffe, for the processes of change had commenced before either of them was born; but the history of their times must always be read as a striking chapter in the history of the new forces that had but recently been loosed in society and were working powerfully to reshape the world.

It was in an age of restlessness, amid the ferment of new life, that Chaucer lived and wrote. Old things and new appear side by side upon his pages, and in his poetry we can study the essential spirit, both of the age that was passing, and of the age that was to come. It is idle to reproach him for the conservatism which is so pronounced a feature of his temperament; and to complain that he shows no clear sense of the irreparable rottenness of mediæval institutions, is simply to complain that he was not a clear two centuries ahead of his time. Among his contemporaries, there must have been many who regarded him as dangerously advanced in his ideas, and not a few must certainly have found his satire less genial and tolerant than it sometimes appears to us.[34] When the facts

[34] Cf. S. H. Cox, *Chaucer's Cheerful Cynicism*, in *Mod. Lang. Notes*, 36. 475–81.

of his career are remembered, the wonder is that he showed any understanding at all of the new spirit, which was at work chiefly among classes in society from which circumstances had held him removed. The courtier who could see clearly enough beyond the comforts of the court circle to perceive the evils which stirred the common man to riot and revolt, the Esquire of the Household who could find a place in his consciousness for the vigorous vulgarities of Alice of Bath, the devout Catholic who could draw such pictures as he drew of corruption in the Church, could not have been exactly a placid conservative, wholly unaware that he was living in an age of new and startling things. In his own development as an artist, he moved steadily away from outworn conventions, introducing new forms of expression and a new spirit into English poetry, and following naturally in the footsteps of the great Italian poets who were the heralds of the Renaissance. He remained to the end an independent and impartial spirit, as the greatest artists always must, too strong to be bondsman either to old tradition or to untried ideals; yet he contrived to accomplish something like a revolution in English poetry. His works stand with Petrarch's and Boccaccio's: in a certain sense, monuments to the lost civilization of the Middle Ages; but, in a far truer sense, the first great works of modern European literature. Other men among his contemporaries are more clearly marked as prophets of the new world, but there is no record of the spirit of this age of transition more perfect than the poetry of Geoffrey Chaucer.

CHAPTER II

THE LIFE OF CHAUCER

ON April 4, 1357, Elizabeth, Countess of Ulster, paid four shillings for a "paltok," or short cloak, made by a London tailor for a young man attached to her retinue, and three shillings for a pair of shoes and some red and black breeches, purchased for the same young man. The petty transactions were duly entered in the account-books of the lady's household; and there the record remained in oblivion, amid a dozen other trivial matters, for nearly five centuries. In 1851, the leaves on which the accounts were written were discovered, lining the covers of a fifteenth-century manuscript. With the lapse of time, the countess's insignificant purchases had become a matter of some importance, for the man for whom the clothes were purchased was Geoffrey Chaucer. This is the earliest of the many references to Chaucer which have been discovered in documents and enrollments covering the years in which he lived.

The Countess of Ulster was the wife of Lionel of Antwerp, third son of Edward III. Just what position Chaucer held in the earl's household we do not know, but it is generally assumed that he was serving as a page in 1357, when he makes his first appearance in history, clad in the new paltok and the red and black breeches. We need not be surprised to discover the son of John Chaucer, London vintner, in the household of Prince Lionel. Chaucer was not of noble birth, and although his father bore arms, an earlier generation would hardly have said the poet was gently born; but there was nothing exceptional, in the fourteenth century, in the appointment of a young man of humble origin to a position in a prince's retinue. The yeomen and esquires of King Edward's own household appear to have been recruited from among the sons of families that claimed no very high distinction of birth; and some of them, like Chaucer, were the sons of London tradesmen. The bourgeoisie of London were already in a position to procure such opportunities for the advancement of their sons.

Geoffrey Chaucer was of the London bourgeoisie born and bred. His family is supposed to have been of French extraction, if only because the name is derived from the French "chaucier," meaning "hose-maker." His immediate family, however, cannot be traced farther from London than Ipswich, where his great-grandfather paid rentals to the Priory of the Holy Trinity in the latter half of the thirteenth century. "Malyn" appears to have been the family name at that epoch, and it has been suggested that the surname Chaucier, or Chaucer, was given to the London branch of the family from their residence among the hose-makers and workers in leather in Cordwaner-street Ward. The earliest record that we have of them shows them connected, in one way or another, with the wine trade.

John Chaucer, the poet's father, appears in the public records at an early age. In December, 1324, when he was not yet in his teens, he was abducted from the custody of his mother and step-father, apparently with a view to marrying him to a young cousin, Joan de Westhale. The abduction seems to have been a high-handed attempt to consolidate the title to certain properties by marrying two of the heirs; but it failed to achieve its object and is of importance only because the records of the case, which speedily found its way into the courts, afford reliable evidence that John Chaucer was born in 1312 or 1313, and that he was still unmarried in 1328. This disposes of an old tradition that his son and heir, Geoffrey Chaucer, was born in 1328.

It has commonly been assumed, though on no very substantial evidence, that the year of the poet's birth was 1340.[1] His father, having escaped wedlock with his cousin Joan, had married a certain Agnes, the niece and heiress of a citizen and "moneyer" of London, by name Hamo de Copton. She seems to have brought no inconsiderable fortune into the family, from the estate of her kinsman, and we find John Chaucer and his wife engaged in many transactions involving real estate in and around London. Among his other pieces of London property, John owned a house in the parish of Saint Martin's in the Vintry, extending from Thames Street to the water of Walbrook. It is highly probable that this was the house in which Geoffrey Chaucer was born.

We have no record of the poet's early years. Miss Rickert thought it possible that he attended the school connected with St. Paul's cathedral, where the almoney library contained many volumes of the classics. A statement by Speght (1598) founded the tradition that Chaucer studied

---

[1] Professor Manly argues, on very reasonable grounds, that Chaucer "was born not earlier than 1343 or 1344." Cf. *Some New Light on Chaucer*, 63–67.

at the Inner Temple, where, according to "a recorde in the same howse," he was "fined two shillinges for beatinge a Franciscane Fryer in fletestreate." A vigorous argument for the acceptance of the tradition is presented by Professor Rickert in the *Manly Anniversary Studies* (20–31). Miss Rickert has discovered that the "Master Buckley," whom Speght cited as his authority, was William Buckley, bencher and keeper of the archives of the Inner Temple,— "the one man in England," as Professor Manly remarks, "whose business it was to have seen such a record, if it existed." The education given at the Temple was an expensive one; but it would not have been beyond the means of a man of John Chaucer's wealth, and it would certainly have offered the most desirable form of training for a young man destined for a career at court. One would be glad to accept the tradition, "Franciscane Fryer" and all, but the point has not quite been proved.[2] After all, we can only guess how and where Chaucer received the education which fitted him for his career as courtier and poet, for we have no certain knowledge about the years of his life, prior to his appearance in the retinue of the Countess of Ulster.

Doubtless he remained in attendance upon the countess in her peregrinations during 1357. The new clothes provided for him in April may have been purchased by way of preparation for his appearance at the court of King Edward, at Windsor, where the countess attended the celebration of the Feast of Saint George. According to the fragments of the household account-books, he re-

---

[2] The case for the tradition is ably argued by Manly, *op. cit.*, 7–18. Cf. E. Rickert: *Chaucer at School, in Modern Philology*, 29, 257–74.

ceived a gift of two shillings on May 20; and on December 20, he was given two shillings sixpence "for necessaries against the feast of the Nativity." After visits at Windsor, Woodstock, and Doncaster, the countess had returned, by December, to her principal place of residence, at Hatfield, in Yorkshire; and there, at the Christmas season, she entertained her brother-in-law, John of Gaunt, Earl of Richmond. This was probably the first meeting between Chaucer and the man who was later to be Duke of Lancaster and the most powerful noble in England. John of Gaunt has taken too prominent a place in some accounts of the poet's life. There is no certain evidence that Chaucer's fortunes depended chiefly on the duke's patronage, but the old tradition of a personal friendship between the two men is entirely credible. In all probability, their friendship began at Hatfield, in the Christmas season of 1357.

The fragments of the countess's account-books furnish no further information about Chaucer, and we lose sight of him until 1359. In that year, Edward III again invaded France. His army, marching in three great columns, moved out of Calais, on November 4, and began its leisurely advance upon Rheims. In the division commanded by the Black Prince was Lionel, Earl of Ulster, and Chaucer was undoubtedly in his train. From testimony which he himself gave, twenty-seven years later, in a famous heraldic suit, we know that he made the campaign of 1359, and that he was taken captive by the enemy. Probably this misadventure befell him while the English army was encamped around Rheims, between December 4 and January 11.

He was not left very long in the hands of the enemy. On March 1, 1360, the keeper of the wardrobe of the king's household recorded the payment of £16 toward the ransom of Geoffrey Chaucer.[3] On being released, Chaucer probably rejoined the army and took part in the futile demonstration against Paris. The expedition was accomplishing little or nothing, and King Edward was soon induced to accept a truce. A preliminary treaty was signed at Bretigny, near Chartres, on May 8, 1360, and Chaucer's first military campaign in France was over. We hear of him, later in the year, carrying letters into England at the command of the Earl of Ulster, who was in Calais during the negotiations for peace.[4]

We now lose sight of the poet until June 20, 1367. On that day, King Edward granted an annuity of twenty marks to his "beloved yeoman, Geoffrey Chaucer." There have been many conjectures as to how Chaucer was employed during this interval of nearly seven years, but none of them is based upon actual evidence. The most reasonable assumption is that he continued in the service of Prince Lionel during the greater part of this period, and that he entered the king's household not long before the annuity was granted him; but it is possible, as Professor Manly argues, that he devoted himself, during this interval, to legal studies in the Temple.

In the meantime, his father had died, his mother had speedily remarried, and Geoffrey himself had taken a wife. On September 12, 1366, an annuity of ten marks was granted by the king to a certain Philippa Chaucer, who is

[3] Life Rec. No. 34. The fact that within two days the king paid a slightly larger sum for the purchase of a horse has not, of course, escaped notice. By now, it has become a fairly venerable jest.

[4] The document on which this statement rests is quoted in fulll in an article by Samuel Moore in *Mod. Lang. Notes*, 27. 79–81.

described as one of the "domicellae" of the queen's chamber. That this lady was the poet's wife is put beyond question by the fact that payments under this grant were repeatedly made through his hands. There has been some romantic speculation about the early years of their intimacy, but the fact is that we know nothing whatsoever, either about their courtship or about their married life. Philippa Chaucer, according to the generally accepted theory, was the daughter of Sir Payne Roet, a knight of Hainaut and king of arms of Guienne in the reign of Edward III. He came to England in the train of Queen Philippa, who was a princess of Hainaut, and it is more than likely that his daughter was named after the queen.[5]

With the death of the queen, in 1369, Philippa Chaucer's services as demoiselle of the chamber were terminated; but she seems to have found employment, soon after, in the household of another member of the royal family. John of Gaunt had lost his first wife, the Duchess Blanche of Lancaster, in the year 1369; and two years later, he contracted a marriage with Constance, daughter of the late King Pedro of Castile and Leon, who brought him the shadowy title to a throne very securely occupied by a usurper. In August, 1372, he granted a pension of ten pounds a year to Philippa Chaucer, in recognition of her services to his second wife. Two years later, on June 13, 1374, he granted an annuity of ten pounds to Geoffrey Chaucer, for his good services, and also for the service which "our well-beloved Philippa, his wife, has rendered to our highly honored lady and mother, the queen . . .

[5] The records concerning Sir Payne Roet have been assembled by Professor Cook in his *Chaucerian Papers* in the *Trans. Conn. Academy of Arts and Sciences,* 23. 55–63. Cf. Manly: *Some New Light on Chaucer,* 49–56.

and to our very dear consort," Constance, Queen of Castile. Several entries in the registers of the Duchy of Lancaster, recording New Year's gifts to Philippa Chaucer, indicate that she continued to hold a position in the duke's household, in attendance upon Queen Constance.[6] Philippa's sister, Katharine Swynford, was the duke's mistress for many years and became his wife in 1396, four years after the death of his second duchess.

This marriage, which was something of a court scandal in its day, took place many years after the death of Philippa Chaucer. Payment of her annuity from the king was made for the last time on June 18, 1387, and it is believed that she died during the latter part of that year. The poet did not marry again. It is difficult to see how this fact, which is certainly capable of more than one interpretation, can be taken as evidence that he was not happy in his marriage with Philippa; and every other bit of evidence, which has been used to support such a theory, is equally unconvincing.

Whether Chaucer's marriage was founded upon love or upon more practical considerations, it is not to be denied that his alliance with the demoiselle of the queen's chamber marks the beginning of his advancement at court. From 1367 onward, we find him the recipient of favors which continued to bring him benefits, in varying degrees, until the year of his death. The nature of these favors will be considered more precisely below. For the present, it is sufficient to point out that they indicate a reasonably successful career at court. For a few years, to be sure, in the trying times at the end of the reign of Richard

[6] Life Rec. Nos. 71, 133, 142, 154. The first such gift is recorded in 1373, the last in 1382.

II, the position of a man dependent upon court favors was a precarious one, and there is evidence that Chaucer found himself in some financial difficulties at that time. During most of his life, however, he must have been in comfortable circumstances. He and his wife, during her lifetime, received payments from the royal exchequer and other sources averaging more than £40 a year; and during most of this time they were entitled to £20 more, each year, under the pensions given them by John of Gaunt. This takes no account of wages which we know to have been paid to Chaucer during special missions abroad, nor of wages and gifts of robes which probably came to him, during part of his married life, as esquire of the royal household. The average income of Chaucer and his wife, stated in terms of American money, at its present purchasing power, could not have been less than $7,500 a year. Between 1374 and 1387, if payments on the annuities from John of Gaunt were regularly made, their known income never fell below £60 a year, and it frequently rose so much higher that their average annual income, during this period, was more than £93, the equivalent, at a conservative estimate, of $12,000.[7]

After his wife's death, we find a very considerable curtailment in Chaucer's income. His wife's annuity, of course, was terminated; and in the year of her death, he disposed of his own pensions from the king, probably in order to realize a sum of ready money, which may or may not have been used for investment in income-bearing property. Even in these leaner years, however, he received payments from the exchequer averaging about £17 a year; and his annuity from John of Gaunt doubtless continued

[7] Manly (*Cant. Tales*, 65) reckons £1 equivalent to £30.

until the duke's death, in 1399. No man with an assured income of £27 a year would have been called destitute in the fourteenth century.

The emoluments that came to Geoffrey and Philippa Chaucer from their services to the royal family cannot be taken as evidence of extraordinary favor. The receipt of annuities was a usual circumstance in the career of an esquire of the king. It has been ascertained that pensions, varying in amounts from ten marks to £86, were awarded to nearly all the esquires whose names appear, with Chaucer's, in the household lists of 1368 and 1369. Positions in the customs, or other lucrative posts, fell to the lot of more than one of these associates of Chaucer; and several of them received grants of wine, such as those given by Edward III and Richard II to the poet. Another form of reward, and one which usually brought in fairly large sums, was the guardianship of a minor, whose lands were held under the king, with special fees upon the marriage of the ward. The largest single sum which Chaucer is known to have received, as a result of his services at court, came to him in this way.[8]

In return for these pecuniary favors, the royal esquires rendered services of many different kinds. The household books of other monarchs, which doubtless furnish an accurate picture of the routine at the court of Edward III or Richard II, show that the duties of the esquires included the making of beds, the setting of tables, and other menial offices; but it seems certain that not all the men who held these positions performed duties of the kind laid down in these books. Special functions, as steward or pur-

[8] For a full discussion of the poet's career at court, cf. J. R. Hulbert's valuable study, *Chaucer's Official Life.*

chaser, as usher of the king's chamber or keeper of his money, as custodian of the great horses or guardian of the royal jewels, are recorded on the Patent Rolls as duties assigned to some of the men who served with Geoffrey Chaucer. Much clerical work devolved upon the officers of the household. The king's business frequently took the esquire away from the court, on errands of sundry sorts, and sometimes carried him abroad, as the bearer of confidential messages or as a member of a special embassy to some foreign potentate. It will be seen that the services which Chaucer rendered, like the rewards which he received, were such as fell naturally to the lot of a man who had chosen a career at court.

Until 1369, there is no certain evidence that Chaucer performed other duties than those involved in the regular peace-time routine of the king's household. In that year, however, the truce with the French was broken, and an English army again invaded France. At the beginning of this fresh outbreak of hostilities, several men of the king's household, including Chaucer, received advances of money, which seem to indicate that they were among those whom the keeper of the king's wardrobe describes as "equitantibus de guerra in partibus Francie." If Chaucer made this expedition, he served under John of Gaunt. Letters of protection, granted July 17, 1368, indicate that Chaucer was about to leave for the continent, through the port of Dover, "ovesqz deux hackeneys vint solds por ses despenses et dis livres en eschange," presumably on the king's business. The considerable sum of money he carried with him suggests a long journey, but nothing is known of his destination.[9]

[9] Edith Rickert: *Modern Philology*, 25, 511, 512.

This may be the first of a series of diplomatic errands, which took Chaucer to the continent eight times during the next decade. In June, 1370, he was granted letters of protection till Michaelmas, as he was about to set forth to parts beyond the sea on business of the king. What this business was, we do not know; but we have proof that he was not long abroad, for it is recorded that he received the semiannual payment of his pension, apparently in person, on November 28.

In 1372, he visited the continent again, going on business of which we have more precise knowledge. This journey was a very important matter in the poet's literary career, for it carried him to Italy and brought him into contact with new forces at work in Italian literature. There has been a tradition that he met Petrarch in Padua, while on this journey, but the only foundation for the theory lies in the words spoken by the Clerk of Oxenford, in introducing his story of Griselda. A much more certain matter than the traditional meeting between the two poets is the very obvious influence which the contact with Italian literature had upon Chaucer's subsequent work. What Petrarch and Boccaccio were doing for the literature of their land, Chaucer was soon to do for English literature.

Needless to say, it was not in the interests of literature that Chaucer was sent to Italy by his royal master. Genoese trade was a matter of more importance to Edward III than the poetry of Petrarch and Boccaccio; and the commission which he sent to Italy, in 1372, went to treat with the duke, council, and citizens of Genoa, with a view to agreeing upon some English port, where Genoese merchants might form a commercial establishment. The three commissioners were appointed on November 12, and we learn from Chaucer's own account of his receipts and expenses for the journey that he set out from London on December 1, and did not return until May 23. His accounts also show us that he was detached from the commission to Genoa, for a few weeks, and journeyed to Florence, on some official business of which we know nothing.[10]

During the three years following this journey to Italy, the poet's fortunes mounted rapidly. It was in 1374, it will be remembered, that he was granted his annuity of £10 by John of Gaunt. In the same year, at the feast of Saint George, King Edward granted him a pitcher of wine, to be received daily, during his life, at the hands of the king's butler in the port of London. Professor Manly puts forward, as a "pleasant query," the speculation "that Chaucer's pitcher of wine, like so many similar grants in later years, may have been a reward for a poem, perhaps celebrating some theme appropriate to the feast." It must not be supposed, however, that this was a special form of royal favor, reserved exclusively for poets. Entries on the Patent Rolls show that daily and annual allowances of wine were bestowed upon others at the court from time to time. This gift, like the others which Chaucer received from the king, doubtless came to him as one of the occasional rewards which an esquire of the household might hope to receive. In all probability, the gift of wine was soon transmuted into an annual money payment. When the grant was confirmed by Richard II, on his ac-

[10] In all probability, he was sent to Florence to negotiate a loan with Florentine bankers. Cf. Cook, *Chaucerian Papers*, in the *Trans. Conn. Academy of Arts and Sciences*, 23. 39–44.

cession to the throne, it was definitely stated that Chaucer was to receive twenty marks a year, in lieu of the wine.

Chaucer was still, in 1374, an esquire of the king's household, but he was not obliged to reside at court. On May 10, he obtained rent-free a dwelling on the city wall, at Aldgate. New duties, shortly to be laid upon him, necessitated a residence in London. On June 8, 1374, he was appointed controller of the custom and subsidy on wools, hides, and wool-fells in the port of London. It was stipulated that he should reside at the port and discharge the duties pertaining to his office in person, writing his accounts "manu sua propria." Frequent absences on the king's business, during the years when he held this office, make it clear that these stipulations were not observed with entire strictness; but it seems certain that for the next twelve years, Chaucer had his residence in London, and that he was occupied, during most of the daylight hours, with duties connected with his office. References in *The Hous of Fame* to the sort of life he was leading, at the time the poem was written, indicate that he was kept all day by the river, over his "rekeninges." [11]

The controller of the customs was appointed as a check on the two collectors, and it was his duty to submit to the exchequer an independent account of transactions at the port. His salary was £10 a year, to be paid him by the collectors out of the receipts at the port; but there is some reason to believe that his earnings were augmented by fees. The office of collector, which carried a nominal salary of £20, was held by men of wealth and importance, like Nicholas Brembre, William Walworth, and John Philipot,—men who could lend the king 2,000 marks or fit

[11] *Hous of Fame*, 641-60.

out a fleet at their own expense. It is hardly credible that
these men would have spent time or energy upon duties
at the customs-house, if the profits from the office had
been limited to the comparatively small sum allowed them
as salary. Collectors and controller alike could certainly
expect to derive additional revenue in fees which do not
appear in their accounts with the exchequer. The only
special emoluments of Chaucer's office, which are entered
on the records, are the king's annual gift of ten marks,
made during his last six years in the office, and a particular grant, on July 12, 1376, of the price of some wool,
forfeited by a London merchant, who had exported it to
Dordrecht without paying custom.

This last gift was a large one, amounting to £71 4s. 6d.,
but it was not the most remunerative of the favors which
came to Chaucer during this period of especial prosperity.
On November 8, 1375, the king made him legal guardian
of young Edmund Staplegate, of Kent, whose father had
held his lands as tenant of the king in chief. A document
dated July 9, 1377, gives us the information that the
young man, before reaching his majority, had paid "Gef-
fray Chausyer" the sum of £104, for his wardship and
marriage-fee. On December 28, 1375, Chaucer was given
the custody of another minor, heir to the late John Solys,
who had held some rents in the county of Kent as sub-
tenant of the king. We have no means of knowing how
much money the poet derived from this second wardship.

Toward the end of 1376, Chaucer was associated with
Sir John de Burlee, Captain of Calais, in a journey on
business for the king; but we do not know where this
business took him, nor what it was. Sir John received £13

6s. 8d., and Chaucer exactly half as much, as wages for this special service.

On February 17, 1377, Chaucer set forth once more on the king's business, going this time to "Paris, Montreuil, and elsewhere," and remaining away from London until March 25. His associate on this journey was Sir Thomas Percy, later Earl of Worcester. Later in the Spring, he was in France again, remaining from April 30 until June 26. Froissart is authority for the statement that Chaucer was one of the envoys from the English court, sent to Montreuil in that year, to treat of peace between England and France and to arrange a marriage between Prince Richard, the heir apparent, and a French princess.[12] The poet's name does not appear on either of two commissions appointed by the king to conduct these negotiations; but his two journeys to the continent in 1377 coincide fairly closely with the two sets of conferences carried on by the royal commissioners in that year; and an entry on the Issue Roll, under date of March 6, 1381, makes it certain that his business, on each of his expeditions, had some connection with the negotiations between France and England. The negotiations failed to arrange a peace, perhaps because the French insisted on the dismantling of Calais; and all thoughts of establishing a peaceful alliance by a marriage between Richard and Princess Marie were ended by her death, which occurred during May, 1377. Possibly Dr. Braddy is right in believing that Chaucer has left us, in the *Parlement of Foules,* a literary monument to the uncompleted wooing in which he bore a hand.

[12] *Chroniques,* VIII, 226. Haldeen Braddy gives a full account of Chaucer's part in the negotiations. (*Three Chaucer Studies,* New York, 1932, II. 28-48.)

When Chaucer returned from the second of these journeys, on June 26, 1377, Edward III was dead, and Richard
II, as yet only ten years of age, sat upon the throne.
The new king, on the first day of his reign, renewed
Chaucer's appointment as controller of customs. Subsequently, he confirmed the poet's annuity of twenty marks
and granted him another twenty marks a year in lieu
of the daily pitcher of wine. Evidently, the change of
monarchs made little difference in Chaucer's fortunes. He
is still referred to as "our beloved esquire" in documents
issued by King Richard, and he seems to have held much
the same position under the new king as that which he
had held under Edward III. The accounts of the keeper
of the wardrobe in 1377 show that he was in that year
still receiving payments of forty shillings a year for his
robes, as "scutifer regis"; and some entries on the Pipe
Roll, belonging to the opening years of Richard's reign,
indicate that he was still entitled to wages within the king's
household. His name, however, does not appear in later
accounts of the royal household.

It is perhaps significant that the new regime speedily
availed itself of Chaucer's services for missions abroad.
In the fourth year of his reign, Richard made him a gift
of £22, stating that the sum was given him in recognition
of his services as envoy to Paris and Montreuil to treat
of peace with France, in the time of Edward III, and
again, in the reign of the present king, to discuss a marriage between Richard and the daughter of the French
king. This gives us definite information about the objects
of Chaucer's journeys abroad in 1377, and may also be
taken as evidence that he was attached in some capacity
to the commission appointed in January, 1378, to renew

the negotiations for peace and for the French marriage.

His next errand abroad grew out of the failure of these negotiations. While a fresh set of envoys in France was trying to arrange a satisfactory peace, Richard's government determined upon another effort at arms and fitted out an expedition to descend upon France. On the same day that some £4,000 were paid to John of Gaunt for his army serving in the wars, moneys were advanced to Sir Edward de Berkeley and Geoffrey Chaucer, sent into Lombardy to the Lord of Milan and to Sir John Hawkwood, the famous English adventurer, doubtless to seek their assistance in the English cause. We have no means of knowing the precise nature of the negotiations entrusted to Chaucer and Sir Edward, nor whether they met with any success. Readers of Chaucer's poetry will be less interested in the business which took him a second time to Italy than in the fact that he was brought once more into direct contact with Italian culture. It is also of interest that the very Lord of Milan, Bernabo Visconti, to whom he was sent as envoy, is one of the men selected by the Monk, in the *Canterbury Tales,* to illustrate the caprice of fortune.

This second Italian journey kept Chaucer away from London from May 28 until September 19, 1378. To the years immediately following his return, belong two documents, bearing upon Chaucer's affairs, which have no connection with his career at court. The first concerns a mysterious matter, which has puzzled the poet's biographers since its discovery. It is a deed, dated May 1, 1380, by which one Cecily Chaumpaigne, daughter of the late William Chaumpaigne and Agnes his wife, releases Geoffrey Chaucer, Esquire, of every sort of action "tam de raptu meo, tam de aliqua alia re vel causa." It is not likely that the word "raptu," as it is used in this singular document, refers to the perpetration of a rape. It would require a rather vicious imagination to conceive of Geoffrey Chaucer, controller of customs at the port of London and envoy extraordinary of the king, departing from an obviously even course of life to accomplish the ruin of this mysterious Cecily. It is far more probable that the action referred to was a civil abduction, such as that of the poet's father in 1324. It is even possible to infer, from the terms of the deed of release, that such an abduction was carried out with the lady's knowledge and consent, for the purpose of removing her from the custody of guardians who were not managing her affairs according to her desires. At any rate, it should hardly be necessary to attempt to clear the poet of the charge, sometimes brought against him on the evidence of this document, of the commission of a physical crime against Cecily Chaumpaigne.[13]

The other document belonging to this period and bearing upon Chaucer's personal affairs, is a release, given by him under date of June 19, 1381, of the house in the Vintry, formerly the property of his father. We do not know whether or not this property came to him on the death of John Chaucer, but it seems unlikely that it was available for his use in 1374, when he leased the house at Aldgate; for a residence in Thames Street in the Vintry would have been more convenient for the controller of customs than a dwelling so remote from the river as Ald-

---

[13] Skeat's suggestion that the "little son Lewis," for whom Chaucer wrote the *Treatise on the Astrolabe,* may have been the son of Cecily Chaumpaigne, has not been generally accepted.

gate. In any case, this is the only document which con-
nects Geoffrey Chaucer with the rather extensive property
held by his father and mother. Most of it, doubtless,
passed into the hands of John Chaucer's widow.

It is possible that Chaucer was led to relinquish the
house in the Vintry by events which he had just witnessed. This was the year of the Peasants' Revolt. Only
six days before this release was signed, the mob had been
raging in the streets of London, destroying not a little
property. Chaucer's business judgment may have told
him that tenements in London were not so stable a form
of wealth as they had seemed. One would like to know
whether such a thought was in his mind, and whether he
himself, in those terrible days, when the mob held possession of the city, was in any sort of peril. His connection
with John of Gaunt might have earned him the enmity
of men who made it their first business, on gaining en-
trance to the city, to burn the duke's palace, and who
slaughtered a Minorite friar, "ob iram scilicet et rancorem
quem in ducem gerebant Lancastriae . . . quia familiaris
ei fuisse dicebatur." [14] There is no way of knowing, however, how Chaucer was occupied while the mob was in
the city, nor what his thoughts may have been on that
tumultuous occasion. Only once, in his writings, does he
refer to the events of 1381, and that single reference is
part of the merry nonsense of the Nun's Priest's Tale. [15]

The Peasants' Revolt, to judge by such evidence as we
possess, did not interrupt the even course of Chaucer's
fortunes. On November 28, 1381, he received a special
reward of ten marks for diligence in his office as con-

[14] *Chron. Ang.*, ed. E. M. Thompson. 294.
[15] *Cant. Tales,* B 4584–86.

troller of customs; and in the Spring of the following year, he was appointed controller of the petty customs in the port of London. As he was allowed to appoint a deputy, it is likely that this second office in the customs was in the nature of a sinecure. The document recording his appointment to the post mentions the "customary wages," but what those wages were has not been discovered.

During the next year, the first custom-house of London was built, "upon the quay called the wool-wharf, in the Tower ward," and here Chaucer must have had an office. His labors at the wool-wharf, however, were by this time drawing to a close.[16a] In 1383 and 1384 he was granted permission to be absent from his office on two occasions for a month or more, to attend to affairs of his own, provided he appoint a sufficient deputy; and in February, 1385, on his own petition, he was given license to exercise his office thenceforward through a permanent deputy.

Chaucer's interests seem to have been turning away from London. On October 12, 1385, he was appointed one of the justices of the peace for Kent. It is generally agreed that he took up his residence in that county sometime during the year 1385. In August, 1386, he was elected knight of the shire for Kent, to attend parliament in October; and in that month, the house over Aldgate, which he had leased for the term of his life, was leased to another man. It is not very surprising to find his

16a In the Spring of 1388, Chaucer was threatened with arrest for a debt to John Churchman, collector of customs, possibly for an account left unsettled. Cf. E. Rickert, *Chaucer's Debt to John Churchman* in *Modern Philology*, 25. 121, 122.

two positions in the customs passing into the hands of other men in December, 1386. Explanations of this loss of office have been sought in the political quarrels of that stormy year. The absence of his patron, John of Gaunt, and the ascendancy of a rival party, under the Duke of Gloucester, may have had something to do with the termination of Chaucer's connection with the customs; but it is not absolutely necessary to believe that he was a victim, on this occasion, of political strife. After all, there is no proof that Chaucer was dismissed from office. It is at least possible that he resigned, without any compulsion, in order to assume duties of a more congenial nature, or because his fortunes were now sufficient to persuade him that he was entitled to a life of comparative leisure. Such an explanation finds support in the fact that he sought permission to appoint a deputy, and that such a privilege was granted him, more than a year before he vacated his office. The appointment of the permanent deputy marks the end of Chaucer's active interest in the customs, and it is probable that the loss of his positions as controller, whether it took place under political pressure or by voluntary act, represented no serious affliction. A large share of his income from the offices, during the last year in which he held them, must have gone to pay the wages of his deputies.

Speculations about the motives governing Chaucer in the conduct of his affairs are doubtless idle, but it is difficult not to connect the significant changes, which he made in his surroundings and in his way of life in these years, with the literary urge which must have been at work within him. Three of his most ambitious works had their inception between 1382 and 1387. The *Troilus and Criseyde* has now been dated, to the satisfaction of most scholars, between 1382 and 1385; the *Legend of Good Women* was probably undertaken in 1385 or 1386; and it has long been agreed that the *Canterbury Tales* were begun as early as 1387. The most significant passages in the history of Chaucer's genius belong to this fifth decade of his life. New ideas and new forms of expression were shaping themselves in his mind with astonishing fertility; new material had found its way into his hands,—much of it, doubtless, on his second visit to Italy in 1378. As he turned this material over in his mind, and as he began the actual labor of composition, he must have found that his duties at the wool-quay grew more and more irksome, and that his residence at Aldgate was not the most suitable place in the world for the writing of poetry which was to follow, however humbly, in the footsteps of Vergil, Ovid, Homer, Lucan, and Statius. With the facts of Chaucer's public career before us, students of his life and works cannot ignore his connection with the world of affairs; but it is possible that too many Chaucerian studies have had both their beginning and their end in considerations of the public events of the fourteenth century, with too little thought for the special circumstance that our study happens to be of a poet. It is rather strange, at least, that reasons for the severance of Chaucer's connection with the customs have been sought more often in the political events of 1386 than in the established facts of Chaucer's career as a poet.

Whether Chaucer shaped his circumstances to answer the demands which his genius laid upon him, or was forced into involuntary retirement by adverse political fortunes, his situation was now more favorable for literary work than it had been for many years. Release from routine duties was accompanied by residence in the country. As justice of the peace, he occupied a position of dignity and importance; yet the duties of the office could not have been particularly arduous. His income was probably sufficient for his needs. We know that in 1385 he and his wife received at least fifty-four pounds, in 1386 fifty pounds, and in 1387 thirty-four pounds, over and above the twenty pounds a year from John of Gaunt. Even if we were certain that he was dismissed from his offices at the customs, we could hardly say that he had fallen upon evil fortunes.

After 1387, however, his situation was materially altered. It was in that year that his wife's annuity was paid for the last time. Probably the sudden alteration in his circumstances, caused by her death, accounts for the fact that he requested the king, in the following year, to transfer his annuity to other hands. The sale of a royal annuity for a sum of ready money was not an unprecedented thing, and Chaucer may have found that this was the only way by which he could meet regular expenses which he had assumed. To realize a large sum on his annuity would carry him along, in the way of life which he had been maintaining, until fresh favors could be obtained.

He had little more than a year to wait before such favors came his way. His annuity was transferred to a certain John Scalby on May 1, 1388. On July 12, 1389, he was appointed clerk of the king's works at Westminster, the Tower of London, the castle of Berkhampstead, and the manors of Kennington, Eltham, Clarendon, Shene, Byfleet, Chiltern Langley, and Feckenham, with the park-

lodges in some of these manors, the park-lodge of Hathe-
bergh in the New Forest, and the king's mews for falcons
near Charryngcrouch (Charing Cross). This was a fairly
remunerative position, carrying a salary of two shillings
a day, or the equivalent of about $5,000 a year.

On the other hand, it was not exactly a sinecure. During
his two years in office, the operations under his direction
called for an expenditure of £1,130, which would amount
to at least $150,000 to-day. Chaucer was instructed, under
the terms of his appointment, to impress workmen of every
sort, to purvey materials and carriage, to pursue and arrest
absconding laborers, to arrest "contrary or rebellious"
persons, to conduct inquisitions in cases of theft of material purchased for the works, and to sell the branches
and bark of trees felled for timber. To be sure, he was
not required to attend to all these matters in person; but
even with a deputy superintending the actual labor, the
general responsibility was upon his shoulders, and much
of the detail, as well, must have required his attention.
The position called for a display of practical ability, and
it must have absorbed much of Chaucer's energies, to the
exclusion of literary work.

Other duties, of kindred nature, were laid upon him,
to encroach yet farther upon his leisure. On March 12,
1390, he was made one of a commission to survey the
walls, ditches, sewers, and bridges, along the banks of the
Thames, between Greenwich and Woolwich, to inquire
by whose default they had been suffered to decay, and to
take steps for their repair. In May, 1390, it was part of
his duties, as clerk of the works, to erect scaffolds for
the king and queen at the jousts in Smithfield; and in
July of the same year, he was appointed to repair Saint

George's Chapel, Windsor, with power to take workmen for that purpose, except in Church lands, during a term of three years.

The official records give us many glimpses of Chaucer during his two years as clerk of the works. We hear of his buying materials for the works at the Tower, at Windsor, on the wool-quay, and elsewhere; we find him drawing on the exchequer for the cost of materials and for the wages of his subordinates; and, on one occasion, we hear of his personally advancing £66,—a sum which was not repaid until more than two years later. The sums which he drew were sometimes paid through his agents, but at other times, he received them with his own hands; and it is certain that he was frequently obliged to carry money about the country in fairly large amounts. This was not an altogether wholesome occupation in the late fourteenth century, as the poet learned to his sorrow. Within four days, during September, 1390, he was held up three times on the highway by gangs of robbers; once, at a place called the Fowl Oak, in Kent; once, at Hatcham; and a third time, near Westminster. In the encounter at the Fowl Oak, he was relieved of £20 of the king's money, but he was officially discharged from repayment of this sum. On that occasion, however, he also lost his horse and "autres moebles"; and in the other robberies, the "notable rogues" deprived him of sums aggregating nearly £20.[16]

This sort of thing was rather expensive, both for the king and for his clerk of the works; and it may well be that one or the other felt that the risks of the position

[16] Life Rec. Nos. 225, 231, 232, 234, 235. Cf. E. P. Kuhl: *Chaucer and the "Fowle Ok,"* in *Mod. Lang. Notes,* 36. 157–59.

were greater than a man of Chaucer's advancing years should be asked to bear. At any rate, the clerkship of the works passed out of Chaucer's hands on June 17, 1391. On that day, he presented his accounts, covering his 706 days in office, and made inventory of the "dead stock," including "bolles, trayes, ladels, rammes, scaffoldhirdles, fryingpannes, aundyrnes . . . i ymaginem eris, ii ymagines lapideas non depictas, vii ymagines factas ad similitudinem Regum," and a long list of other articles, which gives us some notion of the complexity of the operations which had been Chaucer's responsibility for nearly two years. Doubtless it is to the poet's credit that he was gifted with enough practical ability to serve the king in this office, as in others that he held; but it may be permitted us to regret the time and energy which must have run to waste over glass and lead and statues of kings, while the *Canterbury Tales* remained a group of unfinished fragments.

An appointment which came to Chaucer before June 22, 1391, as sub-forester of the king's park in North Petherton, Somersetshire, may have been the reason for his relinquishing the clerkship of the works.[17] The duties of this new position were probably far less burdensome than those he had been carrying as clerk of the works, and the office must have brought with it a comfortable stipend, though we have no means of knowing how large it was. The poet was still entitled to £10 a year under his pension from John of Gaunt, and delayed payments of sums still due him, as clerk of the works, brought him some ninety pounds during 1392 and 1393. At the beginning of 1393, moreover, the king made him a gift of ten pounds, as a

[17] He was made sole deputy forester of the park in 1397 or 1398.

reward for his good services; and on February 28, 1394, a new annuity of twenty pounds was granted him.

Good fortune, it would seem, had not deserted him. Nevertheless, there is some evidence that his way was not altogether smooth during the last decade of his life. It has recently been discovered that in July, 1392, he borrowed the sum of 26s. 8d. from a London merchant named Gilbert Maghfeld (or Maufeld); [18] and more than once, during the next few years, he borrowed small sums from the exchequer against his annuity. In April, 1398, moreover, a certain Isabella Buckholt, widow and administratrix of Walter Buckholt, brought action against him in the Common Pleas, for a debt of £14 1s. 11d. Chaucer promptly took out letters of protection from the king, on the ground that he was under royal appointment to attend to many urgent affairs in divers parts of the realm. Miss Rickert has shown that Buckholt had held a subordinate post under Chaucer as Clerk of the Works, and the suit may well have arisen out of some closed account for services which the man's widow was disposed to reopen.

This action for debt and his repeated borrowings from the exchequer have been made the basis for a tradition that the poet was in serious financial difficulties in the latter years of his life. It is possible, however, that too much has been made of this rather inadequate evidence of financial distress. If Chaucer was in difficulties, his troubles were not so grave as those of the royal exchequer; and a prudent man might well decide, at such a time, that it was a wise course to borrow ahead on an annuity, in order to make sure of receiving at least a part of the sums to

[18] Professors Manly and Rickert published this discovery in a letter to the *London Times Literary Supplement*, August 19, 1926.

which he was entitled.[19] It is evident enough that he was having difficulty in collecting his income, and he may have found it hard to adjust his expenditures to the uncertainties of his financial situation; but there is no reason for believing that he was in a state even remotely bordering upon destitution.

He was prepared, certainly, to meet his situation by availing himself of the favor of the king. In the Spring of 1398, he had found immunity against an action of debt, by securing royal letters of protection. In October of the same year, he sought an increase in his resources by petitioning King Richard, "for God's sake and as an act of charity," to grant him a butt of wine, to be given him yearly by the king's butler. Such petitions for royal favor were not unusual, and the language in which this one was couched was merely the conventional phraseology and should not be taken as evidence of extreme distress. All the evidence, indeed, bearing upon Chaucer's financial situation during the latter years of Richard's reign, shows us a man who was not likely to fall into acute poverty. He was always capable of acting promptly to relieve his own necessity, and his favor at court was still strong enough to render the measures which he took quite efficacious.

The butt of wine, which the king granted immediately on Chaucer's petition, was the last of Richard's gifts to his "beloved esquire." In the following year, Henry IV, son of John of Gaunt, usurped the throne. The new monarch was not likely to neglect the poet, who had been

[19] The exchequer was frequently in arrears in the payment of sums due Chaucer under his annuities. Cf. Life Rec. Nos. 251, 255, 257, 259, 263, 272.

his father's friend, and Chaucer took prompt steps to make sure that he did not. The *Compleint to his Purse,* with its graceful envoy, obviously addressed to Henry of Bolingbroke, met with a satisfactory response. On October 13, 1399, within two weeks of his accession to the throne, the new king granted Chaucer an annuity of forty marks, and confirmed the pension of twenty pounds a year given him by Richard II. Five days later, Richard's pension and the annual gift of a butt of wine were definitely confirmed by letters patent; for the original letters from the deposed king "casualiter sunt amisse." This accident was probably not a piece of carelessness, such as practical men like to discover in poets. The veteran courtier, who had learned caution in these late years of political uncertainty, probably felt that it would do no harm to have new letters, under the seal of the present king.

With his fortunes once more on a firm basis, Chaucer made another change of residence. In December, 1399, he took a lease for fifty-three years on a dwelling in the garden of Saint Mary's Chapel, Westminster Abbey. In this house, Chaucer spent the last months of his life. We know of no further duties that were laid upon him; and if his pensions were not yet paid with entire regularity, the letters patent from the new king, guaranteeing him a comfortable income, must have given him security against financial worry. On June 5, 1400, he received payment from the royal exchequer for the last time. He died, according to the inscription formerly legible upon his tomb, on October 25, and was buried in Westminster Abbey. The Poets' Corner of the abbey has grown up around his grave.

In the next generation, wealth and distinction came to one Thomas Chaucer, traditionally regarded as Geoffrey's son. Only one person [1] who lived during the lifetime of Thomas Chaucer has left us any statement connecting the two men as father and son, and their relationship is asserted in only one legal document that has yet been discovered; [2] but Thomas Chaucer is known to have used Geoffrey's seal, and on his tomb are the arms of Roet, Phillipa Chaucer's family. Such evidence as we have seems to confirm the tradition that Thomas was the poet's son. [3]

Almost nothing is known of "litel Lowis my sone," to whom the *Treatise on the Astrolabe* is dedicated. A document in the Public Record Office shows that he was one of four squires, including Thomas Chaucer, in the garrison of the castle of Carmarthen during the Welsh campaign of 1403. [4] Possibly he met his death in that campaign.

Thomas Chaucer's grandson, John de la Pole, Duke of Suffolk, married Elizabeth Plantagenet, sister to Edward IV, and their son, the Earl of Lincoln, was declared heir apparent by Richard III. With the death of the earl at the battle of Stoke, in 1487, the line became extinct.

[1] Thomas Gascoigne, Chancellor of Oxford University, 1434, 1444. Cf. *Athenaeum* 1888, I. 404, 405.

[2] Cf. J. M. Manly, "Thomas Chaucer, son of Geoffrey," *Times Literary Supplement,* London, August 3, 1933.

[3] See Dr. M. B. Ruud's valuable study, *Thomas Chaucer,* Minneapolis, 1926. Russell Krauss (*Three Chaucer Studies,* New York, 1937, pp. 7–169) supports an earlier conjecture that Thomas was the illegitimate son of John of Gaunt by Phillipa Chaucer.

[4] Cf. J. M. Manly, "Litel Lowis My Sone," *Times Literary Supplement,* London, June 7, 1925; and West Wales Hist., IV, 4, ff.

CHAPTER III

THE LESSER WORKS

"THE ROMAUNT OF THE ROSE"

(Extant in but one manuscript)

Authenticity: Only a part of the translation is now attributed
    to Chaucer.
Date: Early.
Source: *Le Roman de la Rose,* by Guillaume de Lorris and
    Jean de Meun.
Metrical Form: Octosyllabics, the metrical form of the French
    original.

IN the Prologue to the *Legend of Good Women* (F
text, 328-31), the God of Love takes Chaucer to task
for certain of his literary labors:

> "For in pleyn text, with-outen nede of glose,
> Thou hast translated the Romaunce of the Rose,
> That is an heresye ageyns my lawe,
> And makest wyse folk fro me withdrawe."

It was a curious accident of literary history that made the
Roman de la Rose a heresy against the law of Cupid. The
poem was begun, about 1225, by one Guillaume de Lorris,
a poet obviously trained in the traditions of courtly love

and far too conventional to give utterance to any sort of heresy. It was apparently his purpose to set forth, under the veil of allegory, the varying fortunes of a lover throughout the course of his wooing. The choice of a subject, the setting of the poem, the treatment of the allegorical figures, and the whole course of the narrative, as well as the specific directions which the God of Love gives to his prisoner, show that Guillaume de Lorris embraced the traditional ideas of courtly love and had no intention of saying anything in the least degree heterodox.

Guillaume's work, however, was never carried to completion. Whether it was broken off by death or by some other cause, we do not know; for we have no knowledge about the man himself, beyond the bare fact that he lived and wrote in the early part of the thirteenth century. He had written 4,058 verses of his *Roman de la Rose* when he laid down his pen. Some fifty years later, about 1275, another poet took up the work and brought it to a conclusion, adding more than 18,000 lines to those which Guillaume had written. This second poet, Jean de Meun, surnamed Le Chopinel or Le Clopinel, might well be styled a heretic against the laws of love. He was a man of a rationalistic and satiric turn of mind, and his continuation of the *Roman* was carried on in a very different spirit from that which had animated Guillaume de Lorris. A clear, cool rationalism takes the place of the idealism which we encounter in the early part of the *Roman;* and the figure of "Reason," who fills but a minor rôle in Guillaume's allegory and whose counsels have but little effect upon the ardent lover, becomes a dominant character in Jean's portion of the poem. The lover's quest is followed to the end, to be sure, but the action is retarded by long digressions, which are enlivened, in no small measure, by satirical passages directed against women and exposing the folly of love. A jealous husband, a sensual old woman, and a hypocritical churchman bring a discordant note of realism into the dream-garden of Guillaume de Lorris; and the young dreamer, who felt the first pangs of love beside the well of Narcissus and sat attentive at the feet of Cupid, is lost in the more versatile nature of the keen thinker, who speculates shrewdly on all manner of subjects, from the source of true gentility to the duplicity of women in seeking artificial aids for their beauty.

Jean de Meun and Guillaume de Lorris were both genuine poets, each in his own way; and the work which they had fathered so strangely between them enjoyed a well-deserved popularity. The high quality of the poetry was enough to have won many readers for the *Roman de la Rose,* but the accident of double authorship made it more certain that the poem would have a wide circulation in the thirteenth and fourteenth centuries. Reflecting, in the work of Guillaume, the idealism of the age that was passing, and foreshadowing, in the work of Jean, the rationalistic spirit of the age that was to come, it became the most influential poem that had been written in thirteenth-century France. All classes of readers, whether their sympathies were caught by the one poet or by the other, were sure to find something to their taste in the *Roman;* and the bold heresies and fearless witticisms of Jean de Meun were the more striking because they were set off against the work of Guillaume de Lorris, just as the radiant beauty of Guillaume's portion of the poem shone the brighter because it was followed by work which made a very different sort of appeal. The influence of the *Roman* can be traced in virtually every writer of any pretense to learning in the fourteenth century, and the poem must have stimulated thought among a host of other readers who have left no writings behind them. Nearly two hundred manuscripts of the poem have survived, to testify to the popularity which it enjoyed, not only in France but in other countries as well.

The fragmentary translation of the *Roman* into Middle English, which is now printed among Chaucer's works, exists in a single manuscript, preserved in the Hunterian Museum at Glasgow. It was first attributed to Chaucer by Thynne, who included it in his edition of the Works published in 1532, printing it from a manuscript which has not since been recovered; and it has held its place in all subsequent complete editions of the poet. As early as 1868, however, Bradshaw rejected the *Romaunce of the Rose* from the canon, largely on the ground of the inferior quality of its rimes.[1] In 1870, the problem of authorship was raised again, with a fresh complication, by Child, who suggested that the translation might be the work of more than one author, and gave it as his opinion that the part after the break at line 5810 (where more than 5,000 lines of the French original are omitted) was better than the middle portion. He indicated that he was very far from believing that any portion of the translation was Chaucer's.[2]

For a score of years, subsequent to the publication of Child's letter on the subject, scholarship inclined to reject

[1] Furnivall: *Temporary Preface,* 107, 108. Cf. G. W. Prothero: *Memoir of Henry Bradshaw,* 353.
[2] *Athenæum,* 1870, II. 721.

the poem from the canon.[3] In an essay printed in his third edition of the *Prioresses Tale* (1880), Skeat argued against Chaucer's authorship of the translation on the ground that it contained imperfect rimes, of a sort not found in the accepted works, as well as dialectic peculiarities suggesting a northern origin.[4] He was led to modify his position, some years later, by the researches of Lindner, who followed up the suggestion made by Child and demonstrated that the portion of the poem now called Fragment C was certainly not written by the same hand as that which wrote the portion immediately preceding it.[5] Influenced by the studies of Lindner, coming upon his own, Skeat was now ready to admit that Chaucer might have written the latter part of the translation.[6]

In the years that immediately followed, very important light was thrown upon the problem by the German scholar, Professor Kaluza, who showed that the work consists not of two fragments, but of three, with the first break occurring after line 1705. In his book upon the subject, *Chaucer und der Rosenroman* (Berlin, 1893), Professor Kaluza printed the results of his study of the Glasgow translation, in close comparison with the French original, and gave it as his opinion that both Fragment A and Fragment C might well be Chaucer's. His conclusions were not accepted by all Chaucerians. Lounsbury still argued for Chaucer's

[3] In an article published in 1886 (*Englische Studien*, 9. 161–67), Fick endeavored to prove that the entire translation was Chaucer's.

[4] The essay is reprinted in the Chaucer Society's volume, *Essays on Chaucer*, 439–51.

[5] *Englische Studien*, 11. 163–73 (1888). Lindner argued that the first 5810 lines were Chaucer's.

[6] Introduction to *Chaucer's Minor Poems*, first ed., 1888, xxiv, xxv.

authorship of the entire translation; Skeat admitted only Fragment A to the canon; and Professor Koch denied Chaucer's authorship of any of the poem. It is now generally agreed that Fragment A is certainly Chaucer's work, and many scholars accept Fragment C as well. It has been many years since anyone believed that Fragment B was from his pen.

It is not likely that many scholars will accept the following novel solution of the problem, recently put forward by Dr. Brusendorff: "The bibliographical facts about the *Romance of the Rose* would . . . appear to be as follows: originally composed in the Standard English of the late fourteenth century, it has only been preserved in a version, written down in the beginning of the fifteenth century by some person from the North Midlands, who had once learned the translation by heart, and who still knew its first 1800 lines or so almost perfectly; during the next 4000 lines, however, his memory constantly kept failing him, so that at last he had to break off abruptly and start again at an episode which occurred nearly 6000 lines further on in the translation, but which he remembered better, until after some 1900 lines he had to break off finally, still almost 10,000 lines from the end." [7]

In all probability, the translation of the *Roman de la Rose* which the God of Love attributed to Chaucer in the Prologue to the *Legend of Good Women* never was completed. Nothing was more characteristic of the poet than to project vast works which he did not bring to completion, and it is extremely unlikely that he went through with the long task of translating the entire French poem. It is

[7] Aage Brusendorff: *The Chaucer Tradition,* 382. Chapter V of Dr. Brusendorff's book is entitled *The Romance of the Rose.*

the writer's opinion that only Fragment A can certainly be attributed to his workmanship, and it seems entirely natural to suppose that his work upon the translation terminated before he had completed 1800 lines.

Though Chaucer probably never finished his projected translation, it is evident that he had studied the French poem from beginning to end, and its influence upon his work can hardly be exaggerated. Literally hundreds of lines from the *Roman* appear in his own poetry, either in close translation or in paraphrase, and there is not one of his more significant works which does not bear the stamp of the influence of Guillaume de Lorris or Jean de Meun. He must have made the acquaintance of the *Roman* at an early age, when his mind was susceptible to impression and eager for suggestion. The very books which he read were those which the two French poets had read before him, and it is probable that the course of his reading was determined by suggestions which he found in the pages of the *Roman de la Rose*. The mediæval *clarté*, which French critics find in the highest degree in the work of Guillaume de Lorris, reveals its influence upon Chaucer's style throughout his whole career; and the satirical spirit of Jean de Meun contributed much to his most distinctive works. It may very well have been an early reading of the *Roman de la Rose* that first directed Chaucer's genius into the paths of poetry.[8]

The relation which the Middle English translation bears to the French *Roman* (ed. Langlois) is shown by the following table:

[8] The influence of the French poem upon Chaucer's works is fully discussed in D. S. Fansler's *Chaucer and the Roman de la Rose*.

Fragment A 1–1705   French text, 1–1670   Guillaume
Fragment B 1706–4432 French text 1671–4058   Guillaume
         4433–5810 French text 4059–5154   Jean
Fragment C 5811–7696 French text 10681–12360 Jean

An excellent translation of the entire French poem into modern English verse, by F. R. Ellis, included in the Temple Classics, has recently been reissued.

"AN A. B. C."

(Thirteen Ms. copies extant)

Authenticity: Attributed to Chaucer by Lydgate and in four manuscripts, one by Shirley.
Date: Before 1370 (?).
Source: Guillaume de Deguilleville: *Pèlerinage de l'Ame.*
Metrical form: Eight-line stanza, riming *ababbcbc.*

Speght's 1602 Chaucer prefaces this poem with the following heading:

Chaucer's ABC, called *La Priere de Nostre Dame:* made, as some say, at the Request of Blanch, Duchesse of Lancaster, as a praier for her priuate vse, being a woman in her religion very deuout.

Setting aside this very dubious statement, which Skeat characterized as "probably a mere guess," we have no external evidence for dating the poem. It has usually been regarded as an early work, and Skeat hazarded a conjecture that it was Chaucer's "earliest extant complete poem." Professor Koch, on the other hand, is inclined to place the poem at the beginning of Chaucer's "second period," because of the use of the ten-syllable line and the freedom with which the original has been translated.[9]

The *A. B. C.* is an adaptation of a prayer to the Blessed Virgin included in a long French poem, written by a Cistercian monk in the royal abbey of Chalis, Guillaume de Deguilleville, and entitled *Le Pèlerinage de l'Ame* (1330 or 1331). The first part of the work, in which the prayer is interpolated, is called *Le Pèlerinage de la Vie humaine.* The French text of the prayer is included in *The Oxford Chaucer* (1. 60, 261–271), and is printed in the Chaucer Society's One-Text Print of the Minor Poems.

Chaucer's adaptation of his original is decidedly free. Deguilleville wrote in octosyllabics, using a stanza of twelve lines built on two rimes, and Chaucer's change in the metrical form naturally made for freedom of treatment. In general, it may be said that each of his stanzas is an elaboration of a suggestion or two drawn from the French poem, with a few lines, usually at the beginning of the stanza, based rather more closely upon the original. His procedure is well illustrated in the stanza beginning

> Noble princesse, that never haddest pere,

which is based upon the following lines in the French original:

> Noble princesse du monde
> Qui n'as ne per ne seconde
> En royaume n'en enpire,
> De toy vient, de toy redonde
> Tout le bien qui nous abonde,

[9] *Anglia,* 3. 182, 183.

N'avons autre tirelire.
En toy tout povre homme espire
Et de toy son salu tire,
Et en toy seule se fonde.
Ne puet nul penser ne dire,
Nul pourtraire ne escrire
Ta bonté comme est parfonde.

One of the two extant English translations of the *Pèlerinage de la Vie humaine* is attributed to Lydgate. The manuscript in which it is contained leaves a blank for the insertion of Chaucer's translation of the prayer to the Virgin, which Lydgate introduces with these lines:

And touchynge the translacioun
Off thys noble Orysoun,
Whylom (yiff I shal nat feyne)
The noble poete off Breteyne,
My mayster Chaucer, in hys tyme,
Affter the Ffrenche he dyde yt ryme,
Word by word, as in substaunce,
Ryght as yt ys ymad in Fraunce,
Fful devoutly, in sentence,
In worshepe, and in reuerence
Off that noble hevenly quene,
Bothe moder and a maydë clene.

Five manuscripts of the other translation of the *Pèlerinage* include Chaucer's *A. B. C.* at the proper point.

The stanza form used in this poem appears again in *The Former Age, Lenvoy to Bukton,* and the *Monkes Tale.* It is also used, with repeated rimes, in *Fortune* and the *Balade to Rosemounde.*

"COMPLEYNT UNTO PITE"

(Nine Ms. copies extant)

Authenticity: Attributed to Chaucer by Shirley.
Date: 1367–70?
Source: None has been discovered.
Metrical form: Rime-royal, a seven-line stanza riming ababbcc.

The *Compleynt unto Pite* cannot be dated with any certainty, but it may confidently be assigned to the earlier years of Chaucer's career as a poet. Furnivall believed that the poem was "the earliest original work of Chaucer." [10]

No source for the poem has been discovered, although Skeat believed that it would not be surprising "if a French poem of a similar character should one day be found." In view of the almost universal practice of personification, among mediæval poets, it is hardly necessary to seek any source for the central idea of the poem, and few will care to accept Skeat's opinion that the idea of personifying Pity came to Chaucer from Statius: *Thebaid* XI. 458–96. As Professor Lowes has pointed out, the "whole content of the Compleynte is leagues away from the grim and savage struggle in the *Thebaid*." [11]

It is probably unnecessary to warn the reader against accepting the *Compleynt unto Pite* as evidence that the poet had experienced unrequited love. Scholars are now agreed that Chaucer's references to the pangs of hopeless

[10] *Trial Forewords*, 31.
[11] *Modern Philology*, 14. 723. I am not able to follow Professor Lowes in finding in Chaucer's puzzling phrase, "Herenus quene," the "first of his responses to the influence of Dante."

love, in this poem and elsewhere, are conventional rather than autobiographical.[12]

The seven-line stanza, in which the *Compleynt* is written, was one of Chaucer's favorite metrical forms. So far as we know, this represents its earliest use in English poetry.

"THE BOOK OF THE DUCHESSE"

(Three Ms. copies extant)

Authenticity: Mentioned in the Prologue to *The Legend of Good Women* and in the Prologue to the Man of Law's Tale. Attributed to Chaucer by Lydgate: *Prologue to the Falls of Princes.*

Date: 1369–70.

Sources: Part of the Proem based on Ovid: *Metamorphoses* (XI. 410–748), and on Guillaume de Machaut: *Dit de la Fontaine Amoreuse* (542–698). Many details from other sources.

Metrical form: Octosyllabics.

The Book of the Duchesse is the earliest of Chaucer's works to which a date can be assigned with any certainty. It was written as an elegy upon the death of Blanche, Duchess of Lancaster, who died September 12, 1369, and it was probably completed within a few months after her death.[13] Her husband, John of Gaunt, remarried in 1372.

---

[12] The autobiographical interpretation of the poem is presented by Furnivall: *Trial Forewords,* 35, ff. It is contested by Lounsbury: *Studies,* I. 221, ff., and by Sypherd in *Mod. Lang. Notes, 20.* 240–43.

[13] The reader should not overlook the covert allusions to the name of Blanche in line 948, and to the titles of John of Gaunt, Earl of Richmond and Duke of Lancaster, in lines 1318, 1319.

The story of Ceyx and Alcyone is told by Ovid and by Guillaume de Machaut, in the passages indicated above. It has been demonstrated that Chaucer was familiar with both these versions of the story, but it is clear that Ovid was his principal source for this part of his poem. The reader may be interested in comparing Chaucer's description of the House of Sleep with Dryden's translation of the Latin original, which is given below:

Near the Cimmerians, in his dark abode,
Deep in a cavern dwells the drowsy god,
Whose gloomy mansion nor the rising sun,
Nor setting, visits, nor the lightsome noon;
But lazy vapours round the region fly,
Perpetual twilight, and a doubtful sky;
No crowing cock does there his wings display,
Nor with his horny bill provoke the day,
Nor watchful dogs, nor the more wakeful geese,
Disturb with nightly noise the sacred peace,
Nor beasts of nature, nor the tame are nigh,
Nor trees with tempests rock'd, nor human cry,
But safe repose, without an air of breath,
Dwells here, and a dumb quiet next to death.
   An arm of Lethe, with a gentle flow
Arising upward from the rock below,
The palace moats, and o'er the pebbles creeps,
And with soft murmurs calls the coming sleeps.
Around its entry nodding poppies grow,
And all cool simples that sweet rest bestow;
Night from the plants their sleepy virtue drains,
And, passing, sheds it on the silent plains.
No door there was, the unguarded house to keep,
On creaking hinges turn'd, to break his sleep.
   But in the gloomy court was raised a bed,

Stuff'd with black plumes, and on an ebon 'sted;
Black was the covering too, where lay the god,
And slept supine, his limbs display'd abroad;
About his head fantastic visions fly,
Which various images of things supply,
And mock their forms, the leaves on trees not more,
Nor bearded ears in fields, nor sands upon the shore.

Many passages borrowed from the works of Guillaume
de Machaut have been pointed out in the body of the
poem. Professor Kittredge has shown that Chaucer has
drawn especially upon the *Jugement du Roy de Behaingne*
and used the *Remede de Fortune,* the *Dit du Vergier,* and
several of Machaut's minor works. The description of the
hunt and of the walk through the forest, in fact, furnish
the only extensive portion of the *Book of the Duchesse*
which does not betray close imitation of Machaut or of
some other French poet.[14] The opening lines of the Proem
bear a resemblance to some lines in Froissart's *Paradys
d'Amour* and may well have been derived from that source,
since "Eclympasteyre, that was the god of slepes heyre,"
certainly reached Chaucer through Froissart's poem.[15] The
machinery of the elegy—the dream, the ideal landscape,
the singing birds, the veiled hint that the author himself is
languishing in hopeless love—indicates clearly that Chaucer
was at the time very much under the influence of the

[14] *Publ. Mod. Lang. Assn.,* 30. 1–24. Professor Kittredge's
study supersedes the work of Sandras (*Étude sur G. Chaucer,*
89–95).

[15] We do not know where Froissart found his "Enclimpostair."
The priority of Froissart's poem to Chaucer's has been put beyond
question by Professor Kittredge, in an article published in *Englische Studien,* 26. 321–36.

French poetry of courtly love, and it is not surprising to find in the poem so many verbal echoes from Froissart and Guillaume de Machaut. Even less surprising are the many borrowings from the *Roman de la Rose,* which exerted an influence upon nearly everything that Chaucer wrote.

None of these works, of course, may be regarded as the "source" of the *Book of the Duchesse.* The structure of the poem as a whole was probably original with Chaucer. It has been suggested that even here he was indebted to a French poem of the school of courtly love, an anonymous work of the fourteenth century entitled *Le Songe Vert;* but the similarity in structure between the two poems seems to be due rather to the conventions of the type, in which both poets were writing, than to direct borrowing.[16]

Professor Lowes's discovery of the "drye see" and of "the Carrenare" (lines 1028, 1029) is not of the first importance, but the work has been done so vivaciously and with so much of the true scholar's zeal that his article should certainly not pass without comment. It is to be found in *Modern Philology,* 3. 1–46.

The Man of Law, in the *Canterbury Tales,* says of Chaucer that

"In youthe he made of Ceys and Alcion."

It may be that this line merely presents an alternative title for *The Book of the Duchesse,* but it has been taken as evidence that the portion of the poem which tells the story

---

[16] Cf. W. Owen Sypherd: *Le Songe Vert and Chaucer's Dream Poems,* in *Mod. Lang. Notes,* 24. 46–47.

of Ceyx and Alcyone was written as an independent work and was later incorporated in the elegy upon the death of the Duchess Blanche.

The octosyllabic verse, in which the poem is written, had been in use in England for a full century. Such well known poems as *Havelok the Dane* (1270–1280), Robert Mannyng's *Handlyng Synne* (1303), and Richard of Hampole's *Pricke of Conscience* (ca. 1330–1340) were written in this metrical form. Chaucer used the same form later in *The Hous of Fame,* but the earlier poem exhibits far more irregularities, such as the substitution of trochees, the introduction of an extra syllable before the caesura, the violent slurring of syllables, and the appearance of hiatus where elision would be expected. On the other hand, the *Hous of Fame* shows a higher percentage of lines with only one syllable in the first foot.[17] This irregularity is common in Chaucer's verse, and it is safe to say that he did not regard it as an artistic blemish.

"THE COMPLEYNT OF MARS"

(Eight Ms. copies extant)

Authenticity: Ascribed to Chaucer by Shirley and Lydgate.
Date: ca. 1374.
Source: None has been found.
Metrical form: Rime-royal, and a nine-line stanza, riming *aabaabbcc.*

By means of astronomical computation, based on data furnished by the poem, attempts have been made to assign

[17] These statements are based largely upon a study by E. F. Shannon, published in the *Journ. Eng. and Germ. Philology,* 12, 277–94.

the *Compleynt of Mars* definitely to the year 1379, when Mars and Venus were in conjunction on April 14.[18] For a method which aims at precise accuracy, this result is hardly satisfactory, since Chaucer makes it clear, in line 139, that the conjunction which he is describing took place on April 12. Most people of sense will probably agree with Professor Manly that "to draw from the astronomical data any inference as to the year in which the poem was composed would be, to say the least, hazardous." [19]

Equally hazardous is the attempt to date the poem by reference to court scandal, since the evidence that the *Compleynt* rests upon any such basis is not very trustworthy. The poem appears to be nothing more than an ingenious astronomical allegory, used to diversify a highly conventional theme, very similar to that of the typical "aube" or "tagelied." [20] There is every reason to assign it to a fairly early date in Chaucer's poetical career.

Chaucer's acquaintance with the amours of Mars and Venus was doubtless derived from Ovid: *Metamorphoses*, IV. 170–89; but the Latin text certainly cannot be called a source of the poem. The Brooch of Thebes appears in Statius; *Thebaid*, II. 265–98.

Shirley, the fifteenth-century compiler and copyist, appends the following note to his copy of the *Compleynt* in a manuscript preserved in the library of Trinity College, Cambridge:

Thus eondethe here this complaint whiche some men sayne was made by (i. e., about) my lady of York doughter to the

[18] Cf. John Koch, in *Anglia*, 9. 582–84, and in his *Chronology*, 30–33.

[19] *Harvard Studies*, V. 113.

[20] Cf. C. R. Baskerville: *English Songs of the Night Visit*, in *Publ. Mod. Lang. Assn.*, 36. 565–614.

kyng of Spaygne and my lord of Huntyngdoun some tyme
duc of Excestre . . .

In the same manuscript, Shirley introduces the poem as
follows:

Loo yee louers gladethe and comfortethe you of thallyance
entrayted bytwene the hardy and furyous Mars the god of
armes and Venus the double (i. e., fickle) goddesse of loue
made by Geffrey Chaucier at the comandement of the re-
nomed and excellent Prynce my lord the Duc Iohn of Lan-
castre.

"My lady of York" was the Princess Isabel, daughter of
King Pedro of Castile, and sister to the Spanish princess
who was John of Gaunt's second wife. Isabel came to
England in 1372 and was married to John of Gaunt's
brother, Edmund, later Duke of York. "My lord of Huntyngdoun" was King Richard's half-brother John Holland,
later Duke of Exeter. That John of Gaunt should have
commanded Chaucer to celebrate a scandalous intrigue
between his sister-in-law and the king's brother is a
fantastic notion, which probably found its way into Shirley's manuscript through unfounded gossip or through
the copyist's own ingenious imagination.[21]

"THE PARLEMENT OF FOULES"

(Fourteen Ms. copies extant)

Authenticity: Mentioned by Chaucer in the 'Retractation' and
in the Prologue to the *Legend of Good Women.* Ascribed

[21] S. H. Cowling (*Rev. Eng. Studies,* 2. 405–10) believes the
Compleynt of Mars celebrates the amour of John Holland and
Elizabeth, countess of Pembroke, the daughter of John of Gaunt
and the Duchess Blanche. He would date the poem in 1385.

to Chaucer by Lydgate in the Prologue to the *Falls of Princes,* Bk. I, ascribed to Chaucer in three of the Mss.
Date: 1381–2. But cf. Braddy: *Three Chaucer Studies,* II.
Source: No definite source for the poem as a whole. Details from various sources.
Metrical form: Rime-royal.

In 1877, Dr. Koch suggested that the *Parlement of Foules* was an allegory, written to celebrate the betrothal of Richard II and Princess Anne of Bohemia, daughter of the Emperor Charles IV. According to his interpretation of the poem, the "formel" represents Anne, the "royal tercel" who is the first to speak represents King Richard, and the other two contestants are earlier suitors of Anne, William of Bavaria and Frederick of Meissen.[22] It has more recently been suggested that the three suitors were Frederick of Meissen, Charles VI of France, and Richard of England.[23] If we are correct in assuming a connection between the *Parlement of Foules* and the betrothal of King Richard to the Princess Anne, we can date the poem fairly accurately. The marriage of the royal pair took place in January, 1382.

It is to be said, however, that this interpretation of the poem has been vigorously attacked. Professor Rickert accepts the theory that the poem is an allegory, based upon a contemplated marriage in the royal family; but she argues that the lady involved is more likely to have been Philippa of Lancaster, John of Gaunt's daughter, whom the Duke, according to Froissart, wished to marry to his nephew, King Richard. The other suitors, according to

[22] *Englische Studien,* I. 287–89.
[23] Cf. O. F. Emerson in *Modern Philology,* 8. 45–62. Cf. *Mod. Lang. Notes,* 26. 8–12, 109–11.

Miss Rickert's interpretation, were William of Hainaut and John of Blois.[24] Dr. Haldeen Braddy would date the poem in April, 1377, when negotiations, in which Chaucer was himself engaged, were going on for the betrothal of Prince Richard to Princess Marie, daughter of Charles V of France. Professor Manly rejected entirely the allegorical interpretation of the poem, which he regards as an example of the conventional *demandes d'amour,* written to celebrate love on Saint Valentine's day.[25]

The account of the parliament of birds is undoubtedly original with Chaucer, although similar assemblies are described by other mediæval poets. Chaucer's poem certainly owes nothing, unless it be its title, to the fable of Marie de France called "Li Parlemens des Oiseax por faire Roi."

Nevertheless, the poem contains much borrowed material in its other portions. In lines 36–84, Chaucer gives us a synopsis of Cicero's *Somnium Scipionis,* which reached him through the commentary of Macrobius. The original has, of course, been much compressed; but the synopsis gives a very adequate notion of the ideas presented in Cicero's work, and Chaucer has been able, as well, to reproduce some of the actual phraseology and imagery of his original.[26]

In the two lines immediately following the synopsis of

[24] *A New Interpretation of the "Parlement of Foules," Modern Philology,* 18. 1–29.

[25] *What is the Parlement of Foules?* Festschrift für Lorenz Morsbach, 279–90. Answered by Emerson in *Journ. Eng. and Germ. Philology,* 13. 566–82.

[26] A full translation of Cicero's *Somnium Scipionis* is included in Lounsbury's edition of the *Parlement of Foules,* 11–16.

the *Somnium Scipionis,* readers of Dante will recognize the lines which open the second canto of the *Inferno:*

> Now was the day departing, and the air,
> Imbrown'd with shadows, from their toils released
> All animals on earth.

The inscriptions over the gates will also suggest to every reader the characters which Dante saw

> Over a portal's lofty arch inscribed.[27]

The stanza beginning at line 99 is a close imitation of the following lines from Claudian: *In Sextum Consulatum Honorii Augusti Præfatio, 3–10:*

> The huntsman stretches his weary limbs upon the couch, yet his mind ever returns to the woods where his quarry lurks. The judge dreams of law-suits, the charioteer of his chariot, the nightly steeds of which he guides past a shadowy turning-point. The lover repeats love's mysteries, the merchant makes exchange of goods, the miser still watchfully grasps at elusive riches, and to thirsty sufferers all-pervading sleep offers from a cooling spring idly alluring draughts.[28]

Sixteen stanzas of the poem, beginning at line 183, are imitated from stanzas in the seventh book of Boccaccio's *Teseida.* The Italian text, together with a literal translation by W. M. Rossetti, is printed by Skeat (I. 68–73). I reproduce below three stanzas from the translation, containing a part of the description of the Temple of Venus, which Chaucer, as it will be seen, follows very closely:

[27] Cf. *Inferno,* III. 1, ff.
[28] Trans. by M. Platnauer, Bohn Lib. (1922), II. 71.

In mid the place, on lofty columns,
  She saw a temple of copper; round which
  She saw youths dancing and women—
  This one of them beautiful, and that one in fine raiment
  Ungirdled, barefoot, only in their hair and gowns,
  Who spent the day in this alone.
  Then over the temple she saw doves hover
  And settle and coo.

And near to the entry of the temple
  She saw that there sat quietly
  My lady Peace, who a curtain
  Moved lightly before the door.
  Next her, very subdued in aspect,
  Sat Patience discreetly,
  Pallid in look; and on all sides
  Around her she saw artful Promises.

Then entering the temple, of Sighs
  She felt there an earthquake, which whirled
  All fiery with hot desires.
  This lit up all the altars
  With new flames born of pangs;
  Each of which dripped with tears
  Produced by a woman cruel and fell
  Whom she there saw, called Jealousy.

In his treatment of the material borrowed from the *Teseida,* Chaucer shows characteristic independence. He rearranges the order of the stanzas,[29] suppresses some details, and adds others. Particularly interesting is the fact that he supplements Boccaccio's list of famous lovers by add-

---

[29] Lines 183–259 correspond to the *Teseida*, VII. St. 51–60; lines 260-80, to St. 63–66; and lines 281–94, to St. 61, 62.

ing the names of those whom Dante sees in the circle of carnal sinners (*Inferno* V).[30]

The description of the birds which flock about the Goddess Nature is borrowed in large measure from the *De Planctu Naturae* of Alanus de Insulis, a twelfth-century poet, whom Chaucer himself mentions as the source of his description of the goddess (lines 316–18). In the Latin work, however, the birds were represented as part of the embroidery upon the goddess's robe.[31] It is possible that some of the epithets, used to characterize the trees which Chaucer mentions in lines 176–82, were derived from a similar list in Joseph of Exeter's paraphrase of the history of the fall of Troy ascribed to "Dares Phrygius." [32]

"COMPLEINT TO HIS LADY"

(Two Ms. copies extant)

Authenticity: Ascribed to Chaucer in one of the Ms. Apparently regarded as Chaucer's by Shirley, who copies this poem and the *Compleynt unto Pite* under one running title.

Date: 1374, or soon after.

Source: No direct source is known.

Metrical Form: Part I: Rime-Royal; Part II: *Terza rima;* Part III: Ten-line stanza, riming *aabaabcddc* (second stanza imperfect).

[30] Cf. J. L. Lowes, *Chaucer and Dante,* in *Modern Philology,* 14. 705–35.

[31] An English translation of the *De Planctu Naturae,* by D. M. Moffat; has been published in the *Yale Studies in English,* XXXVI.

[32] Cf. R. K. Root: *Chaucer's Dares,* in *Modern Philology,* 15. 18–22.

The use of *terza rima,* which appears for the first time in English poetry in this poem, dates the *Compleint* after Chaucer's first Italian journey (1372–3). As early a date as possible should be assigned to the poem, which is merely a series of experiments in metrical forms, based upon the most conventional of subjects and very much in the manner of such poets as Guillaume de Machaut, whose influence upon Chaucer waned as he grew better acquainted with Italian literature.

A number of lines from this poem found their way later into the *Anelida and Arcite,* one of them exactly as it stands here and others in slightly altered form.

"ANELIDA AND ARCITE"

(The entire poem extant in eight Mss., the "Compleynt" alone in four others)

Authenticity: Ascribed to Chaucer in three Mss., two of them Shirley's. Mentioned among Chaucer's works by Lydgate in the Prologue to the *Falls of Princes,* Book I.

Date: ca. 1380?

Sources: Lines 1–21 based upon Boccaccio's *Teseida,* I. St. 1–3, in reverse order; lines 50–70, upon the same work, II. St. 10–12. Lines 22–46 based upon Statius: *Thebaid,* XII. 519, ff. For the rest of the poem, no source has been discovered.

Metrical form: Rime-royal, except for the "Compleynt," which is discussed below.

The *Anelida and Arcite* is in itself a poem of slight importance, save as it furnishes a very striking example of Chaucer's interest in metrical experimentation; but it has attracted the attention of scholars because it is curiously connected with one of the poet's most important works. Not only does the "fals Arcite" bear the same name as one of the heroes of the *Knightes Tale,* but several stanzas of the *Anelida and Arcite* are derived from the very source from which the story of Palamon and Arcite was taken. The poem breaks off, moreover, upon a promise of just such a description of the Temple of Mars as that which is included in the Knight's Tale.

Stanzas in rime-royal, based upon Boccaccio's *Teseida,* are to be found, not only in this poem, but also in the *Parlement of Foules* and in the *Troilus.* This fact has been used as a foundation for an interesting theory that Chaucer originally projected a translation of the Italian poem in the seven-line stanza. It has even been conjectured that this translation was completed and was the work referred to as "the love of Palamon and Arcyte" in the Prologue to *The Legend of Good Women* (B 420, 421). That Chaucer actually completed any other version of the story of Palamon and Arcite than that which is known to us as the *Knightes Tale* is extremely unlikely, and the theory of an earlier form of that work has now been abandoned. It is clear, however, that the poet had been working over the *Teseida* before the *Knightes Tale* was attempted, and the *Anelida and Arcite* probably represents his first attempt to utilize material from Boccaccio's epic poem. The task must have been undertaken soon after his second Italian journey, at a time when he was still trying to cramp his genius within the conventions of the poets of fourteenth-century France. It was abandoned, it seems to me, because it soon became evident that such diverse material would not blend. At a later time, thoroughly emancipated from the barren notion that every poem must be built around a lover's 'complaint,' Chaucer returned to the *Teseida* and wrote his story of the loves of Palamon and Arcite, which he still later inserted in the *Canterbury Tales,* as the story told by the Knight. A few lines from the *Anelida and Arcite,* altered very slightly, found their way into the later work. Since his attention had been rather closely given to the *Teseida,* at the time when he projected the *Anelida and Arcite,* it is not strange that stanzas from the Italian poem should appear in other works of Chaucer belonging to the same period.[33]

We do not know why Chaucer chose to use the name of Arcite for a false lover in this poem, nor where he found Anelida, "the quene of Ermony." Henry Bradshaw believed that "Anelida" reached Chaucer through a misspelling, in some Latin manuscript, of the name of Anahita, a goddess of Persia and Armenia.[34] It is more probable that he found the name in some old romance.

Professor Tupper's identification of Arcite with the Earl of Ormonde, whose mother was a d'Arcy, and of Anelida with his countess, whose maiden name was Anne Welle, has not gained acceptance.[35] It is true that "Ormonde" was sometimes spelled "Ermonia," in contemporary Latin documents, and that names are to be found for

[33] This view coincides, in general, with that presented by Professor Lowes in *Publ. Mod. Lang. Assn.,* 20. 860, ff.

[34] E. B. Cowell: *Chaucer Essays,* 617–21. But cf. Schick's edition of the *Temple of Glas,* E. E. T. S., Ext. Ser. LX. cxx.

[35] *Chaucer's Tale of Ireland,* in *Publ. Mod. Lang. Assn.,* 36. 186–222.

the count and countess which can be metamorphosed into Anelida and Arcite without great difficulty; but the only evidence that their marriage was not a happy one lies in the existence of two illegitimate children of the earl, and they may very well have been born some years before his marriage to Anne Welle.

Another problem, for which no satisfactory solution has yet been offered, is presented by the mysterious "Corinne," whom Chaucer mentions, in line 21, as one of his authorities. It is possible that he derived the name from "Corinna," a title sometimes given, in mediæval manuscripts, to the *Amores* of Ovid; but there is certainly no evidence that the *Anelida* owes anything to the *Amores*.[36]

The metrical structure of the poem presents some very unusual features. In Stanza 5 of Strophe and Antistrophe, in the "Compleynt," we encounter a four-stress line, which Chaucer does not elsewhere employ in stanza-form, except in the burlesque *Sir Thopas*. Even here, it will be noticed, every fourth line contains five stresses. These two stanzas also afford the only example of Chaucer's use of a rime-scheme modeled on the French *virelai*. Following the pattern of the *virelai*, the two rimes, which are employed in the first eight lines of the stanza, appear in the last eight lines in reverse order; *viz., aaabaaab bbbabbba*.[36a]

[36] Cf. E. F. Shannon: *Source of Chaucer's Anelida and Arcite*, in *Publ. Mod. Lang. Assn.*, 27. 461–85, and his *Chaucer and the Roman Poets*, 15, ff.

[36a] The rest of the "compleynt" is in nine-line stanzas, riming *aabaabbab*. Stanza 6, in Strophe and Antistrophe, employs internal rime, one of the "colours" taught by mediaeval rhetoricians. Cf. E. P. Hammond: *English Verse between Chaucer and Surrey*, 466, 467.

"CHAUCERS WORDES UNTO ADAM"

(One Ms. copy extant)

Authenticity: Ascribed to Chaucer in the Ms., which is Shirley's.
Date: 1386?
Source: None need be sought.
Metrical form: Rime-royal.

The mention of the *Troilus* and of the translation of Boethius is convincing evidence that this stanza was written shortly after the completion of those works, both of which, in all probability, belong to the years between 1380 and 1385.

"THE FORMER AGE"

(Two Ms. copies extant)

Authenticity: Ascribed to Chaucer in both Mss.
Date: ca. 1389?
Source: Boethius: *De Consolatione Philosophiae,* Bk. II. Met. 5.
Metrical Form: Eight-line stanza, riming *ababbcbc.*

We have no means of knowing whether this poem and two others based upon Boethius were written before or after Chaucer's prose translation of the *Consolation of Philosophy.* It seems more probable that they belong to a late period in the poet's career. Only the first four stanzas are based upon Boethius, and we know of no certain source for the rest of the poem.

"FORTUNE"

(Ten Ms. copies extant)

Authenticity: Ascribed to Chaucer in four Mss., two of them
    Shirley's.
Date: ca. 1389?
Source: Based on Boethius: *De Consolatione Philosophiae,*
    Bk. II. Pr. 1, 2, 3, 4, 8.
Metrical Form: Three *balades* with an envoy. Each *balade*
    has three stanzas of eight lines, riming *ababbcbc.* The
    envoy has seven lines, riming *ababbab.* Only ten rimes
    are used in the entire poem.

Henry Bradshaw was the first to trace the ideas in this
poem to their source in Boethius.[37] It is also apparent that
the poem owes something to a passage in the *Roman de la
Rose* (Mid. Eng. trans., 5403–5578), in which Jean de
Meun discusses the benefits which evil fortune confers
upon a man, in unmasking false friends. The heading
"Balades de vilage (i. e., visage) saunz peynture," which
appears in some of the manuscripts, has reference to this
benefit of evil fortune.

There is little profit in searching Chaucer's career for
some particularly severe reversal of fortune, in an attempt
to date this poem; for it is not likely that these well-turned
balades represent the fruit of bitter experience. A poet suffering under grave misfortune might arm himself with
the philosophy of Boethius and argue his case with as
great a show of equanimity as this poem affords; but he
could hardly achieve sufficient detachment to be so deft,
either with his rimes or with his hints. The poem remains,

[37] G. W. Prothero: *Memoir of Henry Bradshaw* (1888), 212.

in general, on a lofty philosophic plane, but it is not without some mundane touches, which strongly suggest the complaint which Chaucer addressed to his empty purse. The envoy makes it clear that we have here just such another graceful petition for royal favor. Attempts to identify the "beste frend," referred to in the refrain of the second *balade,* or the princes addressed in the envoy, have been called idle; but it is the fact that in 1389, or thereabouts, when circumstances made it desirable for Chaucer to secure employment under the Crown, there were sons of Edward III, still living, "three or tweyne"; and Richard the king, on more than one previous occasion, had shown himself Chaucer's "beste frend" in very substantial ways.[38]

"MERCILES BEAUTE"

(Only one Ms. copy extant)

Authenticity: Doubtful.

Date: 1390–93?

Source: Probably derived from French sources.

Metrical Form: Three roundels. The roundel has thirteen lines, riming *abbabababbabb.* The first three lines form a refrain, appearing again at the end; and the first two lines of this refrain are repeated in the middle of the roundel, at lines six and seven.

[38] J. B. Bilderbeck (*Athenæum,* 1902, I. 82, 83) points out that an Order in Council, on March 8, 1390, forbade all royal gifts and grants without the advice of the Council and the assent of the Dukes of Guienne (John of Gaunt), of York, and of Gloucester, *or of two of them.* He argues that the envoy was addressed "half in earnest, half in game" to the Privy Council, at a time when the poet's fortunes needed mending.

This poem, first attributed to Chaucer by Bishop Percy, has been admitted to the canon purely on its own merits, without the support of external evidence.[39] It is to be said, however, that it occurs in a manuscript containing authentic works of Chaucer.

Skeat found a resemblance between these roundels and one by a thirteenth-century French writer, Willamme d'Amiens, but the connection seems tenuous, to say the least. More striking is the similarity, pointed out by Professor Lowes, between *Merciles Beaute* and some poems by Deschamps, an author with whose works Chaucer is known to have been familiar.[40] The audacious line with which the third roundel begins is identical with the first line of the *reponse* of the Duc de Berry to the author of the *Cent Ballades* (1389?):

> Puiz qu'a Amours suis si gras eschapé.[41]

The tone of the poem suggests a date approximating that of the playful *Envoy to Bukton*.

"TO ROSEMOUNDE"

(Only one Ms. copy extant)

Authenticity: Ascribed to Chaucer in the manuscript.
Date: 1390–93?
Source: None has been found.
Metrical Form: A *balade* in three eight-line stanzas, riming on three rimes throughout: *ababbcbc*.

---

[39] The editors of the *Globe Chaucer* do not include the poem.
[40] *Mod. Lang. Rev.*, 5. 33-39.
[41] Cf. W. L. Renwick: *Chaucer's Triple Roundel 'Merciles Beaute,'* in *Mod. Lang. Rev.*, 16. 322, 323.

The *Balade to Rosemounde* was discovered by Skeat, in 1891, on a fly-leaf of a manuscript in the Bodleian. Like the copy of the *Troilus* in the same manuscript, it bears at the end the two words "Tregentil" and "Chaucer." Skeat believed that "Tregentil" represented the name of the scribe.

This poem, like the *Merciles Beaute,* must belong to a period when Chaucer had become thoroughly emancipated from the school of love-poetry represented by his more conventional "compleynts."

"TRUTH"

(Twenty-two Ms. copies extant)

Authenticity: Ascribed to Chaucer in six Mss.
Date: 1386–90?
Source: Possibly based on Boethius.
Metrical Form: A *balade* of three stanzas and an envoy, each of seven lines, riming throughout on three rimes: *abab-bcc.*

Scholars long ago relinquished the sentimental tradition, started by Shirley, that this *balade* of Chaucer was "made on his deeth bedde." A discovery by Professor Rickert makes the tradition even more untenable. She has found, in Sir Philip la Vache, son-in-law to Chaucer's friend, Sir Lewis Clifford, the very person addressed, in the first line of the envoy, as "thou vache." [42] Since the envoy appears in only one manuscript copy of the poem, it is not entirely certain that this "Balade de bon conseyl" was

[42] Edith Rickert: *Thou Vache,* in *Modern Philology,* 11. 209–25.

set down solely for the edification of Sir Philip, and it may be that the last stanza was a later addition by the poet.[43] To classify the *balade,* therefore, with the personal epistles to Scogan and to Bukton is not quite safe; but Miss Rickert's discovery has definitely removed the poem from the dubious company of death-bed utterances.

Like so much of Chaucer's more serious work, the *balade* shows evidence of the influence of Boethius. Dr. Koch finds a possible source in the *Consolation of Philosophy,* Book III. Met. 11, but the resemblances which he points out are very slight. Skeat felt sure that the third stanza of the *balade* was based upon Book I. Pr. 5 in Boethius.[44]

"GENTILESSE"

(Nine Ms. copies extant)

Authenticity: Ascribed to Chaucer by Scogan and by Shirley.

Date: 1390–95?

Sources: Boethius: *De Consolatione Philosophiae,* Bk. III. Pr. 6 and Met. 6. Also *Roman de la Rose,* 18,607, ff.

Metrical Form: Three seven-line stanzas, riming on three rimes throughout: *ababbcc.*

The ideas expressed in this poem are to be encountered frequently in mediæval literature. It is probable that they reached Chaucer through the passages in Boethius and Jean de Meun indicated above. He was to return to

[43] Cf. Koch. *Anglia,* 46. 47–48. Dr. Brusendorff (*The Chaucer Tradition,* 246–50) denies that Chaucer wrote the envoy.

[44] Cf. *Oxford Chaucer,* I. 550–52.

the subject in the tale told by the Wyf of Bath (*Cant. Tales,* D 1109–76).

In one of the manuscripts, Chaucer's poem is inserted in a "Moral Balade," which, according to Shirley, was addressed "to my lorde the Prince, to my lord of Clarence, to my lord of Bedford and to my lorde of Gloucestre, by Henry Scogan, at a souper of feorthe merchande in the vyntre in london at the hous of Lowys Iohan." Henry Scogan was undoubtedly the person addressed by Chaucer in the famous *Envoy,* and the princes named by Shirley were the four sons of Henry IV. In introducing the *Gentilesse* into his "Moral balade," Scogan refers to

> My maistre Chaucier, God his soule have,
> That in his langage was so curyous.

"LAK OF STEDFASTNESSE"

(Twelve Ms. copies extant)

Authenticity: Ascribed to Chaucer by Shirley.
Date: 1386–89?
Source: None has been discovered.
Metrical Form: Three stanzas and an envoy, in rime-royal, using only three rimes throughout.

One of the manuscripts, sometimes attributed to Shirley, says of this *balade* that it was made by "Geoffrey Chaunciers the Laureall Poete of Albion" and that it was sent "to his souerain lorde kynge Richarde the secounde thane being in his Castell of Windesore." Another manuscript calls the poem a "Balade Royale made by oure Laureal poete of Albyon in hees laste yeeres." On this

evidence, the poem has usually been assigned to the latter
years of Richard's reign (i. e., 1397–99), when dis-
sension, oppression, and covetousness were certainly rife
in the land, under the king's feeble and corrupt government. It has been argued, however, that the poem might
have given umbrage to the king, if addressed to him at a
time when his misgovernment was notorious. According
to this view, so proficient a courtier as Chaucer would have
been more likely to address such a poem as this to his
monarch at a period when the government of the land
was in the hands of his none too popular uncles, and
when the people were known to be looking to the young
king to assert himself and put an end to corruption. If
this reasoning is correct, the poem should be assigned to
the years 1386–89.

Skeat's suggestion that the *Balade* was based upon
Boethius, Book II, Met. 8, seems unnecessary.

"LENVOY DE CHAUCER A SCOGAN"

(Three Ms. copies extant)

Authenticity: Ascribed to Chaucer in all three Mss.
Date: 1393?
Source: None need be sought.
Metrical Form: Six stanzas and an envoy, in rime-royal, with
different rimes in each stanza.

From the references to the "deluge of pestilence,"
which the poet attributes to the tears of Venus, the *Envoy to Scogan* has been dated in 1393, when there was an
unusually heavy autumn rainfall. Allusions to advancing
years and a rounding figure make a date as late as 1393

appear correct. At that time, Chaucer was in all probability
residing at Greenwich. From his situation, far down the
Thames from Windsor Castle, he writes his friend, who
was undoubtedly living at the court, to use his influence
to secure favors for the poet.[45]

The friend to whom the epistle is addressed was probably the same Henry Scogan who later incorporated
Chaucer's *balade* of *Gentilesse* in the "moral balades"
which he addressed to the four sons of Henry IV. By his
own account, he was at that time "fader" (tutor) to these
four princes; but what position he held at the court of
Richard II has not been ascertained.

"Lenvoy de Chaucer a Bukton"

(Only one Ms. copy extant)

Authenticity: Marked as Chaucer's in the Ms.
Date: 1393–96.
Source: None need be sought.
Metrical Form: Three stanzas and an envoy, of eight lines
    each, riming *ababbcbc,* on different rimes in each stanza.

In August, 1396, William of Hainaut, led an expedition
into Friesland. According to Froissart, "some men-at-
arms and two hundred archers, under the command of
three English lords," were sent from England, by Richard

---

[45] Such is the usual interpretation of lines 43–46, based on
marginal notes in the manuscripts. Professor Manly suggests that
these notes may belong to a much later period, and that Chaucer
may be referring to a sojourn in Somersetshire, in connection
with his duties as sub-forester of Petherton Park. *Some New
Light on Chaucer,* 38–41.

II, to take part in the expedition. This circumstance has been used to date the *Envoy to Bukton,* on the ground that an allusion to the dangers of being taken prisoner "in Fryse" must have been suggested by this expedition. "The Frieslanders," Froissart tells us, "offered their prisoners in exchange, man for man, but, when their enemies had none to give in return, they put them to death." It has recently been pointed out, by Professor Lowes, that earlier expeditions into Friesland have been recorded, and that an allusion to the perils of being taken prisoner there would have been well understood as early as 1393, and would have been more effective at the time when the expedition of 1396 was being organized than after reports of its success had begun to come in.[46]

Although some scholars argue that "my maister Bukton" was a certain Robert Bukton of Suffolk, it is more generally believed that the poem was addressed to Sir Peter de Buketon, who was King's Escheator for the County of York in 1397. "Peter Bukton came from a community not unknown to the poet as well as to a considerable body of Londoners; . . . he too like Chaucer and his circle was in the Lancashire retinue, and an intimate friend and favorite of Henry, the Earl of Derby (Henry IV); and . . . consequently in view of this close tie between the Earl and the Yorkshireman the Frisian reference is more appropriate to Sir Peter the crusader than to the (seemingly) unadventurous Robert."[47]

[46] J. L. Lowes: *The Date of the Envoy to Bukton* in *Mod. Lang. Notes,* 27. 45–48.

[47] E. P. Kuhl: *Chaucer's My Maister Bukton* in *Publ. Mod. Lang. Assn.,* 38. 115–31.

"THE COMPLEYNT OF VENUS"

(Eight Ms. copies extant)

Authenticity: Ascribed to Chaucer by Shirley.
Date: 1391–94.
Source: Three *balades* of Oton de Granson.
Metrical Form: Three *balades* and an envoy. Each *balade* has
three eight-line stanzas, riming *ababbccb,* on three rimes
throughout. Envoy: a ten-line stanza, riming *aabaabbaab.*

In Shirley's Ashmole manuscript, this poem is headed:

Here begynnethe a balade made by that worthy
Knight of Savoye in frenshe calde Sir Otes
Graunson, translated by Chauciers.

Granson, whom Shirley correctly describes as a knight
of Savoy, had taken an oath of allegiance to the King of
England and received a generous annuity from him. His
three *balades,* here translated by Chaucer, were discovered
some years ago by Dr. A. Piaget. They are printed by
Skeat in the *Oxford Chaucer* (I. 400–404) below the text
of this poem. A comparison of the translation with the
original shows that Chaucer's rendering is rather free,
although he adheres much more closely to his French text
than in his translation of the *A. B. C.*

In one of the manuscripts, Shirley remarks, at the close
of the *Compleynt of Venus,* "Hit is sayde that Graun-
some made this last balade for Venus resembled to my
lady of York, aunswering the complaynt of Mars." Accordingly, it has sometimes been assumed that the princess, to whom Chaucer's envoy is addressed, was Isabel,

Duchess of York, the daughter of King Pedro of Castille. Some manuscripts, however, carry the reading "Princes" in the first line of the envoy, and the connection of the poem with the Duchess of York, like the dubious tradition that the *Compleynt of Mars* was based upon her intrigue with the Duke of Exeter, rests upon very slight evidence. The inappropriate title of the poem may probably be attributed to Shirley.

In 1391, Granson left Savoy, under suspicion of being concerned in the death of Count Amadeus VII, and probably went at once to England. Two years later, upon the confiscation of his estates in Savoy, he was awarded his annuity by Richard II. It seems probable that the *balades* came into Chaucer's hands and were translated by him not long after 1391.

"The Compleint of Chaucer to his Empty Purse"

(Extant in eight Mss., some of which omit the envoy)

Authenticity: Ascribed to Chaucer in three Mss., one of them probably derived from Shirley.
Date: 1399.
Source: Possibly suggested by a *balade* of Eustache Deschamps.
Metrical Form: Balade in three stanzas, in rime-royal; with an envoy of five lines, riming *aabba*.

The envoy can be dated with the closest accuracy. The "conquerour of Brutes Albioun" was Henry IV, who was declared king in parliament on September 30, 1399. On October 13, the new king granted Chaucer a pension of forty marks a year, in addition to the annuity of £20 given him in 1394 by Richard II. The envoy, then, must have been written during the first two weeks of October, 1399. Skeat calls it "almost certainly Chaucer's latest extant composition."

The rest of the poem, on the other hand, may have been in existence before 1399, and it is possible that it had already done Chaucer a service with Henry's predecessor upon the throne,—say in aiding him to secure the pension of 1394. In one of the manuscripts, the poem is called "A supplicacion to Kyng Richard by chaucier"; but as this particular copy includes the envoy, the statement would appear to be a mistake.

Skeat compares this *balade* with one by Deschamps, addressed to Charles VI, but he does not argue that Chaucer owed more to the French poet than the suggestion for his own petition.

"PROVERBS"

(Three Ms. copies extant)

Authenticity: Dubious. Ascribed to Chaucer in two of the Mss.
Date: ?
Source: Probably French proverbial expressions.
Metrical Form: Four-line stanzas, with four stresses to the line, riming alternately.

Although the proverbs were accepted by Skeat, they are of doubtful authenticity. One copy occurs in a Shirley manuscript without anything to indicate that the poems are Chaucer's. They are certainly of little value. The only point about them of particular interest is the recurrence of the idea of the second proverb in the *Melibeus:*

"For the proverbe seith, he that to muche embraceth, distreyneth litel" (*Cant. Tales*, B. 2404).

"AGAINST WOMEN UNCONSTANT"

(Three Ms. copies extant)

Authenticity: Doubtful. No mark of authorship in the Mss.
Date: ?
Source: Idea and refrain from a poem by Machaut.
Metrical Form: Three stanzas in rime-royal, using only three
   rimes throughout.

This poem was first attributed to Chaucer by Stow, in the 1561 Chaucer, and some scholars refuse to accept it as genuine. Skeat, however, included it in the canon. One of the arguments which he used to support the poem's claims to authenticity was the fact that "the general idea of the poem, and what is more important, the whole of the refrain, are taken from Chaucer's favourite author Machault (ed. Tarbé, p. 56); whose refrain is—En lieu de bleu, Damë, vous vestez vert." The point of this line lies in the fact that blue was the color of constancy, green of inconstancy.

"AN AMOROUS COMPLEINT"

(Three Ms. copies extant)

Authenticity: Doubtful. Not ascribed to Chaucer in any of
   the Mss.
Date: ?
Source: None has been suggested.
Metrical Form: Rime-royal.

This poem, first attributed to Chaucer by Skeat, is not of sufficient merit to justify its admission to the canon. Skeat argued for its authenticity on the ground that it is to be found in three manuscripts which contain several of Chaucer's poems, and that it contains lines and expressions closely resembling some which occur in the accepted works. I should be far more ready to attribute these resemblances, not excluding the striking similarity between the first two lines of the last stanza and lines 309–10 of the *Parlement of Foules*, to a natural tendency on the part of an inferior writer to imitate the works of the greatest poet of the age. An argument based upon the inclusion of the poem in manuscripts which contain very large and miscellaneous collections of prose and verse, is hardly convincing. It is to be added that Skeat himself came to be doubtful of the poem's authenticity.

"A BALADE OF COMPLEYNT"

(Only one Ms. copy extant)

Authenticity: Doubtful. No mark of authorship in the Ms.
Date: ?
Source: None has been suggested.
Metrical Form: Three stanzas in rime-royal.

This poem, discovered by Skeat and first printed by him in 1888, has not been generally accepted as authentic, and Skeat himself eventually excluded it from the canon. The fact that it occurs in a Shirley manuscript, without any indication of Chaucerian authorship, is a strong argument against its authenticity.

"WOMANLY NOBLESSE"

(Only one Ms. copy extant)

Authenticity: Ascribed to Chaucer in the Ms.
Date: Early?
Source: No source has been discovered.
Metrical Form: Balade in three stanzas with an envoy. Each
  stanza has nine lines, riming *aabaabbab,* on the same two
  rimes throughout. The envoy has six lines, riming
  acacaa, keeping one of the rimes of the stanzas.

The manuscript in which Skeat discovered this poem
calls it a "Balade that Chauncier made." It is possible that
this manuscript, though not in Shirley's hand, as Skeat
has indicated, was derived from a Shirley copy. With this
much of external evidence behind it, the poem has gained
wider acceptance than some of the others which Skeat
endeavored to add to the canon.

The *Complaint to my Mortal Foe,* and the *Complaint
to my Lode-Sterre,* both discovered by Skeat, and first
printed by him in the *Athenaeum,* in 1894, have not been
generally accepted. Skeat included them in the *Oxford
Chaucer* (IV. xxvii-xxxi), but he himself was not entirely
ready to admit them to the canon.

"BOECE"

(Extant in ten Mss., two containing only part of the
translation)

Authenticity: Mentioned in the Prologue to the *Legend of
  Good Women,* in the 'Retractation' and in the *Words
  unto Adam.*
Date: Shortly after 1380.

Source: The Latin text of Boethius: *De Consolatione Philosophiae,* the commentary of Nicholas Trivet, and a French translation (probably that of Jean de Meun).

Anicius Manlius Severinus Boethius, whom Gibbon called "the last of the Romans whom Cato or Tully could have acknowledged for their countryman," was put to death, by order of Theodoric, in 524 A. D. His most famous work, the *De Consolatione Philosophiae,* was written while he lay in prison in Ticinum, the modern Pavia. No man has expressed more eloquently the comfort which the philosophy of the classic world could bring to a man, even in the sadder days of its decline; and no man ever stood more sorely in need of any comfort he could find. Born in a distinguished Roman family, he had spent his years in the service of the state, recognized in the Senate as its most distinguished member and received by Theodoric on terms of intimate friendship. In 510, through royal favor, he had been made sole consul. He had married the daughter of a senator, and the two sons she bore him had been chosen consuls together in 522. His good fortune had naturally made him the object of many little jealousies, and his fearless opposition to all oppressive or ill-advised measures had won him the ill will of many unscrupulous persons who were in a position to do him injury. Accused of treason to Theodoric, in that he sought to maintain the integrity of the Senate and hoped to restore the ancient liberties of Rome, he was thrown into prison, his goods were confiscated, and he was finally put to death.

The great book which Boethius wrote in prison was not his only contribution to the literature of philosophy. Throughout his life, he had busied himself with the works of the philosophers of ancient Greece, and it had been his ambition to translate all the works of Plato and Aristotle and to quicken the stagnant intellectual life of his century, by streams of thought brought from the pages of Greek speculative literature. Though he never realized this ambition, he did very much to bring the fruits of Greek speculation, in many different fields of thought, within the reach of the readers of his age and of subsequent centuries. His writings include an interpretation of Euclid, a work on music based upon the thought of Pythagoras, an adaptation of the writings of Nicomachus upon arithmetic, and more than thirty books based on the works of Aristotle, who held his place of supreme importance in mediæval thought largely because the translations and commentaries of Boethius made his works accessible.

Of all his writings, no other has the power or beauty of the *Consolation of Philosophy,* and it is that work which accounts for the enormous influence which he exercised over mediæval thought. The book was translated into English, German, Italian, Spanish, and Greek before the end of the fifteenth century, and its influence spread from one end of mediæval Europe to the other, eclipsing that of any other book. King Alfred the Great rendered it into Anglo-Saxon, and there is a tradition that Queen Elizabeth improved her leisure by translating it in her turn.

One factor which contributed to the high esteem in which the *Consolation of Philosophy* was held during the Middle Ages was the belief that Boethius was a Christian and died a martyr to the faith. Under the name of St. Severinus, he was venerated as one of the Great Christian heroes of the pagan world; and in the book which he had written in prison, the Middle Ages believed that they had found an eloquent expression of the power of the Christian religion to bring philosophic comfort to a man in trouble. In this they were mistaken. No book written in the sixth century could have been entirely without traces of the influence of Christianity; but the magnificent lady who comes to Boethius in Book I of his work, to console him as he bewails his misfortune, is not Religion, but Philosophy. She talks with him about the omnipotence of God; she teaches him that the gifts of Fortune are of little value, and that the best happiness of man is to be found in God, who alone is the absolute good; she shows him that evil, so far from flourishing as he supposes, has no real existence at all, since it is no part of God, who alone has true existence; she solves for him the ancient riddle of man's free will and God's foreknowledge, by instructing him in the difference between time, in which man lives, and eternity, in which God sees at once the past, the present, and the future. These are, of course, matters which belong to the philosophy of religion, but they are presented by Boethius in the light of pagan thought, rather than of Christian revelation. His philosophy is a blend of Plato, Aristotle, and the Stoics.[48]

In all probability, Chaucer made the acquaintance of Boethius through the *Roman de la Rose,* and it is possible that he was led to undertake his translation by the suggestion of Jean de Meun that

> 'twould redound
> Greatly to that man's praise who should
> Translate that book with masterhood.

[48] Cf. H. F. Stewart: *Boethius: an Essay* (London, 1891), an excellent study of the subject.

The only direct evidence for dating the translation is the reference in the Prologue to the *Legend of Good Women*. If we are right in dating the earlier version of the Prologue in 1385–6, the "Boece" must have been completed before that date. It has usually been assigned to the period of the *Troilus,* partly on the evidence of the *Words unto Adam,* where "Boece" and "Troilus" are mentioned in the same line, as if they were works which Chaucer's scribe had been copying at the same time, and partly because the influence of the thought of Boethius is so apparent in the *Troilus.*

The problem of the source of Chaucer's translation is more complicated than would at first appear, for his text contains unmistakable evidence that he was working with other appliances before him than the bare Latin text. It now appears certain that he availed himself of a French translation—probably Jean de Meun's—and that many of his interpolations (distinguished in Skeat's text by the use of italics) were derived from a long commentary, by Nicholas Trivet, upon the Latin original.

The translation is disappointing reading for the admirer of Chaucer. Partly because prose was not so happy a medium for his genius as poetry, and partly because his style has been cramped by the difficulties of translating a work which was a little beyond his powers as a Latinist, Chaucer has produced a work that is quite without the ease and fluency which we particularly associate with his writing. Considered as a translation, it comes far from meeting modern standards. "Its inaccuracy and infelicity," says H. F. Stewart, "is not that of an inexperienced Latin scholar, but rather of one who was no Latin scholar at all." This statement is a little severe and takes too little account of the extraordinary difficulties which stood in the path of the translator, in days before the apparatus of modern scholarship had been thought of. Nevertheless, more than a hundred errors have been pointed out in Chaucer's translation. He misses the point of historical allusions; he loses the force of conjunctions, prepositions, and pronouns; he translates interrogatory statements as if they were declarative; he ignores or misplaces negatives and misreads words; and at times he translates so literally that his English is quite without meaning, at least to the modern reader.

But if Chaucer did not succeed in translating the *De Consolatione Philosophiae* to the entire satisfaction of those who would like to find him supreme in every sort of writing, it must be said that he had made the thought of Boethius thoroughly his own. The influence of the pagan philosopher appears again and again in his work, and some of the most serious passages in his poetry have their source in the *Consolation of Philosophy*.[49]

"THE HOUS OF FAME"

(Extant in three Mss., two of 2158 lines, one of 1843 lines)

Authenticity: Mentioned in the Prologue to the *Legend of Good Women* and in the 'Retractation.'

Date: 1374–82.

Source: No source for the poem as a whole. Details from many writers.

Metrical Form: Octosyllabics.

---

[49] The nature of Chaucer's translation and the influence of Boethius upon his works are admirably discussed in B. L. Jefferson's monograph, *Chaucer and the Consolation of Philosophy.*

The lines in which the eagle describes the manner of life which the poet has been leading indicate that the *Hous of Fame* belongs to the period when Chaucer was serving as controller of the customs; i. e., between 1374 and 1385. It is now generally believed that the poem preceded the *Troilus,* and a date not too long after 1374 may be accepted with some confidence.

The *Hous of Fame* reflects Chaucer's widening intellectual interests. The hackneyed mechanism of the "dream school" of poetry, which is utilized at the beginning, was derived from the mediæval French poets who had exercised the strongest influence upon Chaucer at the outset of his career. Chaucer is no longer ready, however, to accept any convention without giving it fresh treatment of his own, and he has enlivened the stale device of the dream by an introductory passage, in which he summarizes, in one long, breathless sentence, the mediæval psychology of dreams, as presented in the commentary of Macrobius upon the *Dream of Scipio.*[50]

The influence of other and greater writers than the French poets of the fourteenth century soon makes itself apparent. The conception, and part of the description, of the House of Fame came from Ovid (*Metamorphoses,* XII. 39-63). Further evidence of Chaucer's familiarity with the same work is to be found in the many allusions which he makes in Book II to myths related by Ovid, and the eagle's reference to the *Metamorphoses* as "thyn owne book" (line 712) may be regarded as reliable evidence that Chaucer actually possessed a copy of this particular work. Familiarity with Ovid's *Heroides,* a work which

[50] Cf. W. C. Curry: *Chaucer and the Mediaeval Sciences,* 233-40.

furnished the material for much of the *Legend of Good Women,* is put beyond question by lines 388–426; and other references point toward the *Ars Amatoria* and the *Ex Ponto.*

Chaucer was undoubtedly well acquainted with Ovid long before the *Hous of Fame* was begun. It is not so clear that his acquaintance with Vergil was of long standing. The fact that he takes occasion to furnish his readers with a digest of the *Aeneid* suggests that Skeat is right in his conjecture that "at the time of writing, Vergil was, in the main, a new book to him." The description of *Fame* herself owes something to Vergil's passage on Fama (*Aeneid,* IV. 176–83). That the lady is endowed with "partriches winges" is due to an unfortunate misreading, either by Chaucer or by the scribe whose manuscript he was following, of Vergil's *"pernicibus alis."*

There can hardly be any question about the source of Chaucer's newly awakened interest in Vergil, for it was undoubtedly Dante who had given him a new sense of Vergil's greatness. No poem of Chaucer's shows more striking evidence of the influence of the *Divine Comedy* than the *Hous of Fame.* Passages translated or imitated from Dante are scattered through the poem, and an attempt has been made to show that certain features of the work, such as the eagle, the desert, and the steep rock, have their source in the *Divine Comedy.* Doubtless, too, much has been made, by certain writers, of accidental similarities between the two poems, and some of the "parallel passages" which have been discovered bear only the most tenuous relation to each other.[51] It is certainly diffi-

[51] Cf. A. Rambeau: *Chaucers Hous of Fame in seinem Verhält-niss zu Dantes Divina Commedia,* in *Englische Studien,* 3. 209–68;

cult to agree with those who argue that this is the poem which Lydgate had in mind when he declared that Chaucer wrote a work which he called "Dante in Inglissh." [52] The one conclusion that can definitely be accepted, out of the theories which have been put forward about the relation between the *Hous of Fame* and the *Divine Comedy,* is that Chaucer must have been reading Dante with unusually close attention at the time when he wrote this poem.

The fact that the *Hous of Fame* breaks off abruptly, upon what appears to be an indication that tidings of great importance are about to be communicated to the reader, has led to some speculation about Chaucer's purpose in writing the poem. Rudolf Immelmann has put forward the theory that the poem was projected as a companion piece to the *Parlement of Foules:* as that poem was written to celebrate the betrothal of Anne of Bohemia to Richard II, so the *Hous of Fame* was undertaken, about December 10, 1381, as a congratulatory poem to be presented to Anne on her arrival in England; and it was left unfinished because the interval before the princess landed (December 18) proved to be too short for the completion of the work.[53] Professor Manly rejects this theory and puts forth one of his own, declaring that he is "disposed to believe that this poem was intended to herald or announce a group of love stories and to serve as a sort of prologue to them." [54]

and C. Chiarini: *Di una imitazione inglese della Divina Commedia,* Bari, 1902. An admirable discussion of Chaucer and Dante is to be found in an article by C. Looten in the *Revue de Littérature Comparée,* V. 545–71.

[52] Prologue to the *Fall of Princes,* 303.

[53] *Englische Studien,* 45. 397–431.

[54] *What is Chaucer's Hous of Fame?* in the *Kittredge Anniversary Papers* (Boston. 1913), 73–81.

Professor Sypherd, on the other hand, rejects every theory which endeavors to discover a hidden significance in the *Hous of Fame,* and argues that the poem is complete in itself, save for a brief conclusion which the poet failed to write. "I shall be satisfied," he says, "to regard it as a love-vision poem, in which the poet realizes to the fullest extent the possibilities of the device of a journey as a reward for his services in the cause of Love. Employing such rich poetic material as the combined classical conception of the goddess of Fama and the abstract idea of worldly reputation, the journey of the 'grete poete of Itaile' through the lower world and to the abode of the blessed, and the conventional device of the love-vision, Chaucer has given us in the *Hous of Fame* a complete poem, rich in thought and fancy, in story and significance." [55]

"THE LEGEND OF GOOD WOMEN"

(Extant in twelve Mss. several of which contain only fragments of the poem)

Authenticity: Mentioned, as "the Seintes Legende of Cupyde" in the Introduction to the Man of Law's Prologue; attributed to Chaucer by Lydgate (*Fall of Princes*).

Date: 1386–95.

Source: Discussed below.

Metrical Form: The heroic couplet, here used for the first time in English poetry.

A manuscript in the Cambridge University Library offers a version of the Prologue to the *Legend of Good*

[55] *Mod. Lang. Notes,* 30. 65–68. An interesting hypothesis by B. H. Bronson is noted under Bibliography.

Women which differs materially from that contained in the other manuscripts. It alters the order of many passages, includes some lines which do not appear elsewhere, and omits lines which are found in other copies of the poem. The most notable singularity of this version of the Prologue is the omission of the "dedication" to Queen Anne, contained in lines B 496, 497:

> And whan this book is maad, yive hit the quene
> On my behalfe, at Eltham, or at Shene.

The unique version of this Cambridge manuscript (designated as the A-text in Skeat's edition) was for many years regarded as the earlier form of the Prologue. It is now the general opinion that this text represents a later recension. The B-text was probably written in 1385 or 1386, after Chaucer had terminated his duties at the Customs House, had left London, and had taken up his residence in the country. References to the *Hous of Fame* and to the *Troilus and Criseyde,* in lines B 417 and B 332, support this date for the Prologue; and the first two hundred lines give the very definite impression that the poet had left the city and was residing in the country.

That the *Legend* was undertaken to please the queen, if not at her specific request, as Lydgate says, seems certain. The identification of Alceste with Queen Anne is not quite so certain, but the respect which the poet shows, both for Alceste and for "hir flour, the dayesye," suggests the devotion of the courtier. The revised text may safely be assigned to a date after 1394, the year in which Queen Anne died. King Richard, in his grief at the loss of his queen, tore down the palace at Sheen, which had been her favorite residence, and avoided everything which might remind him of her. The omission of the "dedication" to Queen Anne from the A-text and the modification of some of the more ardent expressions of devotion to the daisy make it appear likely that Chaucer's revision of the Prologue was undertaken at a time when such pointed references to his "lady sovereyne" would not have been acceptable to the king. The ultimate date for the revised version of the Prologue may be set at 1395.

The use of the conventional device of the dream at once suggests the influence of the French poets of courtly love. The entire Prologue, indeed, is written in the spirit of that school of poetry. We are not only brought at once into the ideal springtime landscape so familiar to readers of the dream poems of the later Middle Ages; the poem reflects the traditions of courtly love in more essential matters than its setting, and concludes by representing the author himself before the bar of a court of love. The charge brought against him is one which can be understood only in the light of the tradition that poets had it as their principal function to glorify love and to sing the praise of women; and the penance laid upon him is intended to bring him back into the fold of conventional love poetry, after his dereliction in writing of Criseyde and in translating a work which contains the satiric utterances of Jean de Meun.

It is hardly necessary to point out the passages which reflect this conventional atmosphere, so frequently encountered in Chaucer's earlier works. Of more significance, perhaps, is the evidence that certain specific poems by fourteenth-century French authors had recently been exerting an influence upon the poet. A literary fad, which has been called the "Cult of the Daisy," had been inaugurated by Guillaume de Machaut, in the *Dit de la Marguerite,* wherein the daisy receives extravagant praise, presumably because the King of Cyprus, for whom the poem was written, was in love with a lady who bore the name of Marguerite. Froissart, in his *Dittie de la Flour de la Marguerite* and his *Paradys d'Amours,* adopted the convention thus inaugurated by Machaut; and Deschamps followed suit in several of his poems, notably his *Lay de Franchise.* That Chaucer was familiar with the marguerite-poems of Deschamps and Froissart has been put beyond question by Professor Lowes;[56] and it is quite possible that the structure of the Prologue to the *Legend of Good Women* was influenced, in some measure, by the *Lay de Franchise* and the *Paradys d'Amours.* It is to be said, however, that no poem which has yet been discovered can be definitely called a source of the Prologue.

For the Legends, on the other hand, various definite sources can usually be assigned.[57] The *Legend of Cleopatra* reveals less direct borrowing than the others. It was probably derived, in part, from the fourth book of the *Epitome Rerum Romanorum* by L. Annaeus Florus, a Roman historian of the second century. It is also possible that Chaucer had seen a Latin translation of Plutarch's *Life of Antony.* The story of Cleopatra is to be found in Boccaccio's *De Claris Mulieribus,* and in his *De Casibus Virorum et Feminarum Ilustrium,* and Chaucer may have consulted these works. The description of the battle of Actium has obviously been influenced by accounts of battles at sea

[56] *Publ. Mod Lang. Assn.* 19. 593–683.

[57] The sources of the Legends are fully discussed by Bech in an article in *Anglia* (5. 313–82), which also considers the relation between the Legends and the similar stories told by Gower in the *Confessio Amantis.*

that had been fought in the poet's own times.

The *Legend of Thisbe of Babylon* is based upon Ovid: *Metamorphoses*, IV. 55–166. Chaucer follows his original very closely; but he fails to tell us that the trysting-tree was "a faire high Mulberie with fruit as white as snow," and he has had the good taste to omit from Thisbe's dying speech her injunction to the tree to bear black fruit henceforward, in token of the tragedy which has taken place beneath its boughs.

The *Legend of Dido, Queen of Carthage* is retold from the *Aeneid* Books I–IV. Chaucer shows characteristic freedom by rearranging his material in chronological order. "Myn autour," from whom he quotes the letter which Dido wrote "before that she deyde," is Ovid (*Heroides,* Epistle VII. 1–8).

The first twenty-eight lines of the *Legend of Hypsipyle and Medea* are undoubtedly original with Chaucer. The rest of the legend is based very largely upon Guido delle Colonne (*Historia Troiana,* Books I and II). The letters of the two heroines are from the sixth and twelfth epistles of Ovid's *Heroides,* in a very much abridged form, which seems to indicate that the poet was growing a little weary of the lamentations and reproaches of Cupid's saints. Although he refers specifically to the *Argonauticon* of Valerius Flaccus, the evidence that he made any use of that work is exceedingly slight.

In the fourth line of the *Legend of Lucretia*, Chaucer refers to "Ovyde and Titus Livius" as if they were his sources. As a matter of fact, his legend is derived almost entirely from Ovid (*Fasti,* II. 721–852), and at times his version is little more than a translation. Livy's account of Lucrece is to be found in Book I, chapters 57–59. The allusion to "the grete Austin," in line 1690, seems to indicate that Chaucer had seen the commentary of St. Augustine upon the story (*De Civitate,* chapter xix).

The *Legend of Ariadne* begins by following, rather closely, the account given by Ovid in the *Metamorphoses* (VII. 456–58, VIII. 6–176); and the ending is obviously based on the *Heroides,* Epistle X. Dr. Meech has shown that the treatment of the story indicates use of the *Ovide Moralisé* or of Filippo's translation of the *Heroides.*

The *Legend of Philomela* is based throughout upon Ovid (*Metamorphoses,* VI. 426–605), but Chaucer has incorporated some suggestions from a work by Chrétien de Troyes which he encountered in the *Ovide Moralisé.*

C. G. Child, in an article in *Modern Language Notes* (11. 476–90), has demonstrated that the *Legend of Phyllis* contains material to be found in Boccaccio's *De Genealogia Deorum.* Similar material, however, appears in Filippo's Italian translation of Ovid (*Heroides,* II), which Chaucer seems to have consulted.

The *Legend of Hypermnestra* is taken from Ovid (*Heroides,* Epistle XIV), but some details may be traced to Filippo's translation. The story also appears in the *Fables* of Hyginus, but there is very little reason to believe that Chaucer consulted this work. Professor Curry, who is perhaps a little too ready to discover a predominant influence of astrology in the shaping of characters in Chaucer's poetry, believes that the poet has sought to "rationalize the life and character of Hypermnestra," according to the scientific method, by providing her with a horoscope which would account for the fact that she alone, among the fifty daughters of Aegyptus, failed to slay her husband at her father's command. "Venus's influence, it would seem, is responsible for Hypermnestra's beauty of person and for the partial suppression of Mars's malice; and Jupiter, joined in some benevolent aspect with Venus, has been most powerful in the creation of her gentle, sympathetic character and her marital fidelity. As the heavens revolve, however, the progress of Saturn into a position of evil aspect results in her untimely death." [58]

The *Legend of Good Women* has been a favorite battle ground of Chaucerian scholarship. The problem presented by the two versions of the Prologue and the difficulty of identifying Alceste, to the satisfaction of minds that are trained to seek scientific precision even in the works of the poets, have between them provided the learned journals with many pages of controversy, to which the present writer will not so much as refer his readers. The important matter of the chronological relation between the two versions of the Prologue has happily emerged from the dust of controversy, and only the most sceptical will care to retrace the steps in the long and arduous struggle which has ended in establishing the priority of the B-version. For the settlement of the other problem, the identification of Alceste, we must await the return to this troubled planet of Geoffrey Chaucer himself, who alone can speak with final authority upon the subject. Nothing short of his word, one would surmise, will put an end to the discussion.

[58] *Chaucer and the Mediaeval Sciences,* 164–71.

"Tretis of the Astrolabie"

(Extant in 24 Mss.)

Authenticity: Ascribed to Chaucer in one of the Mss. and by Lydgate.

Date: 1391.

Source: Based very largely on Messahala: *Compositio et Operatio Astrolabie.*

Chaucer's *Treatise on the Astrolabe* is an attempt to describe in simple English, intelligible to a boy of ten, the structure and use of an instrument employed, from very ancient times, to determine the altitude of the sun and stars and to work out various other problems in astronomy. The Prologue promises five parts, but the work breaks off before the second part is brought to an end.

In the Prologue, Chaucer speaks of treatises on the Astrolabe in Greek, Arabic, Hebrew, and Latin, and professes to be merely "a lewd compilatour of the labour of olde Astrologiens." He makes it very clear, however, that Latin works on the subject formed the principal source of his own treatise; and Skeat, following a suggestion by Henry Bradshaw, discovered the particular work to which Chaucer was chiefly indebted. It was a Latin version of the *Compositio et Operatio Astrolabie,* by Messahala, an Arabian astronomer, who lived in the eighth century. The full text of this treatise is printed in Skeat's edition of Chaucer's Astrolabe, published by the Early English Text Society, in 1872. The first and longer portion of the work, which describes in detail the making of an Astrolabe, has little bearing upon Chaucer's treatise, since the "suffisaunt Astrolabie" which he had given "litell Lowis" was probably procured ready-made; but he has made generous use of the second part, which describes the operation of the instrument. His own Part I is founded very closely upon Messahala, though he has expanded his original frequently for the sake of greater clarity. In Part II, he has drawn about two-thirds of his material from Messahala, sometimes translating almost word for word. The works of other astronomers and astrologians probably furnished him with the rest of his "conclusiouns."

Two references in Part II to "the yeer of oure Lord 1391," make it appear likely that the Treatise was composed in that year. The fact that the tables, which the treatise promised but did not include, were to be calculated "aftur the latitude of Oxenford" has led to the assumption that "litell Lowis" was a student at Oxford. One of the manuscripts has a colophon which states that the Treatise was "compilatus per Galfridum Chauciers ad Filium suum Lodewicum, scolarem tunc temporis Oxonie, ac sub tutela illius nobilissimi philosophi Magistri N. Strode." The colophon, however, is added to the manuscript in a later hand and is probably a mere conjecture.

CHAPTER IV

TROILUS AND CRISEYDE
Sources

THE story of Troilus and his faithless mistress was
first told by Benoit of Sainte-Maure, a French
poet of the twelfth century. His *Roman de Troie* (ca.
1160), a long poem in octosyllabic couplets, was founded
very largely upon two works which mediæval readers
believed to be accounts by eye-witnesses of the siege of
Troy. His principal source was the *Daretis Phrygii De
Excidio Trojae Historia,* which purported to be a translation, by Nepos, of a document discovered by the translator at Athens. No one would now think of attributing
its dull Latin prose to Nepos, nor does anyone believe
that the *Historia* originated with Dares the Phrygian,
described by Homer as a priest of Hephaestus, dwelling
in Troy. (*Iliad* 5.9). Benoit, however, doubtless accepted
the work as a dependable history, and he based the first
three-fifths of his romance very largely upon the account
of "Dares," imitating his source in tracing the story of
Troy back to its most remote origins in the Argonautic
expedition. Out of the fifty-two pages of Latin text, he
spun the first 24,425 lines of his romance.

For the remaining portion of his poem, Benoit drew also

upon another eye-witness account of the siege, the *Ephemeris Belli Trojani,* attributed to Dictys the Cretan, who was supposed to have taken a share in the capture of Troy, among the allies of Idomeneus of Crete. A Latin version of the *Ephemeris,* belonging to the fourth century, A. D., and purporting to be the work of one Septimius Romanus, informs us that the original was a diary kept in Phœnician characters by Dictys, during the siege, and later recovered from his tomb. The story of the diary, of the tin case in which it was buried beside its author, and of the discriminating earthquake which rescued so important a document from oblivion, is obviously a hoax. That the Latin version, however, was actually based upon a Greek original has been put beyond doubt, by the discovery, in 1899, of a papyrus containing a portion of the Greek "Dictys."

In neither of these sources did Benoit de Sainte-Maure find any suggestion of the love-story of Troilus. The young prince himself takes a conspicuous part in many of the battle-scenes of "Dares," who describes him as follows: *"Troilum magnum, pulcherrimum, pro aetate valentem, fortem, cupidum virtutis."* We are also informed that on one occasion, Troilus wounded Diomedes, but there is not the faintest hint that the two were rivals in love. Criseyde, who appears as Briseida in both Dares and Benoit, is thus described by the former: *"Briseidam formosam, non alta statura, candidam, capillo flavo et molli, superciliis iunctis, oculis venustis, corpore aequali, blandam, affabilem, verecundam, animo simplici, piam."* This description is the only reference to the lady in the work of "Dares," who entirely omits the story of Hippodamia, daughter of Brises (Briseis or Briseida), the slave girl who was taken from Achilles by Agamemnon.

"Dictys," on the other hand, relates the story of the daughter of Brises, but he calls her Hippodamia, never employing the patronymic Briseis, or Briseida. Of Troilus, he has less to say than "Dares," but he gives us a brief account of the prince's death and of the mourning which it caused among the Trojans.

Out of such fragmentary references in his sources, Benoit wove the story of the love of Troilus for the faithless Briseida. It is clear that he did not understand the Greek patronymic forms and therefore did not identify Hippodamia, whose story he took over from the pages of "Dictys," with the Briseida whom he found described by "Dares." He seems to have felt that so charming a lady should be provided with a love-story, and he proceeded to invent one for her, quite unconscious of the fact that the heroine of this new amour was the very daughter of Brises, for whose favors he represents Achilles and Agamemnon as contending.

Benoit's account of the loves of Troilus and Briseida is but an episode, woven into his story of the siege of Troy. It occupies, in all, only 1349 lines out of the 30,316 of the *Roman de Troie,* beginning at Line 13,065. The story, as Benoit presents it, runs as follows:

At a conference between the Greeks and Trojans, called at the request of the Greeks, Antenor is exchanged for King Thoas; and Calchas, in debate with Priam, wins assent to his request for the restoration of his daughter, Briseida. The reader gains his first knowledge of the love of Troilus and Briseida from the lamentations of the lovers when they hear of their approaching separation. They spend the night together grieving; and on the next

morning, Briseida takes her departure from Troy, Troilus
leading her horse. The poet pictures her grief but assures
us she will soon be comforted with a new love, pausing,
at this point, to reflect upon the inconstancy of woman.
Diomedes, who escorts Briseida from the walls of Troy
to the Greek camp, begins his wooing, but is met by discreet evasions. Briseida informs him that she is now too
sad to think of love, but assures him that she would hold
no man dearer than Diomedes, if she were to love at all.

In her father's tent, Briseida receives the greetings of
the Greek chieftains; and in three days, Benoit tells us,
she has forgotten her desire to return to Troy. Diomedes,
however, makes but slow progress in his suit. He presents
her with a steed which he has taken from Troilus in
battle; but she receives the gift, at the hands of his messenger, with a speech in which she sings the praises of
Troilus and warns Diomedes that the capture of the horse
will be avenged. Her warning is speedily justified, for
the Trojan Polydamas unhorses Diomedes and seizes his
mount for Troilus.

During a six-months' truce, which presently ensues, Diomedes suffers from the cruelty of Briseida, who becomes
more perverse as she is assured of his love. For many
days, he begs her mercy in vain. Toward the end of the
truce, however, she is persuaded to grant him her sleeve
to carry into battle as a favor. She consents, also, to his
riding the horse which he captured from Troilus; and we
are told that her love for the Trojan prince is *"quassee"*
(*cassée*). Going into battle with Briseida's favor, Diomedes encounters Troilus. Their first combat is interrupted; but in a second encounter, some weeks later,
Troilus wounds his rival so seriously that he is carried

from the field. Pity for the wounded Diomedes completes the conquest of Briseida, who visits him often, to nurse and comfort him, no longer dissembling her love. She realizes that her infidelity to Troilus has destroyed her fair fame, but resolves to be true to her new lover.

Troilus, in despair at her treachery, fights the more fiercely, on that account, and succeeds in unhorsing the great Achilles. In the next battle, however, Troilus is surrounded and unhorsed by the Myrmidons, and before he can rise, he is slain by Achilles. The mourning for Troilus and the lament of Hecuba bring the episode to a close.

The story extends to Line 21,782 of the *Roman,* for it has been frequently interrupted by other matters,—battles, truces, the death and funeral of Hector, the love of Achilles for Polyxena, etc. Troilus, however, takes a prominent part in many of these episodes. His love-story and his exploits together furnish a large part of the interest for nearly 9,000 consecutive lines of Benoit's poem.

GUIDO DELLE COLONNE

A paraphrase of Benoit's *Roman de Troie,* written in Latin prose and entitled *Historia Trojana,* was produced in 1287 by a Sicilian, named Guido delle Colonne. Guido cites Dictys and Dares as his authorities, although his debt to either of them was certainly slight, and makes no mention of the French romance which he was following so closely. It was not until the nineteenth century that the extent of his plagiarism was thoroughly demonstrated. Since he was virtually translating the *Roman de Troie,* with a few abridgments and digressions of his own, it is not surprising that the story of Troilus and Briseida, as he presents it, differs only in unimportant details from the version of Benoit de Sainte-Maure.

BOCCACCIO

About 1338, Giovanni Boccaccio produced his version of the love-story, under the title of *Il Filostrato*. He was indubitably acquainted with Benoit's *Roman* and Guido's *Historia*, and it has been demonstrated that he made use of both, basing his story principally upon Benoit and drawing upon Guido here and there for a few details in language or situation. Boccaccio's version of the story, however, differs from that presented in either of his sources, in the following important matters:

1. The entire interest in the *Filostrato* is concentrated in the story of Troilus and his love, and the events of the siege of Troy are relegated to the background.

2. Boccaccio gives an account of the love of Troilus from its beginnings, whereas both Guido and Benoit begin the episode with the restoration of Briseida to her father, giving us to understand that, at the time, Troilus was her accepted lover.

3. In recounting this added episode in the story, Boccaccio introduces a new figure—a friend of the hero and cousin to the heroine, by name Pandaro—who acts as go-between in the wooing.

4. In the *Filostrato,* the name of the heroine is altered to Criseida (in some of the manuscripts and in the printed editions spelled "Griseida"), perhaps because Boccaccio, familiar with the name and history of Briseis, saw that Benoit had inadvertently attributed two dif-

ferent love-stories to Hippodamia, daughter of Brises.

5. By separating the story from the larger narrative of the siege of Troy, Boccaccio gave it a definite structure of its own and developed its dramatic possibilities much more fully.

The *Filostrato* is written in Italian in *ottava rima*.[1] In the belief that the careful student of Chaucer will wish to have readily available the material for a close comparison between the structure of *Troilus and Criseyde* and that of the *Filostrato*, I append a full summary of the Italian poem:

Canto I. After an invocation to his mistress and an appeal to other lovers to attend his song and to pray the God of Love on his behalf, Boccaccio tells of the siege of Troy and of the desertion of the city by Calchas. Criseida, widowed daughter of Calchas, alarmed at the popular outcry against her father, visits Hector ,and secures his assurance of protection. She returns to her home "e quivi riposossi," loved by all who know her and untroubled by the care of son or daughter. The siege wears on, with varying fortunes, but does not interrupt the religious observances of the Trojans, who pay especial reverence to Pallas. Criseida attends a spring festival in honor of the Palladium, taking her place near the door of the temple (St. 1–19).

Troilo, roving through the temple, pauses occasionally

[1] *Il Filostrato e il Ninfale Fiesolano,* ed. V. Pernicone, Bari, 1937. N. E. Griffin and A. B. Myrick: *The Filostrato of Giovanni Boccaccio* (text and prose translation), Univ. of Penn. Press, Philadelphia, 1929. A translation into English verse by H. M. Cummings was published by the Princeton Press in 1924. See also W. M. Rossetti: *Chaucer's Troylus . . . compared with Boccaccio's Filostrato,* published by the Chaucer Society.

to praise or to disparage the ladies, to ridicule the sighs of some lover, or to comment upon the levity of woman. He acknowledges that he has experienced the folly of love and enjoyed some of its delights, but praises Jupiter that he has escaped. He suddenly catches sight of Criseida, in her black mantle, and is wounded by the dart of Love. Throughout the service, he remains gazing at her; and when she leaves the temple, he departs, a changed man. He returns home with his companions, continuing to jest at love, but soon makes excuse to send them on their way and retires to his chamber, there to muse upon Criseida. He believes that to win her love would be a great good fortune, and resolves to follow where love leads him, concealing his love if possible. In high spirits, he sings and praises Love (St. 20–40).

From day to day, Troilo's love increases so that he thinks of little but Criseida. He thinks no more of fame nor of the danger of the city, but love drives him on to perform such deeds in the field that "gli Greci il temean come la morte." He is robbed of his sleep, loses his appetite, and grows pale with grief, but whether Criseida had knowledge of his sufferings is uncertain. Troilo begins to fear that she will love another. He regrets his former gibes at love and fears the ridicule of his friends if his secret be discovered. He laments that he loves one who is hard as a stone and cold as ice, prays Love for his assistance, and prophesies his early death if he experiences no alleviation of his pain. His torment is multiplied a hundredfold each day (St. 41–57).

Canto II. Troilo is visited, one day, by his friend Pandaro, "un troian giovinetto, d'alto lignaggio e molto coraggioso," who asks the cause of his sorrow. Troilo urges him to depart, lest he witness his friend's death, assuring him that the cause of his distress is not the siege, but a sorrow which he will conceal. Urged by Pandaro, in the name of their friendship, he at length confesses that it is love which troubles him, imploring his friend not to reveal his secret. He has not told Pandaro before, because he could expect no help from one whom he has seen unable to help himself in love. Pandaro acknowledges his helplessness in his own case, but argues that he may be of assistance to his friend, and at last induces Troilo to go so far as to confess that the lady whom he loves is a relative of Pandaro. Assured that his friend would help him, "se quella ch' ami fosse mia sorella," Troilo confesses that he loves Criseida, Pandaro's cousin. Pandaro laughs and bids Troilo be of good cheer, for Criseida is worthy of his love. Only one obstacle does he fear; his cousin is the most correct of women (più che altra donna onesta), but Pandaro will find means, with sugared words, to work his friend's desire, employing all his wit in the enterprise. He knows that such amours are hardly fitting to a lady and that his own reputation, as well as hers, will be lost if the affair is ever discussed by vulgar tongues; but he believes that lovers should follow their desires, provided they act prudently. Since it is his belief that all women are amorous and are restrained only by shame, he would not believe his cousin, even if she were to tell him that she had no desires. He is sure that he can bring the lovers mutual comfort. Troilo is contented, though he has some fears lest Criseida, through timidity, will not listen to her cousin. He assures Pandaro that he desires nothing dishonorable from such a lady and will be content if he is permitted to go on loving her. Pandaro again promises to assume the go-between's labor, of which he promises Troilo the "dolce fine" (St. 1–32).

Parting with his friend, Pandaro goes at once to Criseida. He leads her aside, and, after much pleasant chat, gazes fixedly at her, praises her beauty, and tells her that there is one who loves her. Blushing, she seeks further information. After eulogizing her lover and holding her a little in suspense, Pandaro tells her that it is Troilo who loves her. On the verge of tears, Criseida reproaches him, asking him what treatment she may expect from strangers when her very cousin tries to make her accept the monarchy of Love. She admits that Troilo is great and valorous. Since her husband's death, however, her wishes have been far from love. If she were to give any man her love, it would be to Troilo; but she begs Pandaro to leave her to her lot, suggesting that Troilo can easily find another lady to his liking (St. 33–51).

Pandaro, feeling himself repulsed, rises to go, but turns to assure his cousin that he has given her only such advice as he might have given sister, daughter, or wife. He knows that Troilo is worthy of her love; he is as secret, faithful, and loyal as any man that ever lived. Pandaro reminds her of her widow's weeds and of her wasting youth, warning her that age or death may steal her beauty. This argument takes instant effect. She admits the truth of what he says, and asks him if he really believes that she can still know the joys of love, asking him, also, how he first discovered Troilo's secret. Pandaro smiles and tells her of riding in the woods one day with the prince and hearing him sing of love. His suspicions aroused, he sought an opportunity to talk with him alone and won his secret from him. He declares that he has now come to Criseida out of sheer pity, and asks her if she will let her lover die of unrequited love. She is moved to pity, for—she confesses—she is not so cruel as she appears. She sees where Pandaro's pitying desires will lead her, but she consents to see Troilo, praying that he may be discreet. Pandaro reassures her and takes his leave (St. 52–67).

Criseida retires to her chamber and turns over all his words in her heart. She debates the matter with herself: "I am young, beautiful, charming, and blithe; a widow, rich, noble, and beloved: why should I not fall in love, if I am discreet and keep it hidden? My youth is slipping away; should I waste it miserably? In all this land I know no woman without a lover; shall I lose my time for nothing, since it is no sin to do as others do? Who will want me when I grow old? Regrets will then be vain. This man is fair, noble, wise, of royal blood and high valor. Why not grant him my love? What bliss will I yet have with him, if I love him as he loves me! Furtive love is sweeter than marriage." She considers the other side of the question: the disquiet of love, its sighs and jealousies, the disparity in rank between Troilo and herself, the uncertainty of holding his love, the dangerous prospect of discovery. Nevertheless, she is unable to drive the image of Troilo from her bosom (St. 68–78).

Returning to Troilo, Pandaro, well content, brings him such comfort that the prince revives like drooping flowers at the dawn. As joyful as if a thousand Troys had been given him, he embraces Pandaro, and together they go out, in the hope of catching a glimpse of Criseida.

She is at her window, and Troilo is surprised to find that her looks are not severe or harsh,—for which he praises God and Pandaro. No longer lukewarm, Criseida desires Troilo above every other bliss and regrets that she did not sooner know of his love (St. 79–83).

The lovers see each other from time to time. At first, Troilo is in the highest spirits. He makes lavish gifts and makes his raiment gay. But his love burns more fiercely, and he discovers that he is not content merely with Criseida's great courtesy and with the privilege of gazing upon her. He declares that he would spend a hundred and fifty nights in hell for one night with her. He seeks advice from Pandaro. His friend advises a letter, which he promises to deliver without delay. This counsel pleases Troilo; but, as a timid lover, he fears that Criseida will refuse to receive the letter. Pandaro promises that he will bring a reply from the lady. Troilo, praying that his writing and Pandaro's mission may be fruitful, writes the letter, in which he sets forth his sufferings, praises Criseida's beauty, and tells her that she alone can console him. He bathes the gem of his signet on his tearful cheeks, seals the letter, and kisses it a hundred times or more, calling it blessed because it will reach his lady's hands (St. 84–107).

Pandaro takes the letter to Criseida, who greets him, between fear and desire, with a demand for tidings. He offers the letter, but she will not take it. Bidding him have some regard for her, as well as for the young man, she commands him to take the letter back to Troilo. He comments on the perversity of her sex, and Criseida, with a smile, takes the letter and puts it in her bosom, promising to read it at her leisure. Pandaro takes his leave, and Criseida eagerly seeks an opportunity to read her letter. She resolves to find time and place to extinguish the flame which burns her, lest her face betray her love-lorn condition. She will neither die nor cause another to die, when she has it in her power to heal both. No one could now call her pitiless to Troilo: she longs to be in his arms (St. 108–117).

Pandaro returns and asks Criseida what she thinks of his friend's writing. Under his urging, she writes a reply, in which she assures her lover that she will be glad to content him so far as her honor permits. "I mean to live and die in chastity. If the world were what it should be, it would be well for me to gratify you; but such as it is, so we must accept it. I know your worth so well that I am sure you will see what is meet for me to do. If it were not forbidden, I would gladly do whatever would give you pleasure." She concludes with a prayer that God may content their desires (St. 118–127).

Troilo, on reading her letter, perceives that she loves him, but he is not greatly comforted. He and Pandaro agree that Criseida must change her tone ere long, and Troilo hopes for the hour that will bring the fruition of his suffering. The lovers exchange letters often. Criseida's letters are sometimes mild and sometimes bitter. Pandaro, seeing that Troilo still suffers, seeks out his cousin and begs her to bring her lover better comfort. To her protests that she will preserve the crown of her chastity and will always love Troilo like a brother, he replies with a suggestion that the world takes no heed of what happens when it is asleep. He assures her that no one will know what Troilo does and urges her to tell him when, where, and how she will receive her lover. She bursts into lamentations, saying that the blood freezes in her heart at what he asks of her and regretting that she ever listened to him, when first he planted desire in her heart. She can no longer refuse. She begs Pandaro to take care that all is kept secret. He reassures her. She reminds him that ere long, part of her household will be absent at a festival: she will then be with her lover. Let him be discreet and keep his ardor well hidden (St. 128–143).

Canto III. After a brief invocation to his love, the poet reminds us of Troilo's discontent. Pandaro, returning from his latest interview with Criseida, finds him musing in a temple. Leading him aside, he says: "Friend, so much I felt for you when I saw you so greatly languishing for love, that my heart sustained a great part of your torment; so that I have never rested until I could give you comfort. For you, I am become a go-between; for you, I have cast my honor to the ground; for you, I have corrupted the pure breast of my cousin (de mia sorella) and planted in her heart the love of you. Nor will it now be long before you have the fair Criseida in your arms. But, as God knows, who sees all things, and as you know yourself, not any hope of gain has drawn me on; only the fidelity, which as a friend I bear you, has led me to this labor, in order that you might find mercy. Therefore, I pray that you may act as befits a prudent man. You know that Criseida's fame is hallowed among the people, nor was anything but good ever said of her. If evil should befall her, I fear the great shame that will come to me, 'che parente le sono, e trattator similemente.' Wherefore I beseech you, as strongly as

I can, that all this business may be secret between us. I have removed from Criseida's heart all shame and every thought against you, and have so smitten it, by speaking of your love, that she loves you and is disposed to do whatever it pleases you to command her." Again he promises Troilo that he shall soon have Criseida in his arms, and once more he begs him to be secret, "O my friend, be not displeased if many times I beg this of you; you see well that my prayer is honest" (St. 1–10).

Who could tell the joy which the soul of Troilo felt on hearing Pandaro? The longer his friend speaks, the more his woe goes fleeting. The sighs, which have been his in such abundance, yield place, and the wretched pain departs. His tearful face, now that he hopes for bliss, becomes joyous. And as the new spring, with leaves and blossoms, suddenly reclothes the shrubs, which stood naked in the harsh season, and makes them fair, clothing meadows, hills, and brooksides with herbs and new flowers,—so, filled with new joy, Troilo laughs with countenance serene. Looking Pandaro in the face, he says: "Dear friend, you should remember both how and when you found me weeping, in the bitter time I used to have through love, and how your words sought knowledge of the cause of my distress. You know how long I held myself from revealing it to you, who are my only friend; nor was there any peril in telling you, although through shame I did not. Think, therefore, how I could assent to such a thing,—I, who tremble with fear, whilst I talk with you about it, lest any other hear it. Nevertheless, by that god who governs equally the heavens and the earth, I swear to you—and so may I not come within the hands of cruel Agamemnon—that if my life were eternal, as it is mortal, you could live secure; that to the best of my power, I will keep faith with you; and that the honor of her who has wounded my heart shall be preserved." He begs his friend not to give himself the vile name which should be left to the "dolenti avari," who perform such labors for gold. "And that you may know what good will I bear you, I have a sister Polyxena, more prized for beauty than others, and there is also the fairest Helen, who is my sister-in-law: open your heart, if either of them please you; then let me go to work with her who is your choice." He begs Pandaro to complete the service he has begun (St. 11–19).

The desired moment comes, and Criseida summons Pandaro, but Troilo has gone forth to battle. Pandaro sends a messenger to the prince, who joyfully returns to the city. At nightfall, with great circumspection, he enters Criseida's house and lies in hiding "in certo luogo rimoto ed oscuro." Criseida, who has heard him come, coughs, that he may know she is aware of his presence; then she speeds her maids to bed, declaring that she is too sleepy to stay awake. When all are asleep, she comes down to her lover, torch in hand. She leads him to her chamber, and they retire together (St. 20–32).

"O sweet night and much desired! What a night wast thou to the two joyful lovers! If the cunning of all the poets were mine, I could not tell their joy." The lovers can hardly believe that they are in each other's arms and fear that it is all a dream. Troilo often kisses her eyes, declaring that they hold him prisoner in the net of love. No moment passes without a thousand sighs,—not such as spring from grief, but gentle sighs, such as show the affection which lies within the heart. The poet calls upon misers to reflect that they have never felt such pleasure, in their pursuit of gold, as comes to the man who is favored at once by love and fortune. They may lie and say yes and call love a grievous madness: "God make them sad, and give their gains to lovers." The lovers converse together, telling of their past anguish and ever taking fresh delight in one another. "Ragion non vi si fece di dormire" (St. 33–41).

With the crowing of the cocks, the lovers realize they must part, and they curse the dawn and weep. Troilo wonders what he is to do, if already, at the first step, longing to return so strains him that life endures it not. He seeks assurance that he will stand as continually in her mind as he holds her in his. She urges him to live secure in her love and tells him that she will know no happy hour until he is with her again (St. 42–51).

Troilo returns to his palace. He cannot sleep, but revolves in his mind each word and act of his mistress. Criseida lies thinking of Troilo and giving thanks to Love. Pandaro visits Troilo in the morning and receives his thanks. Troilo assures him that he has raised him from hell to paradise. Though he were to die a thousand times a day, he could not repay his debt, for it is no slight thing which Pandaro has given him. Pandaro again warns him to be secret. Troilo gives his promise, relates his happy adventures, and tells Pandaro that he burns more than ever, though this fire is of another quality. He cannot exhaust the pleasure that he takes in talking about his love (St. 52–63).

After some time, fortune provides another opportunity for a meeting between the lovers. As before, Troilo conceals himself within Criseida's house until she can come to lead him to her chamber. They both confess that their love increases from day to day. When they perceive the signs of hostile day, they part as before (St. 64–71).

Troilo lives in great content, believing that all other men live in sadness, compared with him. Sometimes he leads Pandaro into a garden to listen to his praises of Criseida. He sings to Venus: "O Light eternal, whose joyous splendor makes beautiful the third heaven, from which rain down pleasure, beauty, mercy and love! Beloved of the Sun and daughter of Jove, benign lady of every gentle heart, certain cause of the good which moves me to sweet sighing for my fair estate: ever be thy virtue praised! Heaven, earth, sea, and hell, each in itself feels thy power and clear light. And if I discern the truth, plants, seeds, the grass, birds, beast, and fish feel thy power in the pleasant season; yea, men and gods. Nor does any creature in the world, without thee, avail or endure. Thou first, beautiful goddess, didst move Jove to delight and to the high effects for which all things live and have their being. Thou often makest him merciful to the troublous deeds of mortals; merited weepings thou turnest into glad and delightful feasts; and in a thousand forms thou hast sent him down hither, when, now for one woman, now for another, thou has wounded him. At thy pleasure, thou makest fierce Mars benign and humble, and chasest away all ire. Thou drivest out cowardice and fillest with lofty pride the man who sighs, O Goddess, for thee. Thou makest everyone, according as he desires, deserving and worthy of high sovereignty. Courteous and gentle dost thou make those who are inflamed with thy fire. Thou holdest in unity houses and cities, realms, provinces, and all the world, fair goddess;

thou art the certain cause of friendships and of their precious fruits. Thou alone knowest the hidden qualities of things; whence comes it that thou puttest such meaning into them that thou causest him to marvel who knows not how to estimate thy power. Thou, goddess, settest law for the universe, whereby it maintains itself in being." Troilo continues his song, praising Criseida scarcely less reverently than Venus, and blessing the happy hour when he first saw his lady's eyes. He declares that he will desert riches, war, the pleasures of hunting and of falconry, to devote his heart entirely to love (St. 72–89).

Nevertheless, we are informed that his love makes him more dreaded by the Greeks than before, and that, in times of truce, he goes hawking and hunting, scorning small game and pursuing only bears, boars, and great lions. When he sees his lady, he is as fair as a falcon freed from its hood. All his talk is of love, of fair breeding and full courtesy. Though of royal blood, he makes himself benign to all alike. He holds in detestation pride, envy, and avarice. But such bliss lasts but little while, thanks to jealous fortune! She turns an angry face on Troilo and bereaves him of all the sweet fruits of Criseida's love (St. 90–94).

Canto IV. The siege is still maintained. Hector, with a chosen band, makes a sally, but the Trojans are discomfited and return to the city, leaving Antenor and some others in the hands of the enemy. Priam asks for a truce to discuss an exchange of prisoners. In an assembly of the Greeks, Calchas pleads for the restoration of Criseida: "My lords, I am a Trojan, as you all know; and, if you well remember, it was I who first brought you hope and told you that you will attain victory, and that Troy shall be destroyed and burned. I came to give you counsel and aid, leaving behind all that I had. For that I care little, save for my young daughter, whom I left there,—alas! hard and inflexible that I was! Hitherto I have seen no time to recover her, but now that time has come, if I can obtain this boon. Here are noble barons, Trojans and others, whom you hold as prisoners. Give me but one out of the many, in ransom for whom I may have my daughter back. Console this poor old wretch, who is bereft of all other solace." He assures them that the wealth of Troy is in their hands, and that Hector, chief bulwark of the city, will shortly meet violent death. The old man's prayer takes effect; the Greeks agree to give him Antenor; and he entrusts the business of the exchange to negotiators, who carry the proposal to Priam (St. 1–13).

At a "parlamento," Troilo hears of the proposal and feels his heart transfixed. Full of anguish and fierce dread, he awaits the decision. Love makes him eager to oppose the whole thing, but reason restrains him with the thought that he may make his lady angry. The barons agree that Criseida shall be surrendered. Troilo falls in a swoon, like a lily caught by the plough-share. Priam, Hector, and his brothers do their best to recover him. Revived at last, he makes some excuse and retires to his palace (St. 14–21).

In closed and darkened chamber, he gives vent to his sorrow so violently that he seems a rabid wild-beast. Like a bull, leaping here and there under a mortal wound, groaning miserably, Troilo strikes his head against the wall and beats his face and breast and arms. His eyes, for pity of his heart, weep sorely; his sobs rob his words of meaning; he blasphemes the gods and himself. After his fury has abated a little, and his weeping moderated through length of time, he throws himself upon the bed and laments aloud, accusing Fortune of having no concern save his wretchedness. Had it pleased her to destroy the pride of Ilium, or to bereave him of his father or of Hector; had she carried off Polyxena, Paris, or Helen, and had but left him Criseida, he would not have said a word in complaint. It is her way to show her power by aiming her darts at the things a man most desires. He addresses Love, asking what he can do with his sorrowful life, if he must lose her to whom he has given all himself. Why does not his spirit, wretched and astray, flee from his ill-fortuned body and follow Criseida? His sorrowful eyes, whose only comfort was in Criseida's face, will lose their worth through weeping; in vain will they look on other virtue, since all their weal is taken from them. Who now will give comfort to his pain? If this parting had been delayed till he was better prepared, it had been easier to bear. He curses Criseida's father, as a mis-lived and unsound old man, who was led by madness to desert Troy. He wishes the seer had died on the day of his flight, or that he were now within reach of vengeance. After a thousand sighs and more lamentations, Troilo sends a messenger to summon Pandaro (St. 22–42).

Pandaro has heard the sad tidings and comes to Troilo with dismay upon his face. They weep together. Pandaro seeks to console his friend, on the ground that Troilo has had his desire, whereas he himself has never had a glance from the lady of his love. The city, moreover, is full of beautiful and gracious ladies; if Criseida is lost, they will find many others. As he has often heard it said, new love chases away the old. Let him not think of dying for Criseida. Troilo prays God to slay him before he should commit such an outrage as to change his love. Other ladies may be beautiful, graceful, and courtly, but none can compare with Criseida. He can never vanquish his love, even if he wished to do so. Death alone can part his breast and love, and in the utmost torment of hell, he will wail for Criseida. He bids Pandaro cease speaking of other ladies and asks him why he does not take his own advice and change his love, seeking another who would set his heart at peace. If even Pandaro, who has found love unkind, cannot seek a new mistress, how can he expect Troilo, who has experienced the joys of love, to expel his lady from his heart? Such love as his cannot be driven out. Once more he calls on death (St. 43–62).

Pandaro, seeing that his arguments are vain, now advises the prince to ravish Criseida away. Does he not dare, in his own city of Troy, to steal away a woman whom he loves? Troilo admits that he has considered such a plan but has discarded it, lest he betray his honor and Criseida's reputation. He has also thought of asking Criseida of his father, but this, too, would reveal their love and might not meet with success. So he is left in bewilderment, knowing not what to do and feeling the cause of his torment increasing. Pandaro replies that if he were as inflamed with love as Troilo and had the prince's power, he would do his utmost to carry his lady off. Fortune assists the hardy and rejects the coward. Criseida will not be displeased; and if she is, in short time Troilo will make his peace. Let her do without reputation, as Helen does. Once more he urges Troilo to be valorous and show more spirit, promising him to be with him in any perilous case. Troilo gives his consent to the proposal, on condition that Criseida does not oppose it. Pandaro promises to arrange a meeting between the lovers that evening (St. 63-77).

Swift fame, which reports false and true alike, has fled through Troy, carrying the tidings that Criseida has been exchanged for Antenor. When Criseida hears the news, she fears that it is true, but dares not inquire. But as it happens that one woman goes to visit another in any new situation, if she wishes her well, so many of them come to spend the day with Criseida. They tell her of the pact that has been made and express their feelings on the occasion. One says that she is glad Criseida is returning to her father and can be with him; another says she is not pleased to see her departing; a third declares that Criseida will be able to plan for peace for them all. This and much other feminine chatter Criseida hears as if she were not there. Her face cannot conceal her thoughts of love, and her soul goes seeking Troilo. She tries to rid herself of her callers, but the fools who form a circle round her think she weeps for them, who were wont to be her companions. Each tries to comfort her for something which does not grieve her, as if one were to scratch her on the heels when her head itched. After more vain chatter, they depart and she retires to her chamber. Tearing her hair and beating her breast, she laments her lot. She declares that she was born under an evil aspect of the heavens and laments that she was not stifled at her birth. She wishes she had never seen Troilo, since now Fortune robs them of each other. She believes she will not eat or drink again; and if her soul does not leave her body of itself, she will drive it out with famine. Black clothing shall be a witness to her sorrow. She wonders what her lover can do without her and if he will be able to bear his grief. She curses her father, who in his latest years has wrought such evil things. She accuses heaven of injustice, since she must bear the punishment for another's sin (St. 78–94).

Pandaro finds her weeping and dishevelled, her eyes giving true signs of her suffering. She hides her face with her arms for shame. Pandaro tries to console her, but the sight of her, looking like one who is carried to the grave, reduces him to tears. He gives her definite assurance that the sad news is true and tells her that Troilo finds it so distressful that he is bent on dying in his grief. Pandaro declares that he has wept so much to-day with Troilo that he wonders where all their tears have come from. At last, however, Troilo has somewhat abated his weeping and has a wish to be with Criseida. She declares that knowledge of Troilo's grief is more bitter to her than her own sorrow, since she loves him better than herself. Bidding him come when he will, she falls back, weeping, on her arms. Pandaro urges her to rise up and take some thought for her appearance before her lover comes, for he would kill himself if he knew she were grieving so. He declares that Troilo shall not come if she continues thus. She promises to make the effort, and he takes his leave (St. 95–108).

Pandaro, returning to Troilo, finds him brooding and reproaches him for so paining himself that his eyes seem dead in his head. He reminds him that he has lived without Criseida and asks him if he was born only for her.

He bids him be a man and lay aside his lamentations. He tells him of Criseida's grief and of her promise to receive her lover that evening. When the time approaches, Troilo leaves Pandaro and hurries to Criseida's arms (St. 109–113).

The lovers meet in dumb sorrow. Criseida swoons, and Troilo, finding that she does not hear him call her and that her eyes are closed as if in death, fears that she is dead. He places her recumbent, kissing her and seeking any signs of life in her. Convinced that she has died, he composes her body, as is done with the dead, and draws his sword, resolved to die, that his soul may follow that of his lady and dwell with hers in the nether world. He curses Jove and Fortune and takes a farewell of Troy, of Priam, and of his brothers. As he is about to stab himself, Criseida revives. She sees the sword and demands the reason for its being drawn. He tells her of his resolve, and she declares that she would never have remained in life after him (St. 114–126).

The lovers retire to bed, but now they embrace in sorrow, not in joy. Criseida tells him of her grief when she learned of their approaching separation, but assures him that since her swoon she has not been so desperate and has begun to entertain some thoughts which may be useful to them both. All her kin save her father, she reminds him, remain in Troy. Peace is continually talked of, and if Helen is restored to Menelaus, they shall have it. Then she can return. Even if that fails, she can come back in time of truce, for such visits are permitted to women, and her kinsfolk will invite her. Even when they are both in Troy, they have to pass some days without seeing each other. Whether peace is made or not, she has another hope of returning, for her father will hardly care to keep her amid the armed men of the Greek camp, and where can he send her, save back to Troy? Moreover, Calchas is avaricious and will be glad to have her return to protect the property which he has left behind him (St. 127–136).

Troilo listens attentively, half convinced of all she says. Part of their grief leaves them and hope returns, and they take delight in one another, as the bird delights in his song in the fresh season. But Troilo cannot forget that she must depart. He declares that he will slay himself if she delays her return. He does not feel at all sure that there will be peace, and he is certain that Calchas will never return to Troy. The seer is more likely to wed his daughter to a Greek, telling her that Troy is doomed. Such a thought is more grievous to Troilo than he can say. If she forsakes him, she must consider him dead. Therefore, they must find means of preventing her departure altogether. He proposes that they flee to some other region, where they will be welcomed as lords. Criseida, sighing, replies that all may be as he says; but she swears to him that neither her father's command nor his cajoleries nor a husband can turn her love from Troilo. As for his plan of fleeing away, she does not consider it a wise counsel. He would be deserting his family in time of peril. The real truth of the matter would never be believed, and it would be said that not love, but fear and cowardice, had brought him to such a course. "Reflect, also, that my chastity, held as supreme, would be spotted with infamy; nor would it ever be raised again by excuses, or by any virtue I might work, whatever I might do, though I were to live a hundred thousand years."

She bids him reflect that their love is a delight because of its secrecy, and that their ardor will abate if they possess each other securely. Therefore, she bids him take heart and trust her to return to Troy on the tenth day after her departure (St. 137–154).

Troilo declares he is content, if she will return on the tenth day, but still begs her to find a way of remaining. She reproaches him with lack of faith in her promises and lack of fortitude in bearing his misfortunes like a man. She assures him that she feels their parting as bitterly as he; but sometimes, as he knows, it is useful to wait for a time in order to gain time. He must not think she is so silly as not to be able to find a way of returning. Wherefore she beseeches him, by their mutual love, to take comfort, for she hopes soon to return. She begs him not to be caught, during her absence, by the charms of any other lady. If she learned of such a thing, she would slay herself (St. 155-162).

Troilo replies that he could not do such a thing if he would. He will tell her why he loves her so much: it was not her beauty nor her high birth, nor accomplishment nor riches—though she abounds in these—but her lofty demeanour, her high spirit and chivalrous talk, her manners, nobler than any other's, her ladylike disdain, whereby every vulgar thought or act appeared vile to her. These things neither years nor fickle fortune can take away. Thence it is that he always desires to have her with him. Once more he laments her departure. After much converse and much weeping, as the dawn approaches, the lovers part (St. 163-167).

Canto V. On the same day, Diomede comes to receive Criseida for her father. Troilo stands near by, concealing his sorrow wonderfully, but reproaching himself, under his breath, for taking no action. He asks himself why he does not seize Criseida by force of arms, slaying Diomede, betraying his brothers, and plunging Troy in outcry. Fear lest Criseida be killed alone restrains him. The lady laments her fortune. She turns disdainfully to Diomede and bids him lead her away, taunting him with the honorable exchange the Greeks have made, of a woman for a mighty king. She spurs her horse forward, looking at no one. Troilo, mounted and bearing a falcon on his wrist, accompanies her as far as beyond the walls (compagnia le fece infino fuor di tutto il vallo), and would have gone all the way with her but for fear of discovery. When Antenor has been restored to the Trojans, the lovers part. Troilo whispers Criseida to return, lest he die. He turns and rides away, not speaking to Diomede. The latter perceives their love, but conceals his thoughts. Criseida is welcomed by her father. Her heart suffers from grief, but the poet takes occasion to inform us that she will soon change, abandoning Troilo for a new lover (St. 1-14).

Troilo returns to Troy, seeks his palace, and hides himself in his chamber. He gives way to the grief he has hitherto restrained. He passes the entire day and night in lamentation. He blasphemes the gods, the goddesses, and nature, and curses his father, who had conceded Criseida to the Greeks. He reproaches himself for not having carried his lady off. Turning and tossing on his bed, he contrasts his present woe with last night's joy. Then he held her in his arms and kissed her breast and mouth and eyes; now he is alone, weary and weeping, in doubt whether such a night as the last will ever come again, and spending his embraces on the pillow. His love grows greater as his hope grows less. If his mind is so despondent at her departure, how is he to endure? (St. 15–21).

Pandaro has not been able to visit Troilo that day; but in the morning the prince sends for his friend, that he may lighten his heart a little by talking of Criseida. He begs Pandaro to tell him what he is to do to enable him to bear his misfortune. He never expects to see Criseida again and wishes he had fallen dead before he allowed her to depart. He wonders who sees her now, who sits beside her and hears her voice. Has she forgotten him, now that she is with her father? He tells Pandaro of the wretched night he has passed: of his wakefulness, and of fitful slumbers, in which he has dreamed that he was fleeing, or was alone in some dreadful place, or was in the hands of his enemies. At times, he tells Pandaro, he has trembled so much that he thought he was falling from heights to depths. He admits that he ought to have some hope of Criseida's return, but his heart will not permit him to do so (St. 22–28).

Pandaro asks him if he believes that he is the only one who has ever loved and suffered the pain of parting. He swears by Pallas that others have been as much in love as Troilo, and met with even greater misadventures than his, without giving themselves up to wretchedness. Troilo should do likewise, especially since Criseida has promised to return on the tenth day. That is not a long sojourn. He bids Troilo drive away his dreams and fancies, for they are but wind, proceeding from his melancholia. The dreams and auguries which foolish people look to are not worth a bean (non montano un moco). He begs him to spare himself, to rise up and talk with him of past joys, and to think of those that are to come. The city is great and full of delights, and now is a time of truce. He advises a visit to some pleasant quarter of the city, where some king will entertain them, until the time which his lady fixed has passed. It is not magnanimous to sorrow as Troilo is doing. People will say that he is weeping, like a coward, for the adverse times, and not for love, or that he is feigning to be sick. Troilo protests that his loss is such that he ought not to be blamed if he never did anything but weep. He will try to comfort himself, however, since his friend begs him to do so. He prays God to send the tenth day soon. He asks where they can go for pastime and himself suggests a visit to Sarpedon. He is afraid that Criseida will return in the interval and that he will remain in ignorance of her presence in the city; but Pandaro promises to have a messenger ready to notify him of her return, and the two friends make their way to the palace of Sarpedon (St. 29–40).

The latter entertains them with hunting and feasting, but these things bring little joy to Troilo, who thinks only of Criseida. Every other lady, every pastime, every sweet song is troublous to him, not seeing her in whose hands Love had placed the key to his life. Evening and morning, he sighs for her. He calls her name a thousand times and turns over and over the letters he has had from her. On the third day, he asks Pandaro what they mean by staying there, since they are not tied down and compelled to live and die there. Are they waiting to be shown out? He longs to be off. Pandaro seeks to pacify him, asking him if they came thither merely for fire. The tenth day is not yet come. To leave now might seem a slight to their host. And where could they go, where they would find the sojourn pleasanter? He begs Troilo to stay two days more (St. 41–47).

On the fifth day, they take their leave. Troilo wonders if he will find that Criseida has returned; but Pandaro, who better understands the intentions of Calchas, says otherwise within himself: he believes that the tenth day, the month, and the year will pass before Troilo sees his lady return. Arriving at the palace, they enter Troilo's chamber, to talk of Criseida, but the prince speedily drags his friend forth to gaze at the lady's dwelling, since he can do no better. Seeing the doors and windows locked, he finds his sorrow born anew and can hardly stand or walk. "Alas!" he cries, "how luminous and pleasing was this place, when her beauty dwelt there! But now, without her, it remains dark, nor do I know if ever it will have her again." Riding through the city, he revisits the places which remind him of her. He reproaches Cupid for triumphing over him and acknowledges that his former injuries to love have been well avenged. Since he is now wholly set to serve Love, however, he prays him that Criseida may be as much constrained as he is, so that she will return and put an end to his sorrow. Sometimes he goes to the gate by which Criseida left the city, remembering their parting. To himself, it seems that the color is fading from his face, and he fancies that he is sometimes pointed out as one who is utterly vanquished and perplexed. He finds some respite in singing of his love, showing in verse the cause of his sorrow. He sings of her soft glances, which have led him at last to long for death. He laments, in his song, that Love did not kill him at the very first, and begs for death, that his soul may seek Criseida's embrace.

After his song, he returns to his former sighs. Every night, in his bed, he thinks always of Criseida. He believes he can never reckon out the ten days until her return. The days and nights seem longer than they were wont, and he declares that the sun has entered upon new wanderings. On the morning of Criseida's departure, he had seen the old moon horned; he reflects that when the new horned moon appears, his lady will be back. He gazes on the Greek tents and imagines that the winds which come up to him from the plain are like Criseida's sighs. In such wise he passes his time. Pandaro is always with him, seeking to comfort him and giving him good hope (St. 48–71).

Canto VI. In the Greek camp, Criseida passes her nights in tears, till her cheeks grow thin and pale. She weeps continually, remembering her joys with Troilo and making a bitter fountain of her eyes. No one could be so cruel as not to weep with her. What grieves her most is that she has no one to sorrow with her. She gazes on the walls and palaces and towers of Troy, musing upon the joy and pleasure and sweetness she knew within the city. Now, in sad annoy, she is consuming her dear beauty. She regrets that she did not consent to flee with Troilo. Who could have spoken ill of her for going with such a man as he? She sees now that she has fled the bad only to pursue the worse. Her heart is beggared of joy. But she will do her utmost to flee and return to her lover, as she promised. But from so high and great intent, the poet tells us, a new lover soon turned her. Diomede, he informs us, employed every argument he could to enter into her heart and, in brief time, drove away the thought of Troilo and Troy (St. 1–8).

It is on the fourth day that Diomede calls upon her and

finds her in tears. He fears that his is a vain labor, for it is clear that the lady sorrows for another lover. He tells himself that he must be a sovereign artist to expel the first love from her heart and enter it himself. Being firm in his resolve, however, he makes the attempt. At first, he speaks of the war between the Greeks and Trojans and asks her opinion on the outcome. He asks her if she finds the Greek ways strange. He does not go so far as to ask outright why Calchas delays to give her in marriage (St. 9–12).

Since her heart is still all fixed on Troilo, her replies are not altogether satisfactory to Diomede, but they give him some hope. Growing bolder, he tells her that he has seen her lovely face transformed with sorrow from the day when they left Troy together. He knows not what the cause can be, if it be not love. He advises her to cast her love away, for the Trojans are, as it were, kept in prison by the Greeks, who are not disposed to depart without sacking Troy with sword and fire. Nor should she imagine that anyone within the city will ever find any pity: the Greeks mean to make an example to men in the punishment they bestow on Paris. Though there were twelve Hectors and sixty of his brothers, the Greeks would triumph over them,—if Calchas has not deceived them with ambiguities and delusions. However great the honors which the Trojans wear, they shall soon belong to the Greeks, and death shall certainly be the portion of all who dwell in the city. She must not believe that Calchas would have demanded her from the Trojans if he had not foreseen all this. Diomede himself, he tells her, discussed the matter with him, before the demand was made, and encouraged the seer in his resolve, knowing of Criseida's excellence.

He urges her to dismiss the fallacious love of Trojans, to dispel her bitter hopes, and to recall her splendid beauty; for Troy has come to such a pass that every hope men have there is lost. Even though Troy were to stand, her king and his sons are but barbarians compared with the Greeks, who surpass all other nations. She is now among cultivated men, whereas she has been hitherto among insensate brutes. Let her not believe that the Greeks do not know love, as high and perfect as any among the Trojans. Her virtue and her angelic beauty will find a worthy lover. If it did not displease her, he would be the man, more gladly than he would be king of Greece (St. 13–22).

His face is scarlet, and he drops his eyes. Then he begins to speak again, telling her that he is as nobly born as any man in Troy; for had his father Tideus, who fell at Thebes, but lived, Diomede would now be king of Calydon and Argos—as he hopes yet to be. His father was descended from the gods, and he himself has been held in high honor among the Greeks. Therefore, he begs her to drive away her melancholy and take him as her servant (St. 23–25).

Criseida looks at him with displeasure, for the love of Troilo still has power over her. She tells him that she loves the city where she was born and bred and would fain see it delivered. She knows that the Greeks are valorous and courteous, but the virtue of the Trojans is no less, as Hector has shown them. She declares that she has not known love since her lord and husband died. Neither Greek nor Trojan has she cared for in that way, nor has she desire to give heed to any man. She has well heard that he is sprung of royal blood, and this makes her marvel that he can set his heart on a woman of slight condition, like herself: Helen would be more fitting to his state. For herself, she is in tribulation and not disposed to receive such a declaration as he has made. She does not say this because she is grieved at being loved by him; but the times are ill, and he is now in arms. When the victory has come, which he expects, she will know better what to do. Delights may then please her more, and he can speak to her again. Peradventure, his words will be dearer to her then than they are now (St. 26–31).

Diomede holds her last words dear and takes his departure in high hopes, saying no more for the present. He is tall, handsome in person, young, fresh, and pleasing enough; brave and proud, and as ready with his speech as any Greek whatsoever. His nature is prone to love. Criseida, when he has left her, ponders his words, doubtful whether to approach or to flee him. This cools her ardor to return, and new hopes drive out her torments. And for this reason, she does not keep her promise to Troilo (St. 32–34).

Canto VII. Troilo, on the tenth day, goes to the gates, accompanied only by Pandaro. Everyone whom they see approaching they take to be Criseida, until he comes near enough to be recognized. There they remain till noon, when Troilo declares that she will not now come before meal-time. She would have great trouble in getting rid of her father and has stayed to eat with him. After eating, they return to the gate and wait there till twilight and into the evening, since Troilo insists that her father has prevented her return until the dusk. As it grows dark, he commends her wisdom for waiting until she can come without making people wonder why the lady who was exchanged for Antenor is returning to Troy. He believes he sees her coming, through the dusk, but Pandaro informs him that nothing but a cart is approaching. As the stars begin to appear, Troilo still declares that she will come. Pandaro, however, though he makes a show of believing him, laughs under his breath and tells himself that this poor fellow expects a wind from Mongibello (St. 1–10).

The warders now begin to call the citizens within the gates, as well as the country people with their beasts; and Troilo at last returns inside with Pandaro, when all the sky is thick with stars. He has comforted himself with a lover's vain hopes all through the day, and now tells his friend that they were fools to expect her to-day: she had said she would remain with her father for ten days, and then she would return. Therefore, she ought to come on the morrow. The two spend another fruitless day at the gate, and then, at last, Troilo's hopes begin to weaken. He begins to murmur against Criseida. The third, fourth, fifth, and sixth days, after the tenth, go by. Hoping and not hoping, Troilo sighs in vain expectation of her coming. His tears and lamentations return, and his hopes take flight. Desire and jealousy torment him, so that he grieves night and day. He scarcely eats or drinks or sleeps, and he shuns all feasts and every company. He grows so pale and thin that no one could recognize him, and all the vigor leaves his body. He scorns all comfort. Priam, seeing his condition, sometimes summons him and asks him what it is which weighs him down. Hector and his brothers also question him, but to them all he replies merely that he feels pain about his heart (St. 11–22).

One night, he dreams that he sees the perilous misdeed of her who makes him languish: he seems to be in a shadowy forest, where a great boar is ranging; then Criseida appears beneath the boar's feet, and he sees the beast tear out her heart. Seeing that Criseida does not seem to suffer from this outrage, but rather to be pleased, Troilo is so enraged that his sleep is broken. He sees the meaning of the dream. Summoning Pandaro, he tells his friend that Criseida, whom he trusted beyond all women, has deceived him and given her heart to another. The gods have shown it to him in a dream. He tells Pandaro of the dream and explains that the boar is Diomede, whose grandsire slew the boar of Calydonia, and whose family have always worn a boar as crest. It is now clear to him, he declares, that it is not Calchas who has prevented Criseida's return, but Diomede. "Woe is me, Criseida," he cries out, "what subtle art, what new delight, what alluring beauty, what grudge against me, what just disdain, what misdeed of mine, what dire circumstance could draw thy lofty soul from me to another object? Alas for firmness! Alas for promises! Alas for faith and loyalty! Who has cast ye out of my beloved?" He regrets that he ever let her depart. If he had not listened to her evil counsel, but had broken the pact, when he saw her leaving the city, she would not now be false. But he trusted her and hoped for certain that her faith was sacred, while she spoke ambiguously and covertly. He asks Pandaro what he shall do, since he now feels a new fire in his mind, and he declares that his hands shall lay hold on death (St. 23–32).

He snatches up a dagger, to stab himself, but Pandaro seizes him and restrains his hand. Troilo beseeches his friend to release him, that he may slay himself, and they wrestle with one another for possession of the dagger. The weakened condition of the prince gives Pandaro the victory. He disarms Troilo and persuades him to sit down. He remonstrates with him for believing Criseida false on the evidence of a dream, reminding him that he has told him before that it is folly to regard dreams too closely. It may be that this animal, which Troilo interprets as hostile to his love, will be useful to him and not do him the harm he imagines. He should certainly look into the matter and see if his dream will turn out to be true or false. If it be true that Criseida has deserted him, he ought not to plan deliberately for death, for everyone would blame such an act. He should rather scorn her as she scorns him. It he must die, let him seek death at the hands of the Greeks. When Troilo is to die, he and Pandaro shall go forth together and die doing slaughter upon the enemy (St. 33–45).

Troilo's rage is allayed. He falls to weeping again, and begs Pandaro to be sure of his undying affection. He admits that it was madness which made him seek to kill himself and admires his friend's fortitude in staying his hand. He asks Pandaro to tell him how he may discover the truth about his suspicions. Pandaro advises testing her by writing a letter: if she loves Troilo no longer, they will have no reply; or, if she does answer, they can clearly see whether there is any hope of her return or not. Troilo has not written her since her departure; it may be that she has some very good cause for tarrying. Troilo accepts the advice and writes to Criseida. He commends himself to her great virtue, telling her that she has left him in greater misery than she could believe. Though she has almost become a Greek, still she will not refuse to receive his letter, but will take it and read it to its close. If a servant might complain of his master, he might have reason to complain of her, considering her promises and her oaths to every god, that she would return by the tenth day, whereas she has not returned within forty. But, forasmuch as it behooves him to be pleased with whatever pleases her, he does not dare repine, but as humbly as he can, he writes her to know what her life has been among the Greeks. He fears that her father's cajoleries have been too much for her or that a new love has entered her mind. If she had delayed but two or three days beyond her promise, he could understand her tarrying and could bear his sorrow patiently; but she has stayed so long that he greatly fears some new love is the cause of her delay, and that is a greater grief than any he has known. This dread has brought him to such a pass that he is of no use to Venus or to Mars. Since her departure, his eyes have not ceased to weep, and he has lost the power to sleep or eat or drink. She can imagine what he would do if he were certain of the thing he fears. He is sure that he would kill himself if he knew she had deceived him. Every form of amusement has become hateful to him. The painted flowers and the fresh verdure of the fields cannot withdraw his soul from thoughts of her. He gazes only at that part of the heavens under which he believes her to be dwelling. He envies the hills which surround her, the streams which run down to the sea, because they can be near her. He believes the sun is drawn toward her through the heavens. To hear the place named where she is staying, or to see anybody coming thence, rekindles the fire in his breast. He is sorry for her, amid the armed knights and the clamors of war,—she who lived so delicately in Troy! He begs her to return. He will pardon her the pain he has suffered through her delay and will not ask amends, beyond the sight of her fair face. By the delights they have known together, by their kisses, their embraces, and their sighs, he implores her to return. If, peradventure, something hinders her, let her write him who has detained her beyond the tenth day. If she can give him hope, he will wait. He asks her pardon for the stains of tears upon the letter and concludes with a prayer that God may be with her and hasten her return (St. 46–75).

The letter is sealed and sent, but in vain they wait for a reply. Troilo's grief increases, and his fears, based upon the dream, are strengthened. Deifebo, coming to see him one day, as he lies in his bed, overhears him crying out upon Criseida and guesses his secret. Dissembling his knowledge, Deifebo rouses Troilo by telling him that the truce is ended and by summoning him to battle. Like a famished lion seeking prey, Troilo leaps up and declares that he hates the Greeks and will fight them as he never fought before. Deifebo, who divines the cause of his hatred, seeks his brothers and communicates his suspicions to them. They agree to say nothing to Troilo about the matter but decide to take steps to comfort him. They bid the ladies of the palace visit Troilo, with songs and singers, to help him forget his sorrow (St. 76–83).

Polyxena, beautiful as an angel, sits on one side of him; on the other sits Helen; and Cassandra stands before him. Hecuba, Andromache, and many others of his relatives are there. Each seeks to comfort him, but he does not reply and scarcely heeds them, thinking constantly of Criseida. Cassandra, who, by chance, has heard Deifebo's narrative, taunts Troilo with having given his love to the daughter of a scoundrelly priest. She proclaims scornfully that this son of a high and honored king is grieving because Criseida has left him. Troilo, believing she has learned his secret from some oracle, fears that her words will be believed if he remains silent. He bursts into bitter denials, declaring that he was never in love with Criseida. If he had been, he would not have let her go. He bids Cassandra hold her tongue. He praises Criseida's beauty, gentility, modesty, sobriety of word and deed; and he calls her fair fame as witness to her chastity. If Cassandra demands royal blood of a woman, beyond all these good qualities, let her reflect that it is not crown or sceptre or imperial robes that produce royalty: true royalty is in virtue, not in power. Criseida could better wear a crown than Cassandra. Would God had made him worthy of such a lady! He bids Cassandra be off, with evil chance, telling her to go spin, since she cannot talk sense, and to leave the virtue of others alone (St. 84–101).

Cassandra, abashed, says no more and speedily returns to the royal palace. The other ladies commend the words of Troilo. Having brought him a little cheer, they depart; but they return to visit him frequently while he remains in bed. His grief continues, but he learns to bear it patiently; and his burning desire to show his valor against the Greeks speedily restores his strength. A letter from Criseida brings him protestations of her love, false excuses for her delay, and a request for further time. He has some hope of seeing her again, but knows not when. So he joins battle once more with the foe, and the Greeks pay dear for all his bitter sufferings (St. 102–106).

Canto VIII. Troilo grows inured to his sufferings. He is strengthened, also, by the grief he feels for the death of Hector. His love, however, does not leave him, though hope grows less. He still seeks by every means and art, as lovers do, to get back his sweet and only care, always excusing her for not returning. He sends her many letters, reminding her of their sweet time together and courteously reproaching her for her long sojourn. In times of truce, he sends Pandaro to her. He even has it in his thoughts to go to her himself, disguised as a pilgrim, but he does not know how he could succeed in the counterfeit. From her, he has only fair words and great promises that do not take effect. He begins to suspect the truth and sees that a new love is the reason for her many reckless lies. He fails to see any way, however, of ascertaining the truth of that which his ill-omened dream has already shown him (St. 1–6).

By chance, he learns that what he fears concerning Diomede is the truth. Deifebo returns one day from battle, bearing an ornate vesture, which he has stripped from Diomede in combat. Troilo, admiring the trophy, as it is borne through Troy, catches sight upon it of the brooch which he gave Criseida on the morning when they parted. Now he sees that his dream and his suspicions were true. He sends for Pandaro and reveals Criseida's treachery. "O Criseida mine," he laments, "where is the faith, where is the love, where is the desire, where is the reward, which you promised me at parting? Diomede possesses all, and I, who love you more, through your deceit remain in sorrow and in travail. Who will henceforth believe in the oaths or in the love of a woman, considering your perjury? Alas, I did not know your heart was so hard that I could be dismissed from your mind for another man,—I who have loved you more than myself and always waited for you, though deceived. Had you no other jewel to give to your new lover—Diomede, I mean—save that which I gave you with so many tears, that you might hold me in remembrance in my sorrow, while you were tarrying with Calchas? Nothing but despite has made you do such a thing, to show your mind right clearly. I see you have expelled me wholly from your bosom; and I, against my will, still hold your fair face pictured in my heart, with grievous sorrow. Oh, woe is me, born in an evil hour! This thought slays me and robs me of every hope of future joy, and it is the cause of all my anguish and grief" (St. 7–15).

He swears that he will bring great sorrow upon her, if he can meet with Diomede in the next mêlée; or else Diomede shall slay him, and make her glad. Still, he has hope in divine justice and calls upon Jove not to turn away his eyes, but to cast her away, in whom have been lies and treason and deceit. He now perceives that Pandaro was wrong in blaming him for having faith in dreams, since the gods reveal the truth to mortals in that way, as in others. He prays that Diomede may be sent in his way when first he goes into battle. He does not care though he should die himself, if he may be sure that he will find his rival sorrowing in hell (St. 16–21).

Pandaro listens with sorrow to all this, and knows it for the truth. Torn between love for his friend and shame for Criseida's misdeed, he knows not what to do. At last he speaks: "Troilo, I know not what I ought to say to you. I blame her as much as I can, even as you do, and I do not intend to make any excuses for her great treachery; nor shall I ever go again where she is. What I did aforetime, I did for love of you, laying aside all my honor. If I brought you pleasure, that is very gratifying to me. In what is now going on, I can do nothing more. I am angry at it, like yourself; and if I saw means to amend it, be certain I should be zealous about it. May God do this, who can change all things! And I pray that He may punish her, that she may sin no more" (St. 22–24).

Great are their lamentations, but Fortune holds her course: Criseida loves Diomede, and Troilo remains in sorrow. In battle, Troilo seeks Diomede more than any other, and when they meet, they exchange mighty blows and evil words. But Fortune did not ordain that the one should slay the other. The wrath of Troilo brings much harm upon the Greeks, so that few meet him and escape death; until, after he has slain a thousand men, Achilles, upon a day, kills him miserably (St. 25–27).

Such was the end of the ill-omened love of Troilo for Criseida, and such the end of his wretched grief; such the end of his shining splendor; such the end of his vain hopes in the false Criseida. The poet concludes the canto with an address to young men, warning them that maidens are fickle and delight in many lovers. Many women, proud of their ancestry, are vain and scornful. Boccaccio warns young men against them, and sketches the perfect woman, who discerns what she should shun and what she should seek, and who keeps her promises. He begs his readers to pity Troilo and to pray the God of Love that he may have peace in the region wherein he dwells (St. 28–33).

Canto IX. The poet takes leave of his book, commending it to his lady, for whom it was written (St. 1–8).

CHAUCER'S USE OF THE FILOSTRATO

Chaucer has made the fullest use of the *Filostrato*.

Of the 713 stanzas of the Italian poem, there are less than two hundred which find no verbal echo in the *Troilus*. Some of Boccaccio's stanzas are translated as closely as the exigencies of Chaucer's metrical form permit, some are paraphrased freely, and some furnish a suggestion which Chaucer elaborates at greater length and in his own way. Since expansion is an almost inevitable concomitant of translation, it is not surprising to discover that one stanza of the *Filostrato* often grows into two stanzas in the *Troilus*. Moreover, passages in the Italian poem which Chaucer does not utilize in their context are frequently drawn upon at other points in the narrative, and lines occurring in episodes which are not reproduced in the *Troilus* are sometimes made to do service in very different surroundings. Although a detailed comparison of the two poems shows that not more than one third of the lines in the *Troilus* are translated from the Italian original, the debt which Chaucer owes to Boccaccio is much greater than the actual figures would indicate.

Of more importance than verbal resemblances between the two poems, is the similarity that exists between them in plot and structure. Chaucer has added much of his own to the story which he found in the *Filostrato;* but he has also taken over every important episode in Boccaccio's plot, with the single exception of the scenes in Troilo's chamber, in which the ladies of the royal household seek to comfort the prince and are witnesses to the revelation of his love for Criseida, made under the impulse of Cassandra's taunts. In addition, Chaucer has discarded the following minor features in Boccaccio's narrative:

1. Troilo's declaration, at the opening of the story, that he has already experienced love (*Fil.* I. St. 23–24).

2. The unknown lover who has been haunting Criseida's doors (*Fil.* II. St. 39–40).

3. The swooning of Troilo in the council at which it is decreed that Criseida shall be restored to her father (*Fil.* IV. St. 18–21).

4. Criseida's taunting words to Diomede as she takes her departure from Troy (*Fil.* V. St. 8).

5. Troilo's attempt at suicide when he has told Pandaro of his dream of the boar (*Fil.* VII. St. 33–36).

6. Troilo's suggestion, in his letter to Criseida, that a new lover is detaining her in the Greek camp (*Fil.* VII. St. 58–61).

7. Deifebo's discovery of his brother's secret and the incidents arising out of that discovery (*Fil.* VII. St. 77–103).

8. Pandaro's visits to Criseida in the Greek camp (*Fil.* VIII. St. 3).

The use which Chaucer has made of his Italian original is marked rather by additions and expansions than by omissions. The following important passages in the *Troilus* have no basis in the *Filostrato*:

1. The scene in Criseyde's garden, in which Antigone sings of the power of love; and the subsequent description of Criseyde's falling asleep, as she listens to the nightingale, and of her dream of the eagle (II. St. 117–33).

2. The dinner at the house of Deiphebus and the first meeting of the lovers there (II. St. 194—III. St. 34).[2]

3. The elaborate scheme by which Pandarus brings the lovers together at his house for the consummation of their

---

[2] Doubtless the prominence given to Deiphebus in this episode and the presence of Helen at the feigned sick-bed of Troilus can be traced to the portion of the seventh canto of the *Filostrato* which Chaucer does not include in his narrative.

love, and the subordinate episode of Troilus's feigned jealousy of Horaste (III. St. 74–169).

4. The interview between Pandarus and Criseyde on the following morning (III. St. 223–26).

5. Hector's opposition to the proposal that Criseyde be exchanged for Antenor (IV. St. 26–30).

6. Troilo's soliloquy in the temple (IV. St. 136–55).

7. Diomede's advances to Criseyde as they ride from Troy to the Greek camp (V. St. 14–27).

8. The directions of Troilus to Pandarus with regard to his own funeral (V. St. 43–46).

9. The descriptions of Troilus and Criseyde (V. St. 116–20).

10. Incidents in Diomede's wooing of Criseyde, subsequent to their first interview at the tent of Calchas. Her lament for the loss of her fair name (V. St. 148–57).

11. Cassandra's story of the Calydonian boar-hunt and of the Seven against Thebes, and her interpretation of the dream of Troilus (V. St. 208-217).[3]

12. Criseyde's second letter from the Greek camp (V. St. 228–33).[4]

The most notable illustrations of Chaucer's expansion of episodes taken from Boccaccio are as follows:

1. The first interview between Pandaro and Troilo has been expanded from 264 lines in the *Filostrato* into 515 lines in the *Troilus*.

2. The scene in which Pandaro informs Criseida of

---

[3] In the *Filostrato,* Troilo himself interprets the dream (*Fil.* VII. St. 25–28).

[4] Boccaccio tells us that Troilo received 'parole belle e promesse grandi senza effetto' (*Fil.* VIII. St. 5), but does not say whether these messages came in writing or through Pandaro.

Troilo's love occupies 272 lines in Boccaccio; Chaucer devotes 525 lines to the episode.

3. In the *Filostrato,* Pandaro and Troilo, on one occasion, pass under Criseida's window. This episode, which occupies but eight lines in Boccaccio's poem, seems to have furnished Chaucer with the suggestion for the two striking scenes in which he presents Troilus riding down the street past Criseyde's palace (II. 610–58; 1247–88).

4. The joys of the lovers, on their first night together, as well as their anguish at parting at dawn, are set forth more fully by Chaucer, who devotes 342 lines to the purpose, whereas Boccaccio relates the entire scene, from their meeting to their parting, in 192 lines.

5. The argument between the lovers, on their last night together, is somewhat longer in the *Troilus,* where it extends to 434 lines, than in the *Filostrato,* where it occupies only 320 lines.

It will be seen that the most significant of Chaucer's expansions and additions occur in the portion of the narrative which precedes the winning of Criseyde. This part of the lovers' story, it will be remembered, was original with Boccaccio,[5] for Benoit and Guido had begun the tale of Troilus and Briseida with the restoration of the lady to her father. Chaucer, in his turn, has expanded and developed this interesting portion of the love-story quite as independently as Boccaccio had done before him.

[5] The opening scene of the *Filostrato,* in the temple of Pallas, probably owes something to the scene in Benoit's *Roman de Troie,* in which Achilles falls in love with Polyxena, on seeing her in the throng gathered at the tomb of Hector in the Temple of Apollo. The background of the love-story, including the tale of the treachery of Calchas, is, of course, derived from Benoit and Guido. For certain details in his narrative, Boccaccio may have drawn upon his own *Filocolo.*

It is true that the Italian poet had no original before him, as he wrote the first 2353 lines of the *Filostrato,* whereas Chaucer based his first three books, in part, upon the pioneer work of Boccaccio; but Chaucer has added, to this portion of the narrative, episodes of his own invention, which run to some 1200 lines and which give a very different tone to the story of the wooing of Troilus and Criseyde. He has also expanded certain scenes, for which he found suggestions in the first three cantos of the *Filostrato,* in such a way as to make them virtually his own. By means of these added episodes and the expansion of scenes which he found in Boccaccio, Chaucer has altered the story of the winning of Criseyde, and has infused a new and original spirit into the love-story which Boccaccio had told. It is not my purpose, in this book, to seek to interpret that spirit, nor yet to discuss the question of Chaucer's consistency in his portrayal of Criseyde's character. It is to be hoped, however, that the full account which I have given of Chaucer's debt to the *Filostrato* will enable a careful reader of the *Troilus* to form a just opinion on these critical matters.

CHAUCER'S USE OF OTHER SOURCES

I. OTHER WORKS BY BOCCACCIO

In an illuminating study of the story of Troilus and Criseyde, Professor Karl Young has pointed out certain resemblances between passages in Chaucer's *Troilus* and in a prose romance by Boccaccio, entitled *Il Filocolo.* This romance, which is an elaborate retelling of the famous story of Floire and Blanchefleur, contains a scene in which the lovers, Florio and Biancofiore, are brought together through the good offices of Glorizia, Biancofiore's maid. Florio, having gained admittance to the tower in which his lady is confined, is concealed in an adjoining chamber by Glorizia and watches while Biancofiore and her maids celebrate a gala-day together. At night, Glorizia hides Florio behind the curtains of the lady's bed. Here he listens while Glorizia draws from Biancofiore fresh protestations of her love for him and sorrowful references to his groundless jealousy of another man. When Biancofiore has retired and sunk into slumber, Florio leaves his place of concealment and rouses her from dreams of him. The lovers make their vows before an image of Cupid, Florio places a ring upon his lady's finger, in token of their espousal, and the two then pass the night together.

The general resemblance between this scene and that which sets forth the winning of Criseyde is apparent, and Professor Young finds enough similarity in detail to convince him that Chaucer drew upon the *Filocolo* for the most significant of the episodes which he has added to the story of Troilus and Criseyde. He also attributes a few touches in the portrayal of the character of Pandarus to the influence of the *Filocolo,* which contains two personages, in addition to the maid Glorizia, who are of service to Florio in his love-affair; and he believes that the words with which Criseyde soothes the supposed jealousy of Troilus may be traced to passages in the *Filocolo* dealing with the jealousy which Florio is led to feel by the sight of his lady's veil in the possession of another man. It is entirely possible that Chaucer was familiar with the *Filocolo,* and it may be that the resemblances pointed out by Professor Young between that work and the *Troilus* represent actual borrowings; but the scenes which he brings into comparison differ from one another in so many important respects that not every one will be prepared to accept his conclusions.

It is a more certain matter that the passage in which the poet follows the soul of Troilus in its flight through the heavens is based upon the *Teseida* of Boccaccio (XI. St. 1–3). The influence of the same poem is clearly evident in four other passages in the *Troilus*. We do not know whether or not Chaucer had completed his *Knightes Tale*, which is condensed from the *Teseida*, at the time when he wrote the *Troilus*.

2. BENOIT AND GUIDO

Many of the details which Chaucer has included in his *Troilus*, particularly in the last two books, were derived directly from the sources of the *Filostrato*. Since most of them are to be found both in Benoit's *Roman de Troie* and Guido's *Historia Trojana*, it is very difficult to determine the extent of the debt which Chaucer owes to each of these authorities; but it is clear that he was acquainted with both works, and it is probable that he consulted both of them while writing the *Troilus*. It is from Benoit and Guido, and not from Boccaccio, that the following details are derived:

1. The advances of Diomede, as he conducts Criseyde to her father's tent, and her evasive replies (V. 92-189).

2. The taking of Criseyde's glove by Diomede (V. 1013).

3. The incident of the bay steed, won from Troilus by Diomede, given to Criseyde, and subsequently returned to Diomede (V. 1037–39).

4. The granting to Diomede of a favor to wear in battle (V. 1043).

5. The wounding of Diomede by Troilus, Criseyde's grief at the sight of his wounds, and her nursing of her new lover (V. 1044–50).

6. Criseyde's lament at her own infidelity (V. 1051–85). For a few incidents connected with the background of the love-story, such as the capture of Antenor, the exchange of prisoners, and the death of Hector, Chaucer has gone directly to Benoit or Guido, correcting or supplementing the account given by Boccaccio.

Some details in the description of Diomede, Criseyde, and Troilus are clearly derived from the *Frigii Daretis Ylias* of Joseph of Exeter, a twelfth-century paraphrase, in Latin hexameters, of the *De Excidio Trojae Historia* of "Dares the Phrygian."

3. BOETHIUS

The long passage in Book IV which presents the meditations of Troilus upon the problem of man's freedom is derived from Boethius: *De Consolatione Philosophiae*, Book V. Prose 3. 7–71. The defense of Fortune by Pandarus (I. 841–54), Criseyde's complaint against 'fals felicitee' (III. 813–36), the hymn of Troilus to Love (III. 1744–71), and fifteen shorter passages in the *Troilus* are derived from Boethius; and the influence of his philosophy upon the mind of the poet is made very evident, particularly in the latter part of the poem, by frequent references to the power of Destiny and to the mutability of Fortune.

4. PETRARCH AND DANTE

The love-song of Troilus in Book I (400–420) is translated from the eighty-eighth sonnet of Petrarch. The influence of Dante has been traced in thirteen passages in the *Troilus,* including at least four in which Chaucer follows the phraseology of the *Divine Comedy* rather closely. In one case, he includes in a song in praise of Love some lines which Dante addresses to the Blessed Virgin (III. 1262–67); in another, he follows Dante in representing Fortune as the agency of divine providence (V. 1541–45); and in a third, he models upon Dante the address to the Trinity with which he brings his poem to a close. "The influence of Dante on Chaucer's mind and art," says Professor Root, "is not confined to the passages in which there is definite borrowing of a phrase or an idea. From Italy, and primarily I think from Dante, came the inspiration to tell the story of Troilus in the *bel stilo alto,* to write in the vernacular with the dignity and elevation which mark the great ancients." [6]

5. MINOR SOURCES

In Book V of the *Troilus* (1485–1510) is a summary of the *Thebaid* of Statius, and the book which Criseyde is reading with her ladies appears to be the same work. It is possible that the influence of Statius is to be seen, also, in some of the invocations with which Chaucer begins his books.

[6] *The Book of Troilus and Criseyde,* xlv.

A source for the love-song of Antigone (II. 827–75) has been pointed out in the *Paradis d'Amour* of Guillaume de Machaut. Nineteen passages in the *Troilus* give clear indication of the influence of the *Roman de la Rose,* and there are other passages which seem to reflect, though not so unmistakably, the poet's thorough familiarity with the work of Guillaume de Lorris and Jean de Meun.

It would be impossible, within the space available, to give a complete account of the sources upon with Chaucer drew for the allusions, reflections, and proverbial expressions which are to be found scattered through the *Troilus.* The range of the poet's reading is illustrated by the fact that he derived material, for this poem alone, from the Bible, from Ovid (*Metamorphoses, Heroides, Ars Amatoria, Amores, Remedia Amoris*), from Vergil (*Aeneid, Eclogues*), from Alanus de Insulis (*Liber Parabolarum, De Planctu Naturae*), from Juvenal (*Satires*), Horace (*Ars Poetica*) and Seneca (*Epistles*).[7] Allusions to astronomy, astrology, and other scientific matters can hardly be traced to their sources, but they serve to illustrate the breadth of Chaucer's intellectual interests and the varied nature of his studies.

6. "LOLLIUS"

Twice, in the course of the poem, Chaucer cites, as his authority, an author named "Lollius," whom he also includes, in the *Hous of Fame,* among the writers who sup-

---

[7] It is not certain that Chaucer knew Horace at first hand, and it is probable that the passages which he utilized reached him through quotation by other authors. It is also probable that the comments which he appears to have borrowed from Seneca reached him through intermediate sources.

port the fame of Troy (III. 1468). Scholars have been unable to find any entirely satisfactory explanation for the fact that this unknown writer [8] is given credit as the source of Chaucer's knowledge of the story of Troilus and Criseyde, while Boccaccio, from whom the poem is principally derived, is never mentioned by name. It is possible that a misreading of a line in Horace, which may have reached Chaucer in a corrupt manuscript, gave him the idea that the Maximus Lollius, to whom Horace addresses his Second Epistle, was "Troiani belli scriptor"; [9] but this does not account for the poet's extraordinary attribution of his material to an author whose works he could not have read, for the simple reason that they never existed. If Chaucer was practising a bit of scholarly mystification, in the hope of throwing an air of historical authority about the fictitious tale which he had borrowed from a contemporary author, he succeeded so well in his purpose that scholars have not yet entirely abandoned their search for "myn auctor called Lollius." [10]

DATE OF THE TROILUS

The composition of the *Troilus and Criseyde* must have fallen between 1381 and 1387. When Chaucer says that

[8] The third-century historian, Lollius Urbicus, need hardly be considered in this connection. His works, which have been lost, appear to have dealt solely with contemporary history.

[9] Troiani belli scriptorem, Maxime Lolli,

Dum tu declamas Romae, Praeneste relegi.

[10] The best statement of the conflicting views presented by various scholars on this perplexing problem is to be found in Young: *The Origin and Development of the Story of Troilus and Criseyde,* 189-95.

"oure firste lettre is now an A" (I. 171), he is reflecting
the courtier's feeling for the initial of his queen's name.
Unless this line was inserted as an afterthought, which is
extremely unlikely, we may accept January 14, 1382, the
day on which Richard II and Anne of Bohemia were
married, as the earliest date for the inception of the poem.
Since a thorough familiarity with the *Troilus* is shown by
Thomas Usk, in his *Testament of Love,* which was probably written in 1387,[11] Chaucer's poem must have been in
circulation before that year. The date 1385–6 has now been
generally accepted for the completion of the poem. This
places the *Troilus* immediately before the first version of
the Prologue to the *Legend of Good Women,* in which
the God of Love takes Chaucer to task for the unfavor-
able view of woman presented in his portrait of Criseyde.
The date of 1385–6 finds curious confirmation in the fact
that just such a conjunction of Jupiter, Saturn, and the
crescent Moon in the sign Cancer, as Chaucer describes in
Book III. 624–25, took place in May, 1385, for the first
time in many hundreds of years.

The study of the text of the *Troilus* has revealed the
fact that Chaucer revised the poem extensively, making
such important additions as the soliloquy of Troilus upon
the freedom of the will (IV. 953–1078), and the passage
which describes the flight of the hero's soul through the
heavens (V. 1807–27). There are many other changes, of
less significance, including verbal alterations and the re-
arrangement of material. In some cases, the readings of
the revised version present a freer rendering of the Italian
original, or serve to deepen the serious tone of the poem;

[11] The author was executed for treason, March 4, 1388.

but it is not possible to discover any general principle which governed the poet in making his revision.[12]

It should be added that the *Troilus and Criseyde* is the only one of Chaucer's longer works which he brought to full completion.

[12] For a full discussion of the text of the poem, cf. R. K. Root: *The Textual Tradition of Chaucer's Troilus,* Chaucer Society, 1916.

CHAPTER V

THE CANTERBURY TALES

FROM the most ancient times, the stories that men have told have had a way of drifting together into collections; and when such a series has been the work of a conscious artist, an attempt has usually been made to weave the diverse elements into some unified pattern. In the later Middle Ages, many such collections of tales were produced, and many different sorts of unifying devices were invented to hold them together. It seems to have been Chaucer's ambition, for several years, to use his talents for story-telling in this way. In 1385 or 1386, he had projected one such series of tales, in the *Legend of Good Women;* and there are some who believe that he had previously completed a large part of another, in the collection of tragedies later presented as the *Monkes Tale.* Neither was likely to hold the attention of a poet whose genius was certainly characterized by a love of variety, which made it easier for him to project long works than to bring them to completion; and it is not surprising that he laid the *Legends* aside when a more compelling artistic device took possession of his mind. It was probably in 1387 that he began the *Canterbury Tales.*[1] Material for a collection of stories, which would afford more variety

[1] Cf. Tatlock: *Development and Chronology,* 131–42.

than the monotonous tales of Cupid's saints, was in his possession. It is certain that he had written the story of Palamon and Arcite and the Life of St. Cecilia before 1385 or 1386; [2] and other material, later incorporated in the *Canterbury Tales*, was probably taking definite shape in his mind, if it was not already in its final form. The new scheme for a collection of tales, which were to be told by pilgrims chosen from many walks of life, offered the fullest possible opportunity for the use of all sorts of material, and was not likely to threaten either the author or the reader with monotony.

It is hardly necessary to search for the "source" of the pilgrimage to Canterbury. Actual observation, coupled with the poet's ready imagination, was sufficient to have furnished Chaucer with the device by which he sought to give unity to his great work. We may be certain, at any rate, that no work which has yet been brought to light could have given him more than a bare suggestion for the framework of the *Canterbury Tales*. The *Decameron,* the most brilliant similar collection of stories, was unknown to Chaucer. Another Italian work of far less brilliance, the *Novelle* of Giovanni Sercambi, shows a greater similarity to the *Canterbury Tales*. It tells of a journey taken by a rather large company, who have fled from their native city to escape the Black Death. On their journeying, they are entertained by tales told by the author, who represents himself as a member of the company, and various forms of entertainment are furnished by other pilgrims during the evenings. One of their number, chosen at the outset, acts as leader (*"preposto"*) of the company. Although all the tales of the collection are told by a single narrator, he

[2] Cf. Prologue to the *Legend of Good Women*, B-text, 414–30.

varies the tone of his *novelle* by addressing some of them particularly to various classes among his fellow pilgrims.

The general resemblance between Sercambi's work and the *Canterbury Tales,* first pointed out by Mr. Hinckley, in his valuable *Notes on Chaucer* (1907), has not been generally considered convincing evidence that Chaucer was familiar with this collection of stories; and a full study, by Professor Young, fails to reveal any very close similarity in matters of detail. Since the *Novelle* were written at a later date than 1374, Chaucer could not have encountered the work on his first Italian journey; but it is possible that he saw it, or heard of it, when in Italy in 1378. It is to be noted that he makes no use of any of the *Novelle* themselves, and if he owes anything at all to Sercambi, it is merely a suggestion for a collection of tales told upon a journey and bound together by some account of the journey itself.[3]

The framework of the *Canterbury Tales,* whether original or borrowed, seems to have been adopted because it promised the fullest opportunity for a large and varied collection of stories. When the Host of the Tabard lays his proposal before his guests (A 788–809), he outlines a scheme calling for a hundred and twenty tales.[4] Each of the pilgrims is to tell two stories on the journey to Canter-

[3] R. A. Pratt and K. Young: "The Literary Framework of the Canterbury Tales," in *Sources and Analogues,* 1–81.

[4] Including Chaucer, there were "nyne and twenty" in the company at the Tabard, and a thirtieth pilgrim was added later, in the person of the Canon's Yeoman. In this discussion I ignore the two extra priests of line 164 of the Prologue, because I cannot believe in their existence. It is true that they cannot be altogether explained away, but I am convinced that their presence among Chaucer's pilgrims was due to some sort of inadvertence.

bury and two more on the road back to Southwark. Need-less to say, Chaucer did not complete the ambitious task which he laid upon himself through the mouth of Harry Bailly. In the Parson's Prologue (I 15–25), toward the very end of the journey, we learn that the poet had modi-fied his own plan very considerably, by the time he had brought his pilgrims within sight of Canterbury. We part with the pilgrims before they reach the goal of their pil-grimage, and we hear nothing at all about their return journey. On the way to Canterbury, moreover, no pilgrim, except the poet himself, tells more than one story; and seven of the company tell no tale at all.[5] The *Monkes Tale* and the *Rime of Sir Thopas* are interrupted by the pilgrims, and the *Cokes Tale* and *Squieres Tale* were left unfinished. Of the hundred and twenty tales which Chaucer seems to promise us in the Prologue, only twenty were com-pleted.

There is further evidence of the incomplete condition in which Chaucer left his last great work. The most tantaliz-ing problem of Chaucerian scholarship is the question of the order of the *Canterbury Tales*. It may be said at once that no entirely satisfactory solution of this problem is ever likely to be offered. Scholars are still taxing their ingenuity to supply what Chaucer might or should have written, to make his story of the pilgrimage to Canter-bury complete and consistent; but the lamentable fact re-mains that he never did finish the story, and no amount of juggling the fragments of his unfinished work will ever bring them into a completed pattern. In all proba-bility, he had not himself determined the precise order in

[5] Yeman, Haberdassher, Carpenter, Webbe, Dyere, Tapicier, Plowman.

which the tales in his collection should stand. He had certainly not written all that he originally intended to write,
either to supply the number of tales which the Host's proposal calls for, or to fill the gaps between the stories with
a consistent narrative of the journey to Canterbury. From
the condition of the manuscripts, it may be inferred that
he had experimented with various arrangements of his
completed material, and that he had cancelled certain passages, as new ideas for the interplay of character, along
the Canterbury road, suggested themselves to his mind.
It is evident that some of the tales were thrust into the
collection with very little consideration of their fitness
for the narrators to whom they are assigned; and one of
them appears to have been transferred, as an afterthought,
from one of the pilgrims to another. In short, there is
every indication that Chaucer had not settled in his own
mind the problems of the precise order of the tales and
their assignment among the pilgrims.[6]

The order in which the *Canterbury Tales* stand in
Skeat's edition is that adopted by Furnivall, for the
Chaucer Society, in 1868. It affords a narrative of the
journey to Canterbury which is not complete, of course,
but which can be followed, through the nine fragments
which Chaucer left behind him, without encountering any
serious inconsistency. Since the journey from London to
Canterbury commonly occupied three days and part
of a fourth, Chaucer's pilgrims are assumed to have been

---

[6] In an able and illuminating study, C. R. Kase argues that the
confusion in the arrangement of the Tales "resulted from the difficulties involved in the insertion of Groups DE and G into a framework not entirely prepared for their reception." *Three Chaucer
Studies*, New York. 1932, III. 86. Cf. Tatlock: *The Canterbury Tales
in 1400* in *Publ. Mod. Lang. Assn.*, 50. 100–39.

upon the road during the better part of four days. If they followed the customary procedure, they spent their nights at Dartford, Rochester, and Ospringe.[7] An explicit statement, in the Prologue to the *Tale of the Man of Lawe*, informs us that the second day of the journey fell on April 18. We may, then, outline the progress of the pilgrims as follows:

April 16. Assembly at the Tabard (A 19–34, 747–821).

April 17. Sunrise (about 4.45): the company rises and sets out from Southwark. At a little brook, called St. Thomas-a-Watering, they draw lots (A 822–49). The Knight and the Miller tell their stories. At about 7.30, the pilgrims are passing within sight of Deptford and Greenwich (A 3906, 3907). The Reeve tells his tale and the Cook begins his. Nothing beyond Group A can be assigned to the first day of the pilgrimage. The pilgrims probably pass the night at Dartford, fifteen miles from London.

April 18. 10 o'clock: the telling of tales apparently has not yet begun (B 1–32). To this day belongs Group B (Man of Law, Shipman, Prioress, Chaucer, Monk, Nun's Priest). Line B 3116 indicates that the pilgrims are approaching Rochester, where they doubtless pass the night, thirty miles from London.

April 19. Group C (Physician, Pardoner), which contains no indications of time or place,[8] and Group D (Wife

[7] It was at these three towns that Queen Isabella broke her journey from London to Canterbury in 1358, and King John of France broke his journey at the same towns in 1360. Cf. Littlehales, *Some Notes on the Road from London to Canterbury in the Middle Ages* (Chaucer Society, 1898).

[8] It is impossible to locate the ale-stake, where the Pardoner stops to drink "and eten of a cake," and where, perhaps, he tells his tale.

of Bath, Friar, Summoner) belong to the forenoon of this day. In D 846, 847, the Summoner promises "tales two or thre" before the company shall reach Sittingbourne. In D 2294, he lets us know that he has been as good as his word. The company, then, probably halts for dinner at Sittingbourne, forty miles from London. The afternoon is occupied by Group E (Clerk, Merchant), in which no references to time or place occur. The pilgrims probably pass the night at Ospringe, forty-six miles from London and ten from Canterbury.

April 20. 9 o'clock: the Squire begins his tale at once, "for it is pryme" (F 73). His tale and the Franklin's, which are obviously connected, form Group F. Just after the *Seconde Nonnes Tale* has been told, the Canon and his Yeoman overtake the pilgrims at Boughton-under-Blean (G 556), having seen the company ride forth from their inn-yard in the morning (G 588). The stories told by the Second Nun and the Canon's Yeoman are, therefore, connected and form Group G. It is still morning when the Host tries to rouse the drunken Cook, as the pilgrims pass through a little town called Bob-up-and-down, at the edge of Blean Forest (H 1–19). The Manciple, in lieu of the Cook, tells his story, which forms Group H. At four in the afternoon (I 5), the Parson begins his sermon, which forms Group I.

Although this arrangement of the *Tales* leaves many gaps in the narrative of the journey, it is as satisfactory as any that has been proposed. The principal objection to be offered against it is that it has no authority in the manuscripts. None of the manuscripts presents the fragments in the order adopted by Furnivall and followed by

Skeat. Only one,[9] admittedly inferior in many respects, links the Shipman's Tale with that of the Man of Law, and even in this manuscript, the order of the groups is very different from that presented in Skeat's edition. Some of the best manuscripts altogether omit the Link called the Shipman's Prologue; others use it as a prologue to the *Squieres Tale,* substituting "Squiere" for "Shipman" in line 17; and a few attribute to the Summoner the speech which Selden Manuscript ascribes to the Shipman, but place the Link immediately before Group D. In other words, only one inferior manuscript presents Group B, (Man of Law, Shipman, Prioress, Chaucer, Monk, Nun's Priest) as a unified whole; the others separate the group into two fragments, usually designated by scholars as B[1] and B[2], placing B[2], which includes all the tales in the group except that of the Man of Law, much farther toward the end of the collection.

There is even less authority for one other important peculiarity of the arrangement adopted by Furnivall and followed by Skeat. Group C, (Physician, Pardoner) precedes the Shipman's Tale in all the existing manuscripts, except Selden B 14, in which it is placed between the *Chanouns Yemannes Tale* and the Franklin's Prologue, with an obviously spurious Link, of fourteen lines, connecting the Canon's Yeoman's Tale with the Physician's.

Although the arrangement of the tales arbitrarily adopted by Furnivall is without manuscript authority, it must be said that it removes one glaring inconsistency which appears in the narrative of the journey, as presented by the manuscripts. Group B[2], placed after Group D in the best manuscripts, contains an allusion to the town

[9] Ms. Arch. Selden B 14, in the Bodleian.

of Rochester, which we are told "stant heer faste by" (B 3116). In Group D, on the other hand, there are clear indications, in the words of the Summoner (D 846, 847, 2294), that the company is approaching Sittingbourne. If we adopt the order of the groups presented by the best manuscripts, then, we discover that the pilgrims reach Sittingbourne before they come to Rochester. Since Sittingbourne is ten miles further than Rochester from London, this is palpably absurd, and no one would care to argue that Chaucer intended us to accept an arrangement of the Tales which involved so obvious an inconsistency. Since it is clearly advisable to reject the authority of the manuscripts, in this matter of the relative positions of Group B ^{2} and Group D, the way is opened to some such arbitrary arrangement as that which Furnivall adopted. His arrangement, as has been said, offers a fairly satisfactory solution of the problem, and it remains only to warn the reader that there is no evidence that Chaucer intended to present his material in just this manner.

If it is futile to attempt to arrive at definite conclusions with regard to the arrangement which Chaucer intended to give the Tales, it is even more futile to search for a unifying *motif* in a work which the author left in so fragmentary a condition. It is true that the presentation of diverse views on marriage gives a certain unity to that portion of the poem which begins with the Wife of Bath's Prologue and ends with the Franklin's Tale; and the fact that the stories which belong to this so-called "Marriage Group" appear in close proximity, though not always in the same order, in all the existing manuscripts, lends support to the theory that Chaucer intended to build this part of the *Canterbury Tales* upon the same underlying theme.[10] Attempts to push the matter farther, however, and to find the same unifying idea running through the entire collection, or through any other considerable part of it, are hardly advisable. Others of the *Tales*, to be sure, are concerned with love or marriage; but nine-tenths of the stories of the world are built upon such themes, and it seems quite unnecessary to conjecture that Chaucer's pilgrims told so many tales of love and lust because the poet had determined to utilize this *motif* to unify his collection of stories.

A similar attempt to discover an architectonic unity in the *Canterbury Tales* is that of Professor Tupper, who has developed a theory that Chaucer intended to bind his stories together by utilizing the familiar schematism of the Seven Deadly Sins, and that the *Persones Tale* was to be an epilogue to a collection which the mediæval reader would recognize as a series of practical applications of the ethical ideas universally inculcated by the Church. Professor Tupper's theory has not gained acceptance, partly because of æsthetic considerations, and partly because the schematism which he attributes to the poet does not appear altogether consistent within itself.[11]

[10] Professor Kittredge's lucid exposition of the unity of the "Marriage Group" (*Chaucer and his Poetry*, 185–211) has gained general acceptance, though not without some opposition. Cf. H. B. Hinckley: *Marriage in the Canterbury Tales,* in the *Publ. Mod. Lang. Assn.*, 32. 292–305.

[11] Professor Tupper's articles on the subject are to be found in the *Journal of Engl. and Germ. Philology*, 13. 553–65; 14. 256–70; 15. 56–106; and in the *Publ. Mod. Lang. Assn.*, 29. 93–128. His theory is discussed adversely by Professor Lowes in an article in *Publ. Mod. Lang. Assn.*, 30. 237–371.

THE PROLOGUE

It has generally been assumed that the Prologue to the *Canterbury Tales* was written when the idea of the pilgrimage was first conceived. The vivacity with which the work has been done suggests the zeal of fresh inspiration. The fact that the poet includes descriptions of several persons who do not contribute stories makes it appear all the more likely that the Prologue was written before he had made much progress with his work upon the individual tales. Miss Hammond has put forth an interesting theory, however, that the portraits of the Reeve, Miller, Manciple, Summoner, and Pardoner—the members of the company who furnish most of the dramatic incident upon the journey—were added after the poet had made some progress with his work and had begun to realize the advantages of introducing more dynamic personalities into the group.[12] The theory is decidedly alluring, but it is only a conjecture. The generally accepted belief is that the Prologue was begun before more than two or three of the stories had been written, and that it was completed before Chaucer proceeded further with his collection of tales.

For many years, the composition of the Prologue was assigned definitely to the year 1387, largely on the evidence of the reference (A 277) to "keeping" the sea "bitwixe Middelburgh and Orewelle." The continental port most used by the Merchants of the Staple during the lifetime of Chaucer was Calais; but for a brief period, between 1384 and 1388, the Staple was removed from Calais and established at Middelburgh. Professor Hales, in a paper in the *Athenæum* for 1893 (I. 443, 444), first pointed out these

[12] E. P. Hammond: *Chaucer, a Bibliographical Manual*, 254, ff.

facts and drew the conclusion that Chaucer's Merchant could hardly have been interested in keeping the sea-lanes to Middelburgh free from pirates at any other time. Professor Knott, however, has recently shown that other ports than the legal Staple were frequently used, under special privilege, by English exporters, and that it is not so certain as had been supposed that the reference to Middelburgh belongs to the period between 1384 and 1388.[13] Nevertheless, the traditional date of 1387 is still accepted for the Prologue, although robbed of this supporting evidence. Skeat's argument for dating the fictitious pilgrimage in 1387 may certainly be accepted,[14] but it does not necessarily follow that the Prologue was written in that year.

No source for this, the most distinctive of Chaucer's works, has ever been discovered. No such series of descriptions is to be found in any work of ancient or mediæval literature which could have come to Chaucer's attention. The Canterbury Pilgrims are described so realistically, indeed, that scholarship is at present searching fourteenth-century England, rather than the books which the poet is known to have read, for the originals of the portraits in the Prologue. Harry Bailly, the host of the Tabard, is known to have been an actual person, who sat in Parliament, as representative of the borough of Southwark, in 1376 and 1378; and "Roger Ware of London" and "Roger Knight of Ware" appear in documents of 1377 and 1384–5 in each case identified as "Cook." (Cf. *London Times Literary Supplement,* 1932. p. 761.)

Professor Manly's Lowell Lectures, published in 1926

---

[13] *Philological Quarterly,* I. 1–16.
[14] *Oxford Chaucer,* III. 373, 374.

under the title, *Some New Light on Chaucer,* "exhibit the results of treating Chaucer as one would a modern writer, of believing that behind his most vital and successful sketches lay the observation of living men and women, of assuming that some at least of the definite statements made about them might be true, and then searching the records of his time to discover if by chance one could find persons answering accurately or nearly so to the descriptions he gave of them." Professor Manly's researches have certainly discovered much material which illuminates the descriptions of the pilgrims and adds greatly to one's enjoyment in reading the Prologue. That his results are highly speculative, he is the first to recognize, and he declares that he is "far from believing that Chaucer merely photographed his friends and acquaintances." His arguments, nevertheless, leave one almost convinced that for a few of the Canterbury Pilgrims something like originals have been found. The Reeve, to whom Chaucer gives a local habitation, if not a name, Professor Manly has traced to the Pembroke estates in Norfolk; the Prioress, who speaks French "after the scole of Stratford atte Bowe," he has found faintly foreshadowed in Madame Argentyn, who was apparently nun, if not prioress, at the Benedictine nunnery of St. Leonard's, Bromley, adjoining Stratford-Bow; and he has shown that the title of the Sergeant of the Lawe, together with certain of the facts of his career, must have caused the fourteenth-century reader of the Prologue to scrutinize Chaucer's lawyer very sharply, in the expectation of finding traits that would suggest one man or another among the very limited group of sergeants at law.[15]

[15] Professor Manly's lectures deal also with the Miller, Sum-

Though occasional details in the descriptions may have been drawn from actual persons, it is extremely unlikely, as Professor Manly says, that Chaucer drew his portraits, in any large measure, from people whom he knew. Imagination, working upon contemporary life, was the principal source of his descriptions; and to seek a complete original, either in books or in life, for any one of the Canterbury Pilgrims, is no more profitable than to search for Sir John Falstaff in Elizabethan libraries or taverns. The Prologue to the *Canterbury Tales*, considered as a whole, is an entirely original work.

On the other hand, several details in Chaucer's descriptions of his pilgrims have been definitely traced to other authors. The Prioress's table-manners, for example, are derived from the *Roman de la Rose:*

> " 'Tis well she take especial care
> That in the sauce her fingers ne'er
> She dip beyond the joint, nor soil
> Her lips with garlick, sops, or oil,
> Nor heap up gobbets and then charge
> Her mouth with pieces overlarge,
> And only with the finger point
> Should touch the bit she'd fain anoint
> With sauce, white, yellow, brown, or green,
> And lift it towards her mouth between
> Finger and thumb with care and skill,
> That she no sauce or morsel spill
> About her breast-cloth.
>   Then her cup
> She should so gracefully lift up

moner, Friar, Pardoner, Franklin, Shipman, Merchant, Wife of Bath, Second Nun, Nun's Priest, and Canon. There is also a brief section on "The Others."

Towards her mouth that not a gout
By any chance doth fall about
Her vesture, or for glutton rude,
By such unseemly habitude,
Might she be deemed.
                              Nor should she set
Lips to her cup while food is yet
Within her mouth. And first should she
Her upper lip wipe delicately,
Lest, having drunk, a grease-formed groat
Were seen upon the wine to float." [16]

From the same source come a few lines in the description of Alice of Bath, who, like La Vieille of Jean de Meun, "scet toute la vielle dance."

Faux-Semblant, the hypocrite whose cynical confession is to be found in Jean's portion of the *Roman,* undoubtedly contributed something to Chaucer's satirical portrait of the Friar. Like Faux-Semblant, Frere Hubert prefers to carry spiritual consolation to the wealthy rather than to the poor; and his views on the impropriety of associating with "seke lazars" seem to be derived from the following passage in the confession of Faux-Semblant:

"I love bet the acqueyntaunce
    Ten tymes, of the king of Fraunce,
    Than of pore man of mylde mode,
    Though that his soule be also gode.
    For whan I see beggers quaking,
    Naked on mixens al stinking,
    For hungre crye, and eek for care,
    I entremete not of hir fare.
    They been so pore, and ful of pyne,

[16] Ellis's translation, 14117–40.

They might not ones yeve me dyne,
For they have no-thing but hir lyf;
What shulde he yeve that likketh his knyf?
It is but foly to entremete,
To seke in houndes nest fat mete.
Let bere hem to the spitel anoon,
But, for me, comfort gete they noon.
But a riche sike usurere
Wolde I visyte and drawe nere;
Him wol I comforte and rehete,
For I hope of his gold to gete.
And if that wikked deth him have,
I wol go with him to his grave." [17]

Both of these scoundrels, it will be seen, use the garb of
the mendicant order for mercenary purposes, and both
have been so successful that Faux-Semblant, like Chaucer's Friar, can boast

Miex vaut mes porchas que ma rente.

It should be added that Chaucer's debt to the *Roman,* in
so far as the portraits of the Prologue are concerned, is
not so much a matter of verbal borrowings as of the spirit
which inspired the work. Though Chaucer's satire is more
subtle and, perhaps, more genial, it was from Jean de
Meun that he first learned to use his pen for the unspar-
ing exposure of hypocrisy.[18]

Another possible source for the satirical spirit, which
animates so much of the Prologue, is Langland's *Piers the*

[17] The translation is from the Mid. Eng. *Romaunt,* Lines
6491–6512.
[18] For a further discussion of this matter see D. S. Fansler:
Chaucer and the Roman de la Rose, 162–66.

Plowman. The two works, to be sure, differ from one another in many ways, but they are certainly much alike in their common purpose of illuminating the darker corners of fourteenth-century English life. Chaucer's recreant churchmen, in particular, are close akin to Langland's. His parish priest is the converse of those whom Langland describes as forsaking their parishes to go up to London,

> To sing there for simony, for silver is sweet.

The Plowman is so similar to the "trewe swinker" who has given his name as title to the Vision of William Langland, that it seems rather singular that more attention has not been paid to the resemblance. It is not likely that Chaucer was unacquainted with a work which was famous to the point of notoriety in his day, and it seems more than probable that some of his Canterbury Pilgrims owe a few of their traits to the less full-blooded figures that flit across the fair field full of folk in Langland's Vision.

Professor Curry, in his *Chaucer and the Mediaeval Sciences,* discusses the share which the poet's scientific interests may have had in the creation of some of the characters among the Canterbury Pilgrims. Much of his argument rests upon the incidents of the journey, as well as upon the brief descriptions in the Prologue, but his starting point is usually in those descriptions. He has shown that the portraits of the Miller and Reeve include physical details which the popular science of physiognomy attributed to men of just the traits of character which these two men exhibit; he has brought the portrait of the Pardoner into comparison with other descriptions of the *eunuchus ex nativitate;* and he has explored the medical lore of the Middle Ages to identify the skin-disease of the Summoner and the Cook's "mormal." His analysis of the character of Alice of Bath, in the light of her horoscope, depends more upon the material presented later in the *Canterbury Tales* than upon the description of the lady in the Prologue.[19]

The Ellesmere Manuscript of the *Canterbury Tales* contains individual portraits of the pilgrims, and a manuscript in the Cambridge University Library was similarly embellished, but many of the pictures have been cut away. The illustrations of both these manuscripts are reproduced in the Chaucer Society's six-text edition of the *Tales*. Woodcuts of the pilgrims were included in Caxton's second edition of the *Tales* (ca. 1484), and they were used again in the edition by Pynson (ca. 1492) and that published by Wynkyn de Worde in 1498. A manuscript of Lydgate's *Story of Thebes*,[20] a work which undertakes to give us some account of the return journey of the pilgrims, contains an illumination of the company leaving Canterbury. In more modern times, as well, the Canterbury Pilgrims have furnished a theme for painters and engravers. The best known representations of the Pilgrims are those of Thomas Stothard, exhibited in 1807, and of William Blake, exhibited in 1809.

[19] Professor Curry also discusses the Doctour of Phisyk in the light of mediæval medical science. Much of the material in the book had previously appeared in learned publications. Professor Curry has modified the position taken in his articles on a number of matters.

[20] Ms. Royal 18 D ii, in the British Museum. The illumination is reproduced, as the frontispiece, in Skeat's modernization of the *Knightes Tale,* published in 1904.

THE KNIGHTES TALE

Evidence that a version of the story of Palamon and Arcite by Chaucer was in existence before 1385 or 1386 is furnished by the reference to such a work in the earlier version of the Prologue to the *Legend of Good Women*. It is now generally believed that the work to which Alceste refers, in her defense of Chaucer, was the poem which we know as the *Knightes Tale*. Alterations must have been made, to adapt the story to its position in the *Canterbury Tales*, but it is not certain that the revision was at all extensive. It seems probable that Chaucer had but recently completed the story of Palamon and Arcite when he commenced his *Legend of Good Women*, and that it was lying ready to his hand when he projected his greater series of stories. The poem should be dated not much before 1385. It could hardly have been "knowen lyte" when the Prologue to the *Legend of Good Women* was written, if it had been long in existence.[21]

Like the *Troilus*, which belongs to the same period in Chaucer's literary career, the *Knightes Tale* is derived from Boccaccio.[22] It is a very much condensed version of the story, which is presented at great length and with much epic machinery in the Italian poet's *Teseida*, a work which extends to 9896 lines.[23] A close comparison of Chaucer's

[21] Professor Kittredge has pointed out (*Modern Philology*, I. 1–18.) that a poem written before 1392, by Chaucer's friend Clanvowe, contains quotations from the *Knightes Tale*.

[22] More than a dozen lines in the *Knightes Tale* contain close echoes of expressions used in the *Troilus*. This fact affords further evidence that the two poems belong to the same period. Echoes from the *Knightes Tale* occur in the *Legend of Good Women*.

[23] S. Battaglia (ed.) : *Giovanni Boccaccio: Teseida*, Florence, 1938.

poem with his Italian original shows that "out of 2250 of Chaucer's lines, he has only translated 270 (less than one-eighth) ; that only 374 more lines bear a general likeness to Boccaccio's, and only 132 more, a slight likeness." [24] I reproduce the analysis of the *Teseida,* made by Tyrwhitt, from his "Introductory Discourse to the Canterbury Tales" (ix). It will show what material Chaucer has borrowed from Boccaccio, and how rigorously he has excluded matters which are not directly connected with the story of Palamon and Arcite.[25]

"The Theseida is distributed into twelve Books or Cantoes.

"B. I. Contains the war of Theseus with the Amazons; their submission to him; and his marriage with Hippolyta.

"B. II. Theseus, having spent two years in Scythia, is reproached by Perithous in a vision, and immediately returns to Athens with Hippolyta and her sister Emilia. He enters the city in triumph; finds the Grecian Ladies in the temple of Clemenzia; marches to Thebes; kills Creon, &c., and brings home Palemone and Arcita, who are *Damnati—ad eterna presone.*

"B. III. Emilia, walking in a garden and singing, is heard and seen first by Arcita, who calls Palemone. They are both equally enamoured of her, but without any jealousy or rivalship. Emilia is supposed to see them at the window, and to be not displeased with their admiration. Arcita is released at the request of Perithous; takes his leave of Palemone, with embraces, &c.

[24] F. J. Furnivall: *Temporary Preface to the Six Text Edition,* 104, 105. The figures are based on the collation of the two poems made by Dr. Henry Ward.

[25] An admirably full summary is given by R. A. Pratt in *Sources and Analogues,* 93–105.

"B. IV. Arcita, having changed his name to *Pentheo,* goes into the service of Menelaus at Mycenae, and afterwards of Peleus at Aegina. From thence he returns to Athens and becomes a favourite servant of Theseus, being known to Emilia, though to nobody else; till after some time he is overheard making his complaint in a wood, to which he usually resorted for that purpose, by Pamphilo, a servant of Palemone.

"B. V. Upon the report of Pamphilo, Palemone *begins* to be jealous of Arcita, and is desirous to get out of prison in order to fight with him. This he accomplishes with the assistance of Pamphilo, by changing clothes with Alimeto, a Physician. He goes armed to the wood in quest of Arcita, whom he finds sleeping. At first they are very civil and friendly to each other. Then Palemone calls upon Arcita to renounce his pretensions to Emilia, or to fight with him. After many long expostulations on the part of Arcita, they fight, and are discovered first by Emilia, who sends for Theseus. When he finds who they are, and the cause of their difference, he forgives them, and proposes the method of deciding their claim to Emilia by a combat of an hundred on each side, to which they gladly agree.

"B. VI. Palemone and Arcita live splendidly at Athens, and send out messengers to summon their friends, who arrive; and the principal of them are severally described, viz. Lycurgus, Peleus, Phocus, Telamon, &c. Agamemnon, Menelaus, Castor, and Pollux, &c. Nestor, Evander, Perithous, Ulysses, Diomedes, Pygmalion, Minos, &c., with a great display of ancient history and mythology.

"B. VII. Theseus declares the laws of the combat, and

the two parties of an hundred on each side are formed. The day before the combat, Arcita, after having visited the temples of all the Gods, makes a formal prayer to Mars. The Prayer, *being personified,* is said to go and find Mars in his temple in Thrace, which is described; and Mars, upon understanding the message, causes favourable signs to be given to Arcita. In the same manner Palemone closes his religious observances with a prayer to Venus. His Prayer, *being also personified,* sets out for the temple of Venus on Mount Citherone, which is also described; and the petition is granted. Then the sacrifice of Emilia to Diana is described; her prayer; the appearance of the Goddess; and the signs of the two fires.—In the morning they proceed to the Theatre with their respective troops, and prepare for the action. Arcita puts up a private prayer to Emilia, and harangues his troop publickly; and Palemone does the same.

"B. VIII. Contains a description of the battle, in which Palemone is taken prisoner.

"B. IX. The horse of Arcita, being frightened by a Fury, sent from hell at the desire of Venus, throws him. However, he is carried to Athens in a triumphal chariot with Emilia by his side; is put to bed dangerously ill; and there by his own desire espouses Emilia.

"B. X. The funeral of the persons killed in the combat. Arcita, being given over by his Physicians, makes his will, in discourse with Theseus, and desires that Palemone may inherit all his possessions and also Emilia. He then takes leave of Palemone and Emilia, to whom he repeats the same request. Their lamentations. Arcita orders a sacrifice to Mercury, which Palemone performs for him, and dies.

"B. XI. Opens with the passage of Arcita's soul to heaven,[26] imitated from the beginning of the 9th Book of Lucan. The funeral of Arcita. Description of the wood felled takes up six Stanzas. Palemone builds a temple in honour of him, in which his whole history is painted. The description of this painting is an abridgement of the preceding part of the Poem.

"B. XII. Theseus proposes to carry into execution Arcita's will by the marriage of Palemone and Emilia. This they both decline for some time in formal speeches, but at last are persuaded and married. The Kings, &c. take their leave, and Palemone remains—'in gioia e in diporto con la sua dona nobile e cortese.'"

Evidence of the influence of other writers than Boccaccio is to be found in isolated passages in the *Knightes Tale.* Chaucer shows his familiarity with the *Thebaid* of Statius in the earlier part of the Tale; and, as in the *Troilus,* the deep influence which the philosophy of Boethius had upon his thinking reveals itself in many passages, as the romance darkens into tragedy towards its close. A few expressions borrowed from the *Roman de la Rose* are to be found in this poem, as in virtually everything that Chaucer wrote.

In a chapter on the Knight's Tale in his *Chaucer and the Mediaeval Sciences* (119–63), Professor Curry endeavors "to interpret the technical significance of the astrological references, and their implications, with which the poem abounds and to show that Chaucer, in order to furnish . . . a motivating force for the final stages of the action, has skilfully gone about transferring the power

[26] This passage was utilized by Chaucer in *Troilus and Criseyde,* V. 1807–27.

of the ancient gods of his sources to the astrological planets of the same name; that the real conflict behind the surface action of the story is a conflict between the planets, Saturn and Mars; that the kings Lycurgus and Emetreus are, respectively, Saturnalian and Martian figures introduced to champion the causes of the heroes; and that the illness of Arcite is a malady inflicted upon him by his planetary enemy, Saturn."

THE MILLERES TALE

During the Middle Ages, such stories as those told by the Miller and the Reeve must have circulated in great numbers, both orally and in writing. It is not likely that Chaucer had any written original before him when he wrote the *Milleres Tale,* but it is equally improbable that he invented the incidents of the story. Two different plots, each typical of the mediæval *fabliau,* have evidently been combined to form a single story, and it is possible that the combination of the two was originally made by Chaucer.

Analogous stories have been found, but none of them can be shown to have antedated the *Canterbury Tales.*[27] In a work called the Nachtbüchlein, by a certain Valentin Schumann, which appeared in Germany in 1559, we have a story "von einem Kauffmann der forchte sich vor dem Jüngsten Tage." Alarmed by a sermon preached at the village church, the merchant provides himself with a boat, which he hangs in the rafters of his dwelling and stocks

---

[27] Stith Thompson (*Sources and Analogues,* 106–23) lists ten versions and prints four of them: a Flemish verse *fabliau* (ca. 1400), the Italian *novella,* Schumann's prose tale, and a German analogue in verse by Hans Sachs (1537).

with food, wine, and beer. Every evening, he retires to this place of safety, lest the flood, which he has been told will accomplish the work of destruction at the Last Day, find him unprovided in his bed. His wife, vexed at his desertion, consoles herself with a young clerk and encourages the attentions of the local blacksmith. The latter arrives at her window one night while the clerk is with her and receives much the same welcome as that which is accorded Absolon. He takes his revenge by means of red-hot iron, and the cries of "Wasser! Wasser!" arouse the merchant from his slumbers and bring him crashing to the floor.

In the early part of the sixteenth century, Hanz Folz had used a similar theme for a Shrove-tide play; and toward the end of the next century, the story appeared in Germany once more, this time in a collection of tales issued under the title *Lyrum Larum, seu Nugae Venales Ioco Seriae*. An interesting German variant appears in a bowdlerized version which is included in a modern collection of tales from Schleswig-Holstein and Lauenburg. In this version, a farmer's pretty wife is left solitary by her husband, who has sought safety, as usual, in the rafters of his house. This lady, however, is not to be persuaded to yield greater favors to her suitor, the village smith, than permission to kiss her hand. Irritated at her continued coyness, the smith at last takes revenge upon her by burning her hand with a red-hot iron, which he has held behind his back. She screams for water, and the farmer cuts himself loose, falls crashing to the floor, and breaks his neck. It may be worthy of notice that in all the existing German versions of the story, the husband provides a means of safety against the flood only for himself, leaving his wife to take her chances with the wrath that is to come; there is not the faintest suggestion of the clever motivation, by which the uxorious carpenter, in the *Milleres Tale,* is led on, by his very anxiety for his young wife, to prepare the way for his own undoing.

An Italian story analogous to the *Milleres Tale* appears in a collection of *novelle* by Massuccio di Salerno (ca. 1470), but here there is no mention of the husband and his fear of the flood. A story in the *Decameron* (Day 3, Nov. 4) bears a faint resemblance to Chaucer's story.

It is clear that the *Milleres Tale* and the one-sided quarrel between the Reeve and the Miller, which it provokes, must belong to the period when the *Canterbury Tales* were well under way. The probable date of this portion of the work is 1387–90.

THE REVES TALE

Like the *Milleres Tale,* the story told by the Reeve was undoubtedly derived from some *fabliau,* which reached Chaucer either orally or in writing. Popular stories of revenge taken upon a cheat are common enough in all literatures. Analogues to the *Reves Tale* have been found in several different languages. The closest parallel to Chaucer's story is offered by a French *fabliau,* extant in two manuscript versions, both of which are printed by W. M. Hart in *Sources and Analogues* (124–47). It relates the adventures of two poor clerks, who find themselves in great difficulties during a time of dearth. Having nothing to live on, they determine to borrow some wheat and turn bakers. When they take their wheat to the mill, however, the miller's wife induces them both in turn to go seek her husband in the woods; and while they are gone, the miller and his wife bestir themselves to such advantage that the clerks, on their return, find neither their grain nor their mare. Taking lodging for the night with the miller, they contrive their revenge in very much the same way as that employed by Chaucer's Cambridge students; and before their departure, they recover both their horse and their grain.

In a similar story, which is to be found in two manuscripts in the Bibliothèque Nationale, there is no reference to a miller or to grain to be ground. Two clerks, "who have spent their substance on folly more than on learning," take lodgings with a *villein* named Gombert. Their nocturnal adventures follow much the same course as those set forth in the other *fabliau* and in the *Reves Tale*.

Two versions of the same story occur in German manuscripts, and a Latin version is included in an anonymous tract, entitled *De generibus ebriosorum et ebrietate vitanda,* which was published in 1516. In the Latin version, the two clerks deliberately make the miller's wife and daughter drunk. A somewhat similar story occurs in the *Decameron* (Day 9, Nov. 6), but Boccaccio's version is not so close a parallel to the *Reves Tale* as those found in the *fabliaux,* and it is probable that the resemblance is due simply to the common use of a story which seems to have been widely known and highly popular in the late Middle Ages.

Chaucer uses the following dialectic peculiarities in the speeches of the two Cambridge clerks, to mark their northern extraction: [28]

[28] Cf. *Oxford Chaucer,* V. 121, 122.

(1) *a* for A. S. *ā,* where Chaucer usually has *ō.*

E. g., *na* (*no*), *swa* (*so*), *ham* (*hoom*), *gas* (*gooth*), *fra* (*fro*), *banes* (*bones*), *anes* (*ones*), *waat* (*woot*), *raa* (*ro*), *bathe* (*bothe*), *ga* (*go*), *twa* (*two*), *wha* (*who*). Also, *saule* (*soule*), *tald* (*told*), *halde* (*holde*), *awen* (*owen*).

(2) *a* for A. S. short *a* before *ng.*

E. g., *sang* (*song*), *lange* (*longe*), *wrang* (*wrong*).

(3) *ee* for *oo.*

E. g., *geen* (*goon*), *neen* (*noon*).

(4) Indicative singular and plural in *-es* or *-s.*

E. g., *far-es bo-es, ga-s, wagg-es, fall-es, fynd-es, bring-es, tyd-es, say-s* (4180), *werk-es* (4030), *is I, I is, thou is.*

(5) *Sal* for *shal,* *slyk* for *swiche,* *whilk* for *whiche,* *thair* for *hir* (their), *hethen* for *hennes,* *til* for *to,* *y-mel* for *amonges,* *gif* for *if.*

(6) Dialectic words not used elsewhere by Chaucer. E. g., *lathe,* barn; *fonne,* fool; *hething,* contempt; *taa,* take; *boes,* behoves.

Skeat believed he had identified the scene of the *Reves Tale,* at Trumpington, in "the spot marked 'Old Mills' on the ordnance-map, though better known as 'Byron's pool,' which is the old mill-pool." He also suggested that Chaucer might have learned something of the neighborhood from Lady Blanche de Trumpington, who was associated with Philippa Chaucer in attendance upon Queen Constance.[29]

THE COKES TALE

Chaucer never completed his tale of Perkin Revelour, the idle apprentice. Since the Host later calls upon the Cook for a story (H 11, ff.), it is possible that the poet in-

[29] *Oxford Chaucer,* V. 116.

tended to suppress this fragment entirely. There is nothing in the fifty-eight lines to indicate the course which the plot of the *Cokes Tale* was to take; and it is, of course, impossible to say whether Chaucer was intending to utilize some familiar story or to create an original sketch of actual life, such as he has presented in the *Chanouns Yemannes Tale*.

The *Tale of Gamelyn,* found in many of the manuscripts of the *Canterbury Tales,* following the *Cokes Tale* and sometimes linked with it, is obviously spurious. It was probably written in the fourteenth century, but certainly not by Chaucer. It was first printed among the *Canterbury Tales* by Urry, in 1721.

THE TALE OF THE MAN OF LAWE

From the "wordes of the Hoost to the companye," with which Group B opens, we learn that it is the eighteenth day of April and ten o'clock in the morning. The little sermon on the waste of time, which Harry Bailly delivers, carries the implication that the pilgrims have travelled through "the fourthe party of this day" without making progress in their tale-telling. It would appear, then, that a new day's journey has begun, and that Group B is quite unconnected with Group A. If we accept the arrangement of the *Tales* presented in Skeat's edition, we may regard Group B as an unbroken account of the progress of the company on their second day, carrying them from Dartford to Rochester.[30]

The Lawyer's reference to Chaucer is not to be taken as evidence that the poet was recognized by any of his

[30] But cf. pp. 196–99, above.

fellow-pilgrims. The "murye wordes of the Host to Chaucer," in the prologue to *Sir Thopas,* make it clear that the author has not made himself known to his companions by name. It is natural that the Man of Law, as an educated man, should be familiar with the writings of the most popular poet of the age. He refers, however, to only two of Chaucer's works: the "Ceys and Alcion," which forms part of the *Book of the Duchesse,* and the "Seintes Legende of Cupyde," which is another name for the *Legend of Good Women.* The allusion to the second of these works dates the Man of Law's Tale after 1385–6. That the passage contains references to several stories which are not included in the *Legend* seems to indicate that these words were written at a time when Chaucer was still contemplating further labors upon the theme of Cupid's saints. It is difficult to understand Chaucer's purpose in including such a reference to the *Legend* unless he intended the Lawyer's words to serve as a sort of prospectus of an unfinished work.

A more interesting matter is the covert allusion to Gower's *Confessio Amantis,* which also includes the tale of Constance. The Man of Law commends Chaucer for not soiling his pages with "swiche cursed stories" as those of Canace and Apollonius. Both of these tales of incest are included in the *Confessio Amantis,* and one of them is the last of the many stories related in that lengthy poem. This allusion has the appearance of a good-humored dig at the man whom Chaucer has elsewhere called the "moral Gower." The two poets were writing for much the same reading public, and their friendship must have been seasoned with some little rivalry, which would not necessarily disturb their personal relationship. It would be most natural, therefore, that the less conventional of the two should seize this opportunity to rally his more staid contemporary upon the nature of some of his themes. That Gower did not relish the humor of the allusion to his tales of incest has sometimes been inferred from the fact that he omitted, in his revision of the *Confessio Amantis,* a passage in which he pays high compliment to Chaucer, through the mouth of the Goddess of Love; [31] but it must be said that evidence of a quarrel between the two friends, arising out of this incident, is of the slightest.

The connection with the *Confessio Amantis* helps us to date both the passage which introduces the *Tale of the Man of Lawe* and the Tale itself. Gower's poem was finished in 1390, and the portion containing the tale of Constance could not have been written much before 1387.[32] It is possible that Chaucer had access to Gower's manuscript before the entire work was completed, but it is more likely that he wrote his own version of the tale of Constance after Gower's poem had been given to the public. The *Tale of the Man of Lawe,* then, belongs after 1390.

The outburst against poverty, with which the Lawyer prefaces his Tale, also has its bearing upon the date of the poem. Although the fourth and fifth stanzas accomplish a very deft transition from the subject of poverty to the tale of Constance, the connection seems an entirely artificial one, for the story which the Lawyer is about to tell has only the slightest connection with the condition of indigence. Certainly the least of the evils which assail the saintly Constance is destitution. The stanzas on poverty

[31] *Confessio Amantis,* VIII. 2941, ff.
[32] Works of John Gower, edited by Macaulay, II. xxi, xxii.

appear to have found their way into the *Canterbury Tales* simply because they were a part of a work which Chaucer was engaged in translating. In the revised version of the Prologue to the *Legend of Good Women* (A 414, 415), there is a reference to a translation, by Chaucer

> of the Wreched Engendring of Mankinde,
> As man may in pope Innocent y-finde.

The work referred to is the *De Contemptu Mundi* of Pope Innocent III, and we may accept this passage as evidence that Chaucer had actually undertaken the labor of translating this uncongenial work. Since this lost translation is mentioned only in the later recension of the Prologue to the *Legend of Good Women,* and is the only work which is there added to the list of Chaucer's writings, it is reasonable to assume that the poet had not begun work upon the *De Contemptu Mundi,* and may not have known it at all, when the first version of the Prologue was written, in 1385–6. Doubtless, the prologue to the *Tale of the Man of Lawe* was written at a time when Pope Innocent's words on poverty, in his gloomy treatise *"de miseria conditionis humanae"* were fresh in Chaucer's mind. Further echoes of passages from the *De Contemptu Mundi* are to be found in the Tale itself. When the Man of Law interrupts his narrative, to moralize upon the instability of human happiness (B 421–27, 1134–41) and upon the evil effects of drunkenness and of lust (B 771–77, B 925–31), his words are taken almost literally from Pope Innocent.[33]

---

[33] The passages in the *De Contemptu Mundi* utilized by Chaucer in the Lawyer's Prologue and Tale are given in full by Skeat: *Oxford Chaucer,* III. 407, 408.

Many of the incidents of the story which the Man of Law tells occur in older tales.[34] The rudderless boat, the cruel mother-in-law, the alleged monstrous birth, and other less important elements in the story are to be found, over and over again, in ancient tales. The unaccountable reluctance which Constance shows about revealing her identity suggests the mystery which surrounds the fairy-lovers of folk tales, and the miracles by which the heroine is preserved against the elements and against her foes are a part of the machinery of the typical saint's legend.

The immediate source of the *Tale of the Man of Lawe,* however, is the story of "la pucele Constance," given in the Anglo-Norman Chronicle of Nicholas Trivet. The author, who lived during the first half of the fourteenth century, was an English Dominican, of considerable attainments as a scholar and so voluminous a writer that he left nearly a score of very lengthy works behind him. His account of Constance, written in the French of the English court and extant in eight manuscripts, has been edited and reprinted by Margaret Schlauch (*Sources and Analogues,* 65–81). It may be summarized as follows:

The Emperor Tiberius Constantinus had a daughter, named Constance, whom he caused to be instructed in the Christian faith and in the seven sciences. In her thirteenth year, she converted certain heathen merchants out of the great Saracen land, who had come to Rome, bearing rich merchandise. On their return to their own country, they were accused to the high Sultan concerning their con-

[34] The Chaucer Society, *Originals and Analogues,* prints fifteen stories which contain incidents analogous to those in the Lawyer's Tale. See also the invaluable study of this and kindred stories, *Chaucer's Constance and Accused Queens* (New York, 1927) by Margaret Schlauch.

version. Brought before him, they defended their faith
and spoke in praise of the maid Constance, who had converted them. The Sultan, smitten with love through their
words, sent the merchants back to Rome, with rich gifts,
to ask Constance in marriage. Tiberius gave his consent,
on condition that the Sultan become a Christian and receive baptism. The Sultan accepted the conditions, gave
hostages for the security of Constance, and ceded Jerusalem to the Christians. Thereupon, amid the grief of the
whole city of Rome, Constance was sent from her father's
house among strange barbarians.

The Sultan's mother, who saw her religion menaced,
plotted evil and treason, entering into secret covenant with
seven hundred Saracens, sworn to live or die in this
quarrel. Feigning to become a Christian, she arranged
with her son that she should hold a feast before the wedding. At the height of the festivities, the seven hundred
fell upon the guests and killed them all, male and female,
save only Constance, and three young men, who bore the
tidings to Rome.

Thus Constance remained alone, in the hands of her
enemies. As no promises and no threats could make her
deny her faith, the Sultaness planned a new torment for
her. She caused a ship to be stored with victuals, sufficient
to sustain the life of the maiden for three years; and
when Constance had been placed therein, the boat was
taken out to the high seas and turned adrift, without sail
or oar.

But God, who steered the ship of Noah, sent a favorable wind, which drove the ship ashore in Northumberland, near a castle, on Christmas Eve, in the eighth month
of the fourth year. Elda, warden of the castle, came down

to Constance and asked her of her condition. Speaking to him in his native tongue, she made such answers as satisfied him, though she did not tell him who she was; and he received her into the castle. Hermingild, his wife, perceiving her noble and virtuous life, was much smitten with love of her and was converted to Christianity through her teaching.

One day, a blind Briton met Hermingild and Constance, as they walked beside the sea, and besought Hermingild to make the sign of the Cross upon his eyes. Encouraged by Constance, she complied with his entreaty, and he was immediately enlightened and saw well and clearly. This miracle led to the conversion of Elda, and the man whose sight had been restored was sent into Wales, to fetch a bishop to baptize the household, to the number of four score and eleven. Shortly after, Elda went to his lord, King Alle, and told him of Constance; whereupon the king was very desirous of seeing her.

During Elda's absence, a Saxon knight, whom he had left in charge of the castle, tempted Constance to sin. Repulsed for the third time, he sought revenge. At daybreak, when Hermingild and Constance were soundly asleep, he cut the throat of Hermingild, his lady, as she lay beside Constance, sleeping in the same bed; and when he had accomplished the crime, he hid the bloody knife behind Constance's pillow. So the wretch endeavored to lay the crime upon Constance; and although Elda defended her, he swore upon the Gospel that she was the murderess. Hardly had he spoken when a closed hand, like a man's fist, appeared before Elda and all who were present, and smote such a blow on the nape of the fellow's neck, that both his eyes flew out of his head, and the teeth out of his mouth, and he fell smitten to the earth. And thereupon, a voice said in the hearing of all, "Against the daughter of Mother Church thou wast laying a scandal; this hast thou done, and I have held my peace."

Some days later, King Alle arrived at the castle and passed sentence of death on the fellow. Taken with love for the maid Constance, the king accepted baptism and married her. Then, after half a year, news came to Alle that the Scots had warred upon his lands, and he gathered his host and took his departure for Scotland, giving his wife in ward to Elda, constable of the castle, and to Lucius, Bishop of Bangor. Now Domild, the king's mother, had great disdain that her son had forsaken his religion for the love of a strange woman, whose lineage he did not know. When God and nature would, Constance was delivered of a male child, a beautiful child and great, and at his baptism he was named Maurice. Elda and Lucius sent word to the king, but their messenger went by way of Knaresborough, where Domild lived, that he might tell her the news. She feigned very great joy in the sight of the people; but that night, she made the messenger so drunk with an evil drink that he lay as if insensible and as a dead man. Then she opened the messenger's box and substituted counterfeit letters, in which Constance was declared to be an evil spirit, and the son born of her body to be a monster, hideous and doleful. On the morrow, the messenger went his way, being charged to return by the same road.

When the messenger was come to the king, he told him the true and joyful news; but the counterfeit letters gave his tidings the lie, and the king bade him say no more of his wife or of the child. In his reply to the letters of Earl Elda and Bishop Lucius, the king bade them keep his wife safely till his return. The messenger, returning to Domild, was again made drunk, and once more the queen opened and read the letters he was carrying. Ill pleased with their contents, she substituted other letters, under the king's seal, in which Elda and the Bishop were commanded, on pain of death, to prepare a ship and store it with provisions for five years, and to banish Constance and her son therein.

These letters so saddened Elda and the Bishop that Constance, perceiving their manner quite changed, feared that her lord was dead and begged them to tell her all the truth. But when they had shewed her the king's letter, she accepted her lord's decree with resignation, being full of God and ready for all His will and ordinances. On the fourth day, she was exiled, with Maurice, her sweet son.

Her ship was guided by God into the Spanish sea and came to land under the castle of an admiral of the paynims. She was brought up from her ship to the castle and well refreshed with meat and drink; after which, the Admiral gave her in charge to his seneschal, Thelous, who was a renegade from the Christian faith. Thelous confessed to Constance his sin in renouncing his faith and begged to go with her to some Christian land. But when they were upon the high seas, being tempted by the devil, he endeavored to entice her to sin. Having turned aside his purpose for the moment, by reminding him of the presence of her child, she presently begged him to look out for land; and when he was most intent, she came privily behind his back and pushed him into the sea.

King Alle, on his return from Scotland, learned that his wife had been banished, for which he and his men were treated with great disdain by all they met. Arrived at his castle, he summoned Elda and Lucius and asked them what made them write such treasonable letters. They showed him the counterfeit letters which they had received under his seal. Whereupon, the messenger was examined and acknowledged his drunkenness at Domild's court. The king went straightway to his mother and commanded her to show the letters which she had treacherously counterfeited. Overtaken with sudden fear, she begged for mercy and confessed her crime; but the king would have no mercy upon her, but hewed her to pieces as she lay in her bed.

In the fifth year of her exile, Constance met with a great Roman fleet, riding at anchor in a haven. The mariners brought the lady and her child to a palace, where she found a senator, named Arsenius, whom she knew, though he did not recognize her. He informed her that the fleet had been sent by the emperor against the Saracens, who had murdered his daughter. The senator and his host had found the bodies of all the murdered Christians, but had not found the body of the emperor's daughter. Arsenius took her to Rome and commended her to his wife, Helen, who was Constance's cousin. Constance and her son remained twelve years with Arsenius, and he and his wife, who had no children of their own, looked upon Maurice as their son and heir.

Then King Alle made a pilgrimage to Rome to get absolution from the Pope for the slaying of his mother; and when he was seven days' journey from the city, he sent Elda forward to find honorable quarters. Elda chose the castle of Arsenius. When Constance heard the news, she swooned for secret joy. Arsenius and the chivalry of Rome went out to meet the king. Constance instructed her son, who was then in his eighteenth year, that when he should go to the feast with his lord the senator, he should leave all other things and put himself before the king of England; for he greatly resembled his mother. King Alle, struck with the lad's resemblance to his wife, asked him whose son he was. When he heard that the lad's name was Maurice, he asked whether he might see the youth's mother. So when he was come to the senator's palace, his wife appeared; and Alle embraced her and cried out, "I have found my wife."

Forty days thereafter, Constance besought her husband to invite the emperor to a feast, and Maurice was charged with the message. At first, the emperor would not consent to come, but when Maurice besought him by the love he bore the soul of his daughter Constance, he yielded. King Alle and his company went forth to meet the emperor; and Constance made herself known to her father, who was so overwhelmed with joy that he well nigh fell from his horse. Then, with good right, they made great joy, and Constance told her father all her adventures.

Trivet concludes his narrative by relating how Tiberius, on account of his great age, made Maurice co-emperor with himself, and how Alle died in England, nine months after his return, and how Constance died a year later, "in the year of the incarnation five hundred eighty four, on St. Clement's day." [35]

[35] This summary is based upon that printed by the Chaucer Society, along with the original text of Trivet's narrative and the translation by Edmund Brock, in their volume of *Originals and Analogues*, 2-53.

It will be seen that Chaucer has followed with great fidelity the account given by Trivet, condensing the story skilfully, but omitting nothing of importance. He has, moreover, included in his 1029 lines, about 350 which represent contributions of his own.[36] These additions include such striking passages as the lament of Constance on leaving her father's house, the two speeches of the Sultan's mother to her henchmen, Constance's invocation to the Cross, the effective simile of the pale face in the crowd, and Constance's pathetic speech on leaving Northumberland.

Several small details in the *Tale of the Man of Lawe* were derived, not from Trivet, but from Gower's version of the story of Constance, which is to be found in the second book of the *Confessio Amantis*. It is clear that both poets went independently to Trivet; but in nearly a score of passages, Chaucer introduces expressions which represent slight departures from his principal source, and which he found in Gower.[37] It is possible, of course, that Gower, and not Chaucer was the borrower; but if that be the case, the borrowing was done with singularly poor discernment, for the account in the *Confessio Amantis* is quite without the humanizing touches which Chaucer has added to the story.[38]

---

[36] The passages are: Ll. 190–203, 270–87, 295–315, 330–43, 351–71, 400–10, 421–27, 449–62, 470–504, 631–58, 701–14, 771–84, 811–19, 825–68, 925–45, 1037–43, 1052–78, 1132–41 (Brock.)

[37] Cf. Skeat: *Oxford Chaucer*, III. 414–17.

[38] For Professor Curry's interpretation of the Tale, in the light of astrological lore, cf. *Chaucer and the Mediaeval Sciences*, 171–94. In an article in the *Journal of Eng. and Germ. Philology* for January, 1927, Dr. J. T. Curtiss disputes Professor Curry's findings.

THE SHIPMANNES TALE

The passage which links the Lawyer's Tale with the Shipman's affords so natural and so dramatic a transition from one story to the other, that one would prefer to ignore the evidence of the manuscripts and to accept the "Shipman's Prologue" as it stands in Skeat's edition. There is every appearance of dramatic purpose in the sudden intrusion of the Shipman—with his black record as thief and pirate, and with the grossly immoral tale he has to tell—as the defender of this respectable company against the terrible calamity of listening to heresy from the lips of one of those dangerous radicals, the Lollards. It is difficult to believe that it was only a scribal error which placed the Shipman's name in line 1179, but the reader should be warned again that its occurrence there has the authority of only one manuscript, and that the arrangement which places the Shipman's Tale after the Man of Law's is largely arbitrary.[39]

It is clear enough that Chaucer's own plans for the story which the Shipman tells underwent a change in the course of his labors over the *Canterbury Tales*. The use of pronouns of the first person in lines 1202, 1204, 1208, and 1209 is evidence that the tale was originally written for a woman, and it is generally agreed that it was the poet's first intention to assign it to the Wyf of Bath. When he found a story for her that better suited his purposes, he was left with an unassigned tale, which he transferred to another narrator without making the necessary revision. It is possible that the disagreement among the

[39] Cf. pp. 198–99, above.

manuscripts, with regard to the so-called "Shipman's Prologue," arose from the fact that the poet's own papers exhibited some confusion in the assignment of this story to a fresh narrator.

No direct source has been discovered for the *Shipmannes Tale*. The fact that Chaucer locates his story in France may indicate that he was drawing his material from some French *fabliau*. A similar story occurs in the *Decameron* (Day 8, Nov. 1), but the difference in the scene of the action, which is laid in Milan, as well as in some of the details, makes it clear that Chaucer was not, in this instance, drawing upon Boccaccio. The latter's version and one of Sercambi's *novelle* which tells a similar story are printed by J. W. Spargo in *Sources and Analogues*, 441–46.

There is no evidence by which the *Shipmannes Tale* can be dated, but it is safe to assume that it was not written until the *Canterbury Tales* were projected, and it probably belongs to the period when the work was a comparatively new undertaking, i. e., between 1387 and 1390. It must obviously have been written before the *Tale of the Wyf of Bathe*.

THE PRIORESSES TALE

No immediate source for the *Prioresses Tale* has been discovered. Many years ago, Tyrwhitt conjectured, "from the scene being laid in Asia," that the tale was based upon "one of the oldest of the many stories, which have been propagated, at different times, to excite or justify several merciless persecutions of the Jews, upon the charge of

murthering Christian children." [40] The earliest known
story of such a murder goes back to the fifth century and
is not likely to have had the slightest influence upon Chaucer. It was not until the twelfth century, moreover, when
the worship of the Blessed Virgin was at its height, that
her miraculous power became associated, in popular tales,
with boy-martyrs, who were supposed to have been
tortured or slain by the Jews. The dark superstition,
which laid the charge of these atrocities upon the Jews,
had been given fresh impetus, two centuries before Chaucer's day, by the martyrdom of St. William of Norwich,
a lad of twelve, who was believed to have been lured into
a Jew's house and crucified, during Passion Week in the
year 1144. As rumors of the fate of St. William passed
through England and Europe, other tales of boy-martyrs
came into popularity. The most famous was that of St.
Hugh of Lincoln, whom the Prioress mentions by name
at the conclusion of her story of the little clergeoun.
Chaucer may well have heard one of the ballads written
upon the martyrdom of this boy, who, according to the
chronicle of Matthew Paris, was murdered at Lincoln by
the Jews, in the year 1255.

Professor Carleton Brown has shown that the particular story which formed the basis for the *Prioresses Tale*
was in existence, in all probability, before the year 1200.
He has assembled thirty-three versions of the legend,
ten of which are found in manuscripts of the thirteenth
century. He divides these versions into three groups, according to certain differences of treatment which seem
to have developed as the story came down through the
centuries, passing over many different lands and incor-

[40] *Introd. Disc.*, xxxii.

porating details which were doubtless borrowed from other stories or from oral traditions.[41]

Group A, which includes the oldest versions of the story, is well represented by the following tale, found in a thirteenth-century manuscript at Vendôme:

"There was a poor widow in England, who had one little son. At school, among other matters, he learned by heart that responsorium of the Blessed Virgin called *Gaude Maria;* and he used to sing it as he passed through the streets. It chanced, however, that one day, in passing through the Jewry, he was singing, according to his custom; and when he sang *'Erubescat iudeus,'* etc., one of the Jews called him privily into his house. When the boy had come running cheerfully in, the Jew shut the door and struck him with an axe and killed him. Then he cast the body in a trench, near the threshold of the house, and filling up the trench, made it even with the rest of the floor. When the boy did not appear in the evening, his mother watched sadly till the dawn; and then she set out to seek him. After she had spent some days in searching, it chanced that at last she came into the Jews' street. While she was wandering hither and thither, suddenly the boy began to sing the *Gaude Maria,* in a higher and sweeter voice than ever before. His mother and other people heard him, and in great astonishment, they burst into the Jews' houses, searching every nook and cranny. At length they came to the house of the murderer, and here they heard the lad's voice very close at hand. Breaking open the door, they began to overturn the house in

---

[41] Most of the material presented in this section is drawn from Professor Brown's valuable study, *The Miracle of Our Lady told by Chaucer's Prioress,* published by the Chaucer Society in 1910. Cf. *Sources and Analogues,* 447–85.

their search; and hearing him singing under their very feet, as it seemed, they dug and found him, alive and sound; but they found some scars upon his head. They asked him what had happened to him, and he made answer: 'When I came into this house, I felt very sleepy and dropped off to sleep. And when I had slept a very long time, the Blessed Virgin came to me, rousing me and scolding me, and said, "How long are you going to sleep, and why do you not rise up and sing my responsorium as you were wont to do? Wake up at once and sing." And lo! at her command, I roused myself straightway and sang, as you have heard.' "

Within this group, the story invariably terminates happily, with the restoration of the boy to life through the intervention of the Blessed Virgin. In the ten manuscripts of Group B, as well, the miracle is wrought to the same conclusion. The mother, however, now drops out of the story, and the little boy becomes a chorister who assists the priest at the service of the Church. Instead of passing through the streets, the chorister sings only in the church, and the Jews who take offense at the song, hear it as it is sung during the services. In the versions of Group B, moreover, the boy, on being restored to life, usually reappears at the church, where his voice is once more heard singing as before. The tale frequently concludes with the conversion of the Jews, who are the first to perceive that a miracle has been wrought.

The following version of the story, to be found in a thirteenth-century manuscript in the British Museum, is typical of Group B:

"In a church where it was the custom to sing the responsorium, *Gaude Maria* each day, a certain scholar, on account of the sweetness of his voice, was frequently bidden sing the verse in which are the words, *Erubescat iudeus infelix*. The Jews, therefore, passing before the church on the way to their vineyards, and taking offense at the words, cautiously conducted, or rather, enticed the lad to their vineyards and killed him. As soon as they were gone, the most glorious Virgin Mary restored the lad to life and bade him boldly sing her praise again. The Jews, hearing the same voice once more and recognizing it, were smitten with wonder, and secretly they put questions to the boy; and he told them that it was he whom they had slain, but he had been healed and restored to life by the Queen of Heaven. On hearing this, the Jews, in no small number, were converted, to the glory of the Blessed Virgin."

Within the third group, there are greater variations than within the others, but the ten manuscripts that Professor Brown has classified in Group C agree in certain peculiarities not to be found in other versions. Some other song—the *Ave regina* or the *Alma redemptoris*—has been substituted for the *Gaude Maria;* the place of the burial of the boy's body has undergone a change; and, most important of all, the addition of a funeral scene substitutes a tragic for a happy ending. The searchers do not find the boy alive; they find only his dead body, but this, through the miraculous power of the Blessed Virgin, continues to sing.

One of the versions of Group C is a tale, told in English verse, of a Paris beggar-boy murdered by the Jews. It is included among the Miracles of the Virgin in a fourteenth-century manuscript in the Bodleian. After explaining that the boy supported his father and his mother by his begging and singing, the poem continues as follows: [42]

> The child non othur Craftus couthe
> But winne his lyflode with his Mouthe:
> The Childes vois was swete and cler,
> Men lusted his song with riht good cher;
> With his song that was ful swete
> He gat Mete from strete to strete.
> Men herked his song ful likyngly:
> Hit was an Antimne of vre lady,
> He song that Antimne eueri-wher,
> I-called Alma Redemptoris Mater,
> That is forthrihtly to mene:
> Godus Moder, Mylde and Clene,
> Heuene yate and Sterre of se,
> Saue thi peple from synne and * we.   * woe
> That song was holden deynteous,
> The child song hit from hous to hous.
> Ffor he song hit so lykynglye,
> The Iewes hedde alle to hym Envye.
> Til hit fel on Aseters-day
> The Childes wey thorw the Iewerie lay:
> The Iewes hedden that song in * hayn,   * hate
> Therfore thei schope the child be slayn.
> So lykingly the Child song ther
> So lustily song he neuer er.
> On of the Iewes Malicious
> * Tilled the child in-to his hous.   * enticed
> His Malice there he gan to * kuythe: * reveal
> He Cutte the childes throte alswithe.
> The child ne spared nout for that wrong,

[42] I reproduce the Chaucer Society text, emended after comparison with Carleton Brown's (*Sources and Analogues*, 470–74).

But neuer the latere song forth his song;
Whon he hedde endet, he eft bi-gon,
His syngyng couthe stoppe no mon.
Ther-of the Ieuh was sore anuyet,
Leste his Malice mihte ben a-spyet.
The Ieuh bi-thouhte him of a gynne:
In-to a * gonge-put fer with-Inne   * privy
The child a-doun ther-Inne he throng.
The child song euere the same song,
So lustily the child con crie
That song he neuer er so hyghe,
Men mihte him here fer and neer:
The Childes vois was so heigh and cleer.
The Childes moder was wont to a-byde
Euery day til the Non tyde,
Then was he wont to bringe heom mete,
Such as he mihte with his song gete.
Bote that day was the tyme a-past.
Therfore his Moder was sore a-gast.
With syk and serwe in eueri strete
Heo souhte wher heo mihte with him mete.
Bote whon heo com in-to the Iewery,
Heo herde his vois so cler of cry.
Aftur that vois his Modur dreuh;
Wher he was Inne therbi heo kneuh.
  Then of hire child heo asked a siht.
The Iew * with-nayted him a-non riht,   * denied
And seide ther nas non such child thrinne.
The childes Moder yit nolde not blinne,
But euer the Moder criede in on.
The Ieuh seide euere ther nas such non.
  Then seide the wommon thou seist wrong,
He is her-Inne, I knowe his song.
The Ieuh bi-gon to stare and swere
And seide ther com non such child there.

But neuer the latere men mihte here
The child song euere so loude and clere,
And euer the lengor herre and herre,
Men mihte him here bothe fer and nerre.

The Modur coude non othur won:
To Meir and Baylyfs heo is gon,
Heo pleyneth the Ieuh hath don hire wrong
To stelen hire sone so for his song;
Heo preyeth to don hire lawe and riht,
Hire sone don come bi-fore heore siht,
Heo preyeth the Meir par Charite
Of him to haue freo * lyuere.   * delivery

Thenne heo telleth the Meire a-Mong
Hou heo lyueth bi hire sone song.

The Meir then hath of hire pite,
And sumneth the folk of that Cite.
He telleth hem of that wommons sawe,
And seith he mot don hire the lawe,
And hoteth hem with hym to wende,
To Bringe this wommons cause to ende.

Whon thei cum thider, for al heore noyse
Anon thei herde the childes voyse,
Riht as an Aungeles vois hit were,
Thei herde him neuer synge so clere.
Ther the Meir maketh entre,
And of the child he asketh lyuere.

The Ieuh may nought the Meir refuse,
Ne of the child hym wel excuse,
But nede he moste knouleche his wrong,
* A-teynt bi the childes song.   * convicted

The Meir let serchen hym so longe,
Til he was founden in the gonge,
Fful depe I-drouned in fulthe of fen.
The Meir het drawe the child vp then,
With ffen and ffulthe riht foule * bi-whoruen   * enwrapt

And eke the childes throte I-coruen.
Anon riht, er thei passede forthere,
The Ieuh was Iugget for that Morthere.
And er the peple passede in sonder,
The Bisschop was comen to seo that wonder.
    In presence of Bisschop and alle I-fere
The child song euere I-liche clere.
The Bisschop serchede with his hond:
With-inne the childes throte he fond
A lilie flour, so briht and cler
So feir a lylie nas neuere seyen er,
With guldene lettres eueri-wher:
Alma Redemptoris Mater.
Anon that lilie out was taken,
The childes song bi-gon to slaken,
That swete song was herd no more.
But as a ded cors the child lay thore.
    The Bisschop with gret solempnete
Bad bere the cors thorw al the Cite,
And hym-self with processioun
Com with the Cors thorw al the toun.
With prestes and clerkes that couthen syngen,
And alle the Belles he het hem ryngen,
With torches Brennynge and clothus riche,
With worschipe thei ladden that holi liche.
In-to the Munstre whon thei * kem,   * came
Bi-gonne the Masse of Requiem,
As for the dede Men is wont.
But thus sone thei weren i-stunt,
The Cors a-Ros in heore presens,
Bi-gon then Salue sancta parens.
    Men mihte wel witen the sothe ther-bi:
The child hedde i-seruet vr swete ladi,
That worschipede him so on erthe her
And brouhte his soule to blisse al cler.

> Therfore I rede that eueri mon
> Serue that ladi wel as he con,
> And loue hire in his beste wyse:
> Heo wol wel quite him his seruise.
> Now, Marie, for thi Muchele miht
> Help vs to heuene that is so briht.

None of the extant versions of the story represents the source of the *Prioresses Tale*. Professor Brown believed that the only version which "could possibly be considered the direct source" is one first pointed out by A. C. Friend in a thirteenth-century manuscript in Corpus Christi College, Oxford (*Sources and Analogues,* 467–68).

There is no means of dating the *Prioresses Tale* with any exactitude, but the perfect workmanship of the poem indicates a date fairly late in Chaucer's career. The Tale has always been dated after 1385, and there is every reason to believe that it was written with the Prioress particularly in mind.

THE RIME OF SIR THOPAS

"The Rime of Sire Thopas," says Tyrwhitt, "was clearly intended to ridicule the 'palpable-gross' fictions of the common Rimers of that age, and still more, perhaps, the meanness of their language and versification." [43] The reader who wishes to discover, at first hand, what sort of work it was that Chaucer was ridiculing, would do well to consult one or another of the "romances of prys" to which the poet himself refers in lines B 2087–90. Not all six of the heroes whom he mentions have been fully identified, but the adventures of four of them are set forth

[43] *Introd. Disc.,* xxxiii.

in poems which are available in modern editions.[44] Unfortunately, these romances are too long for full quotation here; and a summary would hardly be to the purpose, since much of the humor of Chaucer's burlesque lies in the fact that he has appropriated lines and phrases from different romances and woven them into the nonsense of *Sir Thopas,* sometimes repeating them just as he found them, at other times altering them just enough to make them ridiculous.

It should be understood, however, that the fragment represents burlesque rather than parody. Although there is much verbal imitation of the rimed romances, this does not exhaust the ridicule which Chaucer is heaping upon them. "He introduces details exactly in their manner; he burlesques incidents and speeches from them; he employs their tricks of expression; and, above all, he reproduces perfectly the jog-trot of their movement."[45] In short, he is exposing, with a very deft hand, the banality of a popular form of contemporary literature.

The *Rime of Sir Thopas* belongs unquestionably to a late period in Chaucer's career. Only the master craftsman can appropriate the ineptitudes of an inferior art and turn them to ridicule so effectively. The very unevenness

[44] *Horn Childe,* in Ritson's Metrical Romances, III. 282, ff.; *Sir Guy of Warwick,* edited by Zupitza, and *Sir Bevis of Hampton,* edited by Kölbing, for the Early English Text Society; and *Libeaus Desconus,* edited by Kaluza (Leipzig, 1890). The collection, *Middle English Metrical Romances,* edited by W. H. French and C. B. Hale (New York, 1930), presents a wide variety of works within the general type.

[45] T. R. Lounsbury: *Studies in Chaucer,* II. 201. Mrs. Loomis, in her lively chapter on the *Thopas* in *Sources and Analogues* (486–559), quotes passages from many romances to illustrate the sort of thing Chaucer was burlesquing.

of the meter is evidence that the poet had attained such mastery over his medium that he could trifle with the laws of rhythm. He has his sport with rime, as well, arranging his stanzas in eight different rime-schemes and anticipating later writers of burlesque by the use of unusual and occasionally suspicious rimes.[46] If it be true, as Skeat conjectured, that "Chaucer may himself, in his youth, have tried his hand at such romance-writing in all seriousness," he had long outlived the season, by the time he wrote *Sir Thopas,* when he could regard this kind of writing with any seriousness at all.[47]

THE TALE OF MELIBEUS

Stinted of his tale of Sir Thopas, the poet offers the company "a litel thing in prose," which runs to the length of 922 lines. So acute a critic as the late Professor Ker characterized the *Tale of Melibeus* as "perhaps the worst example that could be found of all the intellectual and literary vices of the Middle Ages, bathos, forced allegory, spiritless and interminable moralizing"; and as "a desperate suggestion," he offered the conjecture that the tale was a "mischievous companion to the Rime of Sir Thopas." [48]

Modern readers of the tale—if there be any—may

[46] Thrice he achieves a rime only by disregarding etymology and dropping a final -*e:* in B 1971 (*plas* for *place*), B 2021 (*gras* for *grace*), and B 2092 (*chivalry* for *chivalrye*).

[47] I cannot accept Miss Winstanley's theory that Sir Thopas was intended as a satire against Philip Van Artevelde, the burgher of Ghent. See her edition of the tale, (Cambridge, 1922), lxviii–lxxvii.

[48] Introduction to the Chaucerian selections in Craik's *English Prose,* Vol. I.

choose between Professor Ker's "desperate suggestion" and a belief that Chaucer was unable to escape, on this occasion, some of the most deadly literary vices of his age. A theory which endeavors to take up a middle ground between the two alternatives holds that the *Melibeus* was an early work, belonging to the period between 1373 and 1378, and that it was originally written, in all seriousness, at a time when Chaucer was not likely to have perceived its faults. If this conjecture be accepted, it is quite possible to argue that this tale, like the other which Chaucer attempted to tell, was included in the *Canterbury Tales* as a burlesque upon a popular type of literature. If it was intended as a joke, however, it must be said that it was a pretty heavy one. "In this age of levity," said Tyrwhitt, during the days of Dr. Johnson, "I doubt some Readers will be apt to regret, that he did not rather give us the remainder of *Sire Thopas*."

Setting aside all considerations of Chaucer's probable attitude toward such unpromising material, and examining the actual evidence for dating the tale, we find that it cannot be assigned to any very early date. Professor Tatlock has shown that the omission, in Chaucer's translation of his French original, of the phrase "doulent la terre qui a enfant à seigneur" clearly dates the tale after the death of the Black Prince (July 8, 1376), which left the youthful Richard heir to the throne. He has also pointed out what appears to be conclusive evidence that the *Melibeus* follows the *Troilus* and the *Knightes Tale*. Complete lines from each of these poems have been incorporated in the prose of the tale; and in each case, Chaucer is adding something which he did not find in his original. Unless these lines are later interpolations, then, it is clear that the *Melibeus* must be dated after 1386, and that it was not written until the *Canterbury Tales* had been begun.[49] It is possible that it was not originally assigned to the poet himself, and there is an interesting theory that it was intended for the Man of Law, who goes out of his way to tell us, before he begins his tale, that he speaks in prose (B 96).

In extenuation of Chaucer's literary sin, in writing the *Melibeus,* it is to be said that very little of the work is his own. The tale is a close translation, with a few independent additions, of a French treatise, entitled *Le Livre de Mellibee et Prudence*. This work, in turn, is a free adaptation, by a fourteenth-century French friar, of a Latin work by Albertano of Brescia, called the *Liber Consolationis et Consilii*. Albertano was a judge at Brescia, in Lombardy, and lived in the first half of the thirteenth century. The quotations and sententious expressions, with which his *Liber Consolationis* is studded, were drawn from a multitude of sources.[50] Though the modern reader may not relish the *Melibeus,* the work upon which it was based was undoubtedly well thought of, both before and after Chaucer's day. Four French translations were made of Albertano's *Liber Consolationis,* and the one used by Chaucer retained its popularity into the fifteenth and sixteenth centuries, when it was twice printed. Although Chaucer's "litel thing in prose" may be, as Professor Ker has called it, "a lump of the most inert first matter of mediæval pedantry," it was probably not so unpala-

[49] Cf. Tatlock: *Development and Chronology,* 188–97.

[50] Pointed out by Sundby in his edition of the work, published by the Chaucer Society in 1873.

table to the taste of the fourteenth century as it is to our own.

The French text of Friar Renaud de Louens based on a fourteenth-century manuscript, is printed with a valuable introduction, by Professor J. Burke Severs in *Sources and Analogues*, 560–614.[51]

THE MONKES TALE

The *Monkes Tale* has sometimes been regarded as one of the works written before the *Canterbury Tales* were projected and worked into the new scheme through literary economy on the part of the poet. There is no such convincing evidence for the independent existence of the *Monkes Tale* as there is in the case of the story of Palamon and Arcite and the Life of Saint Cecilia, both of which are mentioned in the Prologue to the *Legend of Good Women;* but scholars have shown great ingenuity in finding arguments to support their conviction that a work which modern taste finds so inferior could not have been written after Chaucer's genius came to full maturity. The most cogent argument which they have been able to bring forward, in support of their contention, is the treatment of Brutus and Cassius as one and the same person (B 3887). It seems hardly possible that Chaucer could have fallen into such an error after reading Dante's *Inferno* (Canto XXXIV).[52]

The most serious objection to the theory that the

[51] See also Prof. Severs' study in *Publ. Mod. Lang. Assn.*, 50. 92–99.

[52] The same error occurs in the Old English translation of Boethius, *De Consolatione*, Book II. Met. 7.

Monkes Tale is one of Chaucer's earlier works lies in the fact that the Tragedy of Barnabo deals with events which took place as late as 1385. This portion of the tale must have been written, at the earliest, not much before the *Canterbury Tales* were begun. To reconcile this fact with the theory of an earlier, independent existence of the collection of tragedies, it has been argued that the tales of Pedro of Spain, Pedro of Cyprus, Barnabo, and Ugolino were added at the time when the collection was revised and inserted in the *Canterbury Tales*. The fact that these four tragedies are placed at the end of the collection in some of the best manuscripts gives support to this conjecture; and the severe criticism of the *Monkes Tale,* offered by the Knight and the Host, bears out the theory that the poet himself had come to recognize the artistic inferiority of such a series of *exempla*. "The Monk's Tale," says Lounsbury, "is introduced as a specimen of these collections of stories, and largely and perhaps entirely for the sake of satirizing, or at least of censuring, the taste that created and enjoyed them." [53]

It is clear, certainly, that Chaucer realized that some of his contemporaries would consider the *Monkes Tale* "nat worth a boterflye," and it may be that the harsh strictures passed upon the work by Harry Bailly represent the poet's mature opinion upon a work of his earlier years. It is even clearer that he did not find the labor of writing "tragedies" so congenial that he cared to continue the series. The reader should be reminded, however, that men so far in advance of the age as Petrarch and Boccaccio were far from taking Harry Bailly's view of this species of composition, that Lydgate's *Fall of Princes,*

[53] Cf. *Studies in Chaucer,* III. 332–34.

written in the generation after Chaucer's, held its popularity through two centuries, and that a similar work, the *Mirror for Magistrates,* with all the faults of the *Monkes Tale,* won distinction more than a hundred and fifty years after Chaucer's death. If we are to accept Lounsbury's conclusions, therefore, we must believe that Chaucer was two centuries ahead of his times in censuring the taste that created and enjoyed such works as these.

The series of tragedies seems to have been suggested to Chaucer by a similar work by Boccaccio, written under the impulse of a temporary conversion from more frivolous literary pursuits, and entitled *De Casibus Virorum et Feminarum Illustrium.* Boccaccio's work includes accounts of Adam, Samson, Zenobia, and Croesus, and it is entirely possible that they furnished Chaucer with suggestions for his own stories of the same personages. Other sources, however, can be shown to have contributed more than the *De Casibus Virorum* to the *Monkes Tale.*

The expulsion of Lucifer from the Heavens and the Fall of Man in Adam were stock examples in mediæval moralistic literature, and it is hardly necessary to seek specific sources for the brief account which the Monk gives of their change of fortune, though it is worth remarking that Boccaccio, like Chaucer, reproduces the traditional notion that Adam was created in a field where Damascus afterward stood.[54] The account of Samson was taken from Judges, XIII–XVI. The opening, though like Boccaccio's, appears to follow Vincent of Beauvais.

The *Hercules,* too, owes more to other sources. The story was undoubtedly familiar to Chaucer, through the

[54] Miss Aiken (*Speculum,* 17. 56–58) believes Chaucer found this detail in Vincent of Beauvais' *Speculum Historiale.*

Metamorphoses (Book IX) and the *Heroides* (Epistle IX) of Ovid, before he came upon it in Boccaccio's *De Casibus Virorum,* or in the same author's *De Mulieribus Claris* (cap. xxii). The passage describing the labors of Hercules is derived from the *De Consolatione Philosophiae* of Boethius (Book IV. Met. 7).

The *Nabugodonosor* and the *Balthasar* are doubtless derived from the Book of Daniel, I–V. Miss Aiken argues that certain misstatements about Daniel himself may be due to Chaucer's misreading of passages in the account of the prophet given by Vincent of Beauvais.

The story of Zenobia was originally told by Trebellius Pollio, a writer of the age of Constantine, in his *Triginta Tyranni;* but Chaucer's source was undoubtedly Boccaccio, who relates the history of the Queen of Palmyra, both in the *De Casibus Virorum* (VIII. cap. 6), and in the *De Mulieribus Claribus* (cap. xcviii). Why Chaucer refers to Petrarch as an authority upon the story (B 3515), remains unexplained.

"Peter, king of Castile, born in 1334, is generally known as Pedro the Cruel. He reigned over Castile and Leon from 1350 to 1362, and his conduct was marked by numerous acts of unprincipled atrocity. After a destructive civil war, he fell into the hands of his brother, Don Enrique. A personal struggle took place between the brothers, in the course of which Enrique stabbed Pedro to the heart; March 23, 1369 . . . It is remarkable that Pedro was very popular with his own party, despite his crimes, and Chaucer takes his part because our Black Prince fought on the side of Pedro against Enrique at the battle of Najera, April 3, 1367; and because John of Gaunt married Constance, daughter of Pedro, about

Michaelmas, 1371." (Skeat: *Oxford Chaucer,* V. 238). Since Philippa Chaucer was probably in attendance upon Queen Constance, it is safe to assume, with Furnivall, that "Chaucer almost certainly had the account of Pedro's death from his daughter, or one of her attendants."

The second stanza refers to two men who brought on the murder of Pedro, by luring him to the tent of his brother. The first is Bertrand du Guesclin, whose arms show a black eagle on a field argent, with a bend dexter, gules, across the shield, appearing to restrain the bird from flying away. The other is Oliver Mauny, of a well-known Breton family, whose name is barely concealed under the expression "wikked nest" (OF. *mau ni,* i. e., *mal nid*). Furnivall gives the following concise account of their share in the murder of King Pedro:

"After the battle of Monteil, on March 14, 1369, Pedro was besieged in the castle of Monteil near the borders of La Mancha, by his brother Enrique; who was helped by Du Guesclin and many French knights. Finding escape impossible, Pedro sent Men Rodriguez secretly to Du Guesclin with an offer of many towns and 200,000 gold doubloons if he would desert Enrique and reinstate Pedro. Du Guesclin refused the offer, and 'the next day related to his friends and kinsmen in the camp, and especially to his cousin, Sir Oliver de Mauny, what had taken place.' He asked them if he should tell Enrique; they all said yes; so he told the king. Thereupon Enrique promised Bertrand the same reward that Pedro had offered him, but asked him also to assure Men Rodriguez of Pedro's safety if he would come to his (Du Guesclin's) lodge. Relying on Bertrand's assurance, Pedro came to him on March 23; Enrique entered the lodge directly afterwards, and after a struggle, stabbed Pedro, and seized his king-dom." (*Notes and Queries,* 4th Series, 8. 449).

It is hardly necessary to search for sources of the *De Petro Rege de Cipro* and the *De Barnabo de Lum-bardia,* for the facts of the careers which they set forth were matters of common knowledge in Chaucer's day. Pierre de Lusignan came to the throne of Cyprus in 1352, distinguished himself by his conquest of Satalie, of Layas in Armenia, and of Alexandria, which he won, and im-mediately abandoned, in 1365.[55] He was assassinated in 1369. Dr. Braddy has suggested that Chaucer's account of the assassination may be derived from *La Prise d'Alex-andrie* by Machaut. With Bernabo Visconti, Duke of Milan, Chaucer must have been personally acquainted, for the commission to Italy, on which the poet served in 1378, was sent to treat with Visconti.

The *De Hugelino,* as Chaucer himself informs us, is derived from Dante (Inferno XXXIII). A translation by Courtney Langdon is reproduced below:

> From him we had departed now, when two
> I saw, so frozen in a single hole,
> that one man's head served as the other's cap.
> And as because of hunger bread is eaten,
> even so the upper on the other set
> his teeth, where to the nape the brain is joined.
> Not otherwise did Tydeus gnaw the temples
> of Menalippus out of spite, than this one
> was gnawing at the skull and other parts.
> "O thou that showest by a sign so beastly
> hatred toward him thou eatest, tell me why,"
> said I to him, "on this express condition,

[55] Cf. *Cant. Tales,* Prologue, A 58, 51.

that shouldst thou rightfully of him complain,
I, knowing who ye are, and that one's sin,
may quit thee for it in the world above,
if that, wherewith I speak, be not dried up."

From his grim meal that sinner raised his mouth,
and wiped it on the hair of that same head,
which he had spoiled behind. He then began:
"Thou wouldst that I renew a hopeless grief,
the thought of which already breaks my heart,
before I speak of it. But if my words
are likely to be seeds, and bear the fruit
of infamy upon the traitor whom I gnaw,
speaking and weeping shalt thou see together.

I know not who thou art, nor by what means
thou'rt come down here, but when I hear thee speak,
thou truly seemst to me a Florentine.
Know, then, that I Count Ugolino was,
and this man here Ruggieri, the Archbishop;
and now I'll tell thee why I'm thus his neighbor.

That, as the outcome of his evil thoughts,
I, trusting him, was seized, and afterward
was put to death, there is no need to say;
but that which thou canst not have heard, that is,
how cruel was my death, thou now shalt hear,
and whether he have wronged me thou shalt know.

A narrow slit within the moulting-tower,
which bears, because of me, the name of Hunger,
and in whose walls still others must be locked,
had through its opening shown me many a moon
already, when I had the evil dream,
which rent apart the curtain of the future.
This one therein a lord and huntsman seemed,
chasing the wolf and wolflings toward the mount
which hinders Pisans from beholding Lucca,

with bitches lean and eager and well trained;
for he had set before him in his van
Gualandi with Sismondi and Lanfranchi.
After a little run both father and sons
seemed weary to me; then methought I saw
their flanks torn open by sharp-pointed fangs.
  When, just before the morning, I awoke,
I heard my children, who were with me there,
sob in their sleep, and ask me for their bread.
Cruel indeed thou art, if, thinking what
my heart forebode, thou grievest not already;
and if thou weepest not, at what art wont
to weep? Awake they were, and now the hour
was drawing nigh when food was brought to us,
hence each, by reason of his dream, was worried;
and then I heard the dread tower's lower door
nailed up; whereat, without a word, I looked
my children in the face. I did not weep,
so like a stone had I become within;
they wept; and my poor little Anselm said:
'Father, thou lookest so! What aileth thee?'
But still I did not weep, nor did I answer
through all that day, or through the following night,
till on the world another sun had dawned.
Then, when a little beam had made its way
into our woeful prison, and I perceived
by their four faces, how I looked myself,
I bit in anguish both my hands. And they,
thinking it done because I craved to eat,
immediately stood up, and said to me:
'Father, much less shall we be pained, if us
thou eat; thou with this wretched flesh didst clothe us,
do thou, then, strip it from us now.' Thereat,
to sadden them no more, I calmed myself;
through that day and the next we all kept mute.

Ah, why, hard earth, didst thou not open up?
 Then Gaddo, when the fourth day we had reached,
stretched himself out at length before my feet,
and said: 'My father, why dost thou not help me?'
And there he died; and, ev'n as thou seest me,
between the fifth day and the sixth I saw
the three fall one by one; and, blind already,
I gave myself to groping over each,
and two days called them, after they were dead;
then fasting proved more powerful than pain."
 When he had spoken thus, with eyes awry,
he seized again the wretched skull with teeth,
which for the bone were strong as are a dog's.

Although the Monk cites Suetonius as if that writer
were the source of the account he gives of Nero, the citation is misleading; for this tragedy appears to be derived almost entirely from Jean de Meun (*Roman de la
Rose,* 6184, ff., 6406, ff.) and from Boethius (*De Con-
sol. Phil.,* Book II. Met. 6 and Book III. Met. 4). The
passages from Boethius may be consulted in Chaucer's
own translation. Jean de Meun's account of Nero, which
is too long to be reproduced here, agrees with Chaucer's
in including the rape of the emperor's sister and in the
motives alleged for the deaths of Agrippina and Seneca.
The only details clearly derived from Suetonius are in
lines 3663–66. These illustrations of Nero's extravagance, however, are to be found in Vincent of Beauvais.

The *De Oloferno* is based upon the apocryphal Book of
Judith; and the *De Rege Anthiocho* is paraphrased from
2 Maccabees, IX. 7, 28, 10, 8, 7, 3–7, 9–12, 28.

No definite source for the *De Alexandro* has been
pointed out. The story must have been very familiar to

Chaucer, for many Alexander romances were in circulation during the Middle Ages. As the Monk observes,

> The storie of Alisaundre is so comune,
> That every wight that hath discrecioun
> Hath herd somwhat or al of his fortune.

The allusion to "Machabee" (B 3845) shows that Chaucer had come across the reference to Alexander in 1 Maccabees I. 7, and suggests a reason for the juxtaposition of Alexander and Antiochus in this singularly eclectic series.

As authority for his story of Julius Caesar, Chaucer refers us to Lucan, Suetonius, and Valerius (Maximus). Probably he drew upon mediaeval sources, not yet fully identified, rather than upon the authors he names.[56a] Miss Aiken offers evidence that he consulted Vincent of Beauvais (*Speculum Historiale*, caps. 35, 41, 42).

The *Cresus*, like the *Nero*, was derived principally from Jean de Meun (*Rom. de la Rose*, 7225–7358), who, in turn, was apparently following Vincent of Beauvais (*Speculum Historiale*, III. 17). The opening stanza appears to have been based upon Boethius (*De Consolatione*, Book II. Pr. 2).

Prof. Root (*Sources and Analogues*, 615–44) prints the material from Boccaccio, Dante, Boethius, and Jean de Meun which Chaucer must certainly have used in writing the *Monkes Tale*.

The metrical form of the *Monkes Tale* is the eight-line stanza, riming *ababbcbc*. It is not used elsewhere in the *Canterbury Tales*.

[56a] Lines 3901–3905 derive ultimately from Valerius.

In the Prologue to his *Fall of Princes,* Lydgate refers to Chaucer's *Monkes Tales* in the following lines:

> My mayster Chaunceer with his fressh comodyes,
> Is ded, Allas, Cheef Poete of breteyne,
> That whylom made ful pitous tragedyes:
> The Fal of Prynces he did also compleyne
> As he that was of makyng souereyne;
>   Whoom al this lond shulde of ryght preferre,
>   Sith of your language he was the lodesterre.

The Nonne Preestes Tale

The story of the cock and the fox, which forms the nucleus of the tale which Chaucer assigns to the Nun's Priest, enjoyed great popularity in the Middle Ages. Originally a fable, told to point a moral, it had found its way into the famous beast-epic built around the fascinatingly wicked character of Reynard the Fox. Slightly different versions of the story are to be found in the French *Roman de Renart* and the German *Reinhart Fuchs,* but neither of them appears to have been Chaucer's immediate source.

In the *Roman de Renart* (II. 25–468), the story runs as follows: [56]

Renart betakes himself to a village, where he expects to find food. Here, near a wood, the well-to-do peasant Constans des Noes has his dwelling, which is abundantly supplied with all kinds of food. But the yard is fenced in

[56] In this summary, and that of the version in *Reinhart Fuchs,* I follow Miss Kate Petersen: *On the Sources of the Nonne Preestes Tale* (Boston, 1898), 47–63. I have made a few slight changes, for the sake of compression.

with strong and pointed stakes and with a thorn-hedge; and here the peasant keeps his hens.

Renart comes, but he can neither jump the fence nor crawl under it. He crouches in the road and ponders. Noting a broken paling, he gets over it and hides himself in a heap of cabbages, which are growing near the break in the fence. The hens have seen him, however, and flee. Chantecler, the cock, comes proudly by and asks them why they flee. Pinte replies that they have seen a wild beast. Chantecler tries to quiet their fears, but Pinte has seen the cabbages moving. Chantecler, assuring her that she is safe in the yard and bidding her go back there, returns himself to his old place. He does not know what hangs over his head, and like a fool, he fears nothing.

He goes to sleep and dreams that a creature holds out to him a red fur coat, with an opening at the neck made of bone, which Chantecler is forced to put on; but it is so narrow at the throat that he is greatly oppressed and can hardly wake from his dream. He apprehends trouble and waking calls upon the Holy Spirit. Then he goes quickly to the hens, draws Pinte aside, and tells her that he is afraid of being betrayed in some way. She rebukes him for faintheartedness. He tells her his dream in detail and conjures her, by the faith she owes him, to tell him if she knows what it signifies. Pinte says that the terrifying thing which Chantecler saw in his dream is the fox, and so she explains the details of the dream. She advises him to go back to his place, for the fox is lurking about.

Chantecler, indignant at Pinte's fears, refuses to accept her interpretation of the dream. He goes back to his former place and again goes to sleep. The fox, seeing that Chantecler is asleep, steals upon him and makes an attempt to seize him. Chantecler saves himself by springing aside. Renart then tries to beguile Chantecler, begging him, as his cousin, not to flee, and the cock is instantly satisfied. Renart asks him if he still remembers his father, Chanteclin, and praises the latter as a good singer, who sang with closed eyes. Chantecler begins to doubt Renart's sincerity; but when the latter appeals to their blood relationship and begs him to sing, he is beguiled into believing him. As he sings, however, he keeps one eye open to watch the fox. Renart reminds him that Chanteclin always shut both eyes; and, without distrust, Chantecler does the same. Then Renart seizes him by the neck and flees. Pinte sees it and laments.

It is evening, and the peasant's wife wishes to get in her hens. She misses Bise and Rosette; she calls Chantecler and sees the fox carrying him off. She pursues, but cannot overtake him. She cries "Harou!" and the peasants hear it and come up. She tells them of the cock's misadventure and Constans scolds her. They see Renart, as he goes through the opening in the fence, and give chase, loosing the dogs.

Chantecler, in his peril, prompts the fox to gibe at his pursuers. As soon, however, as the fox opens his mouth to say the cock's words, "Malgrez vostre . . . ," Chantecler escapes and flies upon a tree. Renart is very sad at this, and when Chantecler mocks him, he invokes shame upon the mouth that speaks out of season. Chantecler, for his part, says, "Misfortune come upon the eye of him who sleeps at the wrong time!" He will have nothing more to do with Renart, and the fox goes off, hungry and complaining.

The version in the German *Reinhart Fuchs* (11–176)

is similar in general outline, but it is much briefer. It may be summarized as follows:

Near a village dwells a well-to-do peasant, Lanzelin, who has grain and corn enough. His wife is called old Ruotzela. The fox often steals her hens because the yard and garden are not fenced in. Ruotzela scolds her husband for it, and he builds a fence. Here, he thinks, the cock and hens will be safe.

One day, at sunrise, Reinhart goes to the barnyard after Chantecler. He finds the fence too close and too high for him, but with his teeth he pulls out a slat and crawls through the hedge. Pinte perceives it, wakes Chantecler, and with her companions flies upon a beam. Chantecler bids the hens return to their former place, for in the enclosed garden they are safe. He himself, however, has had a bad dream: it seemed as if he were in a red fur coat, with an opening at the neck made of bone. He apprehends trouble and calls upon the Holy Spirit.

Pinte has noticed something suspicious among the cabbages and fears trouble for Chantecler. He, however, laughs at women's fears and ridicules the interpretation of dreams, remarking ironically, "This is indeed true, that dreams often explain themselves seven years after." Pinte charges him, for his children's sake, to take care of himself and to fly upon the thorn-bush. Chantecler follows her advice.

Reinhart determines to bring him down by guile. He asks Chantecler whether he is Sengelin. "No," replies Chantecler, "that was my father." Reinhart deplores the death of Sengelin and praises his manners. Trust among kindred, he says, is a joy, but Chantecler is too reserved. Sengelin was a friend of Reinhart's father and never sat so high in his presence; rather, he flew to welcome him, late or early, and he sang to him with both eyes closed.

In order to be just as affable as his father, Chantecler begins to beat his wings and flies down from his thorn-bush. He sings with both eyes closed, and Reinhart, seizing him by the head, makes straight for the woods, while Pinte laments, and Lanzelin comes up at the cry of the hens. Chantecler prompts the fox to speak, and as soon as Reinhart opens his mouth, flies upon a tree. He mocks Reinhart, saying that the way seemed long to him and he does not care to repeat the journey. Reinhart invokes shame upon him who makes a reply to his own hurt or who speaks at the wrong time. Chantecler answers, "It is good to be on one's guard at all times." The fox goes off, hungry and cross.

It will be seen that the *Nonne Preestes Tale* has much in common with each of these versions of the story. There are enough important differences in detail, however, to make it clear that neither the *Roman de Renart* nor the *Reinhart Fuchs* offers the version which served as the immediate source of the Tale; and some scholars have accepted Miss Petersen's theory of a "lost version" of the epic story, which "was very similar to the original of *Reinhart Fuchs*, but which, at the same time, treated certain abridgments of the present *Reinhart Fuchs* version with the greater fullness that is found in the *Renart* account." [57]

Chaucer probably found in his source a bare suggestion for some of the embellishments with which he has ex-

[57] For Miss Petersen's reconstruction of this lost original, see her monograph (88–90). Her theory is disputed by Professor Sisam in his admirable edition of the Tale (Oxford, 1927).

panded the simple beast-fable into the *Nonne Preestes Tale*. The setting, the dialogue between the cock and the hen, the lamentations of Pertelote and her sisters were evidently worked up from scanty suggestions in the earlier version; and the mock-heroic atmosphere which pervades the *Nonne Preestes Tale* is also a heritage which the story derives from its parentage in the beast-epic, though the hand of a great artist has much enhanced the value of this feature of the tale.

Other works than the fable of the cock and fox made contributions to the gallimaufry which the Nun's Priest served up to his fellow pilgrims at the conclusion of the second day of their journey. The discussion of dreams is not without its reference to the famous commentary of Macrobius upon Cicero's *Somnium Scipionis*,[58] but the scientific and philosophic lore displayed by Pertelote and Chauntecleer was not derived solely from Macrobius. Miss Petersen argues that much of the material for this discussion upon dreams, including the two stories quoted on the authority of 'oon of the gretteste auctours that men rede,' was drawn from the *Super Libros Sapientiae* of Robert Holkot, an English Dominican, Professor of Theology at Oxford, who died in 1349. He left behind him a large number of biblical commentaries, of which the best known was his stupendous work upon the Wisdom of Solomon, consisting of two hundred *lectiones* on the nineteen chapters of the Wisdom. "Nor was he only a candle, or domestic light," says Thomas Fuller, "confined

[58] In the ninth chapter of his *Chaucer and the Mediaeval Sciences* (219–32), Professor Curry discusses the scientific aspects of Chauntecleer's dream.

within the walls of his own country; but his learning was a public luminary to all Christendom." [59]

Chaucer does not, like Lydgate, make specific reference to Holkot's commentary, but Miss Petersen makes out a fairly strong case for his familiarity with the work upon the Wisdom of Solomon. It seems clear, however, that he was aware that the two striking examples which Chauntecleer offers of the importance of dream-warnings occur in Cicero; for it is hardly likely that he would apply the term "one of the greatest authors that men read" either to Holkot or to Valerius Maximus, whom Holkot cites as his authority for the stories. [60] The two examples are to be found in Cicero's *De Divinatione,* but in spite of Chauntecleer's explicit statement that his second story occurs "right in the nexte chapitre," they are related, in reverse order, in the same chapter (Book I. cap. 27).

Chauntecleer has other authorities than Cicero to marshal in support of his faith in dreams. He alludes to the dream of Nebuchadnezzar (*Daniel* IV. 25) and to those which Joseph interpreted in Egypt. He speaks of the dream of Andromache, which is mentioned by "Dares Phrygius" in his eye-witness account of the siege of Troy; and he refers to the warning of treachery which came to St. Kenelm in a dream. His array of imposing authorities thoroughly eclipses Madame Pertelote's single learned citation. Her one authority is Dionysius Cato, from whose *De Moribus* she quotes a single distich:

> Somnia ne cures; nam mens humana quod optans
> Dum vigilat, sperat, per somnum cernit ad ipsum.

[59] *Worthies of England* (1840), II. 514.
[60] They occur in the *Facta et Dicta* of Valerius. Book I, cap. 7.

In other portions of his story, as well as in the discussion between Chauntecleer and Pertelote, the Nun's Priest frolics among the learned. He toys a while with the weighty subject of predestination, but abandons it light-heartedly to such authorities as St. Augustine, Boethius, and Bishop Bradwardine.[61] He touches on the dangerous subject of woman's baleful counsel, but, remembering the lady Prioress, takes shelter hastily behind a reference to authors who "trete of swich matere." He refers his audience to a ponderous Latin work called *Physiologus de Naturis XII Animalium,* by one Theobaldus, which has a chapter concerning sirens. He pays his respects to one of the most wooden of mediæval rhetoricians, Geoffrey of Vinsauf, whose *Nova Poetria* contains a lament for Richard I in Latin hexameters, set forth as a specimen of the truly plaintive style and embellished with a notable complaint against Friday, which begins:

> O Veneris lacrimosa dies! O sydus amarum!
> Illa dies tua nox fuit, et Venus illa venenum.

He shows his acquaintance with literature of a lighter sort, not only by throwing a very convincing atmosphere of chivalric romance around Chauntecleer and his "faire damoysele Pertelote," but by his specific reference to

> the book of Launcelot de Lake
> That wommen holde in ful gret reverence.

He casually burns Rome, Carthage, and Troy to illuminate his barn-yard tragedy; and he likens the villain of his

[61] Died 1349, of the Plague. He was Chancellor of the University of Oxford, Archbishop of Canterbury, and author of *De Causa Dei.*

story to three of the darkest traitors in history or legend. His passing allusions wander from the *Aeneid* to the *Mirror of Fools*.[62] In short, Chaucer's tale of the cock and the fox is one of the most learned of his works.

Scholars have not always been willing to accept the *Nonne Preestes Tale* for what it is,—a sprightly bit of nonsense, not without its touches of satire, of burlesque, and of parody, to be sure, but told simply for the sake of its own merriment. The latest attempt to find a hidden meaning beneath the surface of the tale is that of Dr. Leslie Hotson, who believes that the story contains covert allusions to the murder of the Duke of Gloucester at Calais in September, 1397.[63] One of the assassins was a certain Nicholas Colfox, a henchman of Thomas Mowbray, who contrived the murder; and Dr. Hotson believes that this man's connection with the crime accounts for Chaucer's use of the word "colfox," which has not been found elsewhere in English. Dr. Hotson's theory is an interesting one, and he has found very ingenious arguments to support it; but most readers of the *Nonne Preestes Tale* will be reluctant to believe that its merry nonsense is in any way connected with so grim a business as the murder of the Duke of Gloucester.

[62] The *Burnellus seu Speculum Stultorum* of Nigellus Wireker. Burnellus the Ass, dissatisfied with the length of his tail, travels from the medical school of Salerno to the University of Paris in the hope of finding means of increasing its proportions. On the road he encounters another traveller, who tells him the story of the cock who took revenge upon a certain young Gundulfus for breaking his leg with a stone. On the morning of the day when Gundulfus was to be ordained and to receive a benefice, the cock postponed his crowing to so late an hour that the household overslept, and the young man lost his benefice.

[63] *Colfox vs. Chauntecleer*, in *Publ. Mod. Lang. Assn.*, 39. 762–81.

THE PHISICIENS TALE

The position of Group C, in most of the manuscripts and in the black-letter editions of the Tales, is directly after the *Chanouns Yemannes Tale;* and two spurious prologues, in very halting verse, have been supplied to link the *Phisiciens Tale* with what immediately precedes. In the most reliable manuscripts, however, the story told by the Doctour of Phisyk follows the *Frankeleyns Tale.* The position which Group C occupies in Skeat's edition was arbitrarily adopted by Furnivall, for no very satisfactory reason, and was followed by Skeat only under protest.

Chaucer may have read the story of Virginia in Titus Livius, whom the Physician cites as his authority in the first line of the tale. He certainly knew the version to be found in the *Roman de la Rose* (ed. Langlois, 5589–5658), and possibly he cited Livy as his authority simply because Jean de Meun had done so before him: *"Si con dit Titus Livius."* On the other hand, it was little more than the bare framework of the story which he borrowed from Jean de Meun. Some of his lines and phrases are literally translated from the French original, but they are few and far between; and the spirit in which he has told the story is so very different from that which pervades the narrative in the *Roman de la Rose* that the slight verbal resemblances are the only evidence of his indebtedness to Jean de Meun. In the *Roman,* the story is introduced as an example of corruption among judges.[64]

[64] Prof. Shannon (*Sources and Analogues,* 398–408) argues for Chaucer's use of Livy as well as Jean. He prints both the Latin and the French texts. For a translation of Jean's version of the story, cf. R. K. Root: *The Poetry of Chaucer,* 221–22.

Chaucer's additions to his original are many and significant. Nearly a half of the *Phisiciens Tale* has been told before he reaches the point at which Jean de Meun begins the tale. The dialogue between Virginia and her father, moreover, is Chaucer's own contribution. These additions decidedly alter the tone of the story, shifting the emphasis from the false judge, in whom Jean de Meun is principally interested, to the character of the maiden Virginia, who holds the center of the stage in the *Phisiciens Tale*.

It seems possible that Jean de Meun knew less of the original version of the story in Livy than did Chaucer. At any rate, his narrative differs from Livy's in introducing certain sensational features, which make the act of Virginius appear more barbarous. It is probable that these alterations in the story represent the accretions of tradition rather than the invention of Jean de Meun. The story is to be found in the third book of Livy.

It has been conjectured that the passage in the *Phisiciens Tale* (C 72, ff.), addressed to

> ye maistresses in your olde lyf,
> That lordes doghtres han in governaunce,

may have been suggested to the poet by the fact that his wife's sister, Katharine Swynford, was governess to the young daughters of John of Gaunt, from before 1369 to 1382. Professor Tatlock, going a step farther, argues that the whole passage on the behavior of young girls, particularly the lines which discuss the dangers of too early an introduction to the distractions of mixed society, were suggested by the misbehavior of one of Katharine Swynford's young charges, Elizabeth, the second daughter of John of Gaunt and Blanche of Lancaster, born about

1368.[65] This young lady had been betrothed, in 1380, to the Earl of Pembroke, who was then only eight years old. About 1386, according to one of the chroniclers,[66] she was introduced at court and launched upon a career of gaiety, which terminated in her elopement to Spain with the notorious John Holland, half-brother to King Richard and later Duke of Exeter. The eloping pair returned to England in 1388. It seems more than likely that this court scandal was in the poet's mind at the time when he wrote the passage in question. The *Phisiciens Tale* may well be one of the earliest of the *Canterbury Tales,* and it is possible that it was written soon after the return of Holland and his bride had rekindled the gossip which this liaison had caused.

The story of Virginia is related by Gower in the *Confessio Amantis* (VII. 5131–5306), but there is no evidence that either poet borrowed from the other.

THE PARDONERS TALE

The Prologue to the *Pardoners Tale,* with its cynical confession of rapacity and dishonesty, is, so far as we know, entirely original with Chaucer. Satirical sketches of recreant churchmen are common enough in later mediæval literature, and some suggestions for the portrait of the Pardoner may have come to Chaucer through his reading; but the character as a whole is probably his own conception. It is not without the exaggeration allowed to poets and satirists, but it appears to have been founded on the

---

[65] *Development and Chronology,* 150–56.

[66] Malverne's continuation of Higden's *Polychronicon,* Rolls Series, 1886, IX. 96, 97.

truth. Contemporary documents, including a papal letter by Boniface IX, written in 1390, have been brought together, in support of Chaucer's fidelity to the truth, by Dr. J. J. Jusserand, in his essay on "Chaucer's Pardoner and the Pope's Pardoners" in the Chaucer Society's volume, *Essays on Chaucer* (423–36).

The story which the Pardoner tells is founded on a very ancient and popular tale. Like so many of the tales current in mediæval Europe, it is of oriental origin. The earliest known version is a Hindoo story, found in the Játaka-book, and is told of a certain Bráhman, who was the teacher of the Buddha in one of his earlier incarnations. The Bráhman, Vedabbha by name, is taken prisoner by thieves as he and his pupil are travelling through a forest. Disregarding the advice of Gautama, the Bráhman repeats a certain spell, which causes a rain of the seven kinds of precious things to fall from heaven. By means of the wealth which he secures in this way, he gains his liberty, but remains in company with the thieves. Another company of robbers, however, set upon them and take them all prisoner. Members of the original company explain to their captors that Vedabbha has power to call down wealth from heaven. Setting free their other prisoners, the new band of thieves now seize the Bráhman and command him to procure them treasure. He explains that his skill has efficacy only when the moon is in conjunction with the lunar mansion, and that such a conjunction will not occur again for another twelvemonth. Whereupon they cut him in two with a sharp sword and leave him by the road. Pursuing the other company of thieves, they fall upon them and kill them all. Then they divide among themselves into two bands and fight on until only

two men remain alive. The two survivors hide their wealth
in a thicket near a village, and one remains guarding it
while the other goes to the village for rice. The latter,
having eaten his fill, brings back poisoned rice to his
companion. No sooner has he returned than the other falls
upon him and cuts him in two with his sword. Then the
single survivor eats the poisoned rice and falls dead on the
spot.

From India, the story worked its way slowly westward.
The Chaucer Society, in its volume of *Originals and
Analogues* (129–33, 415–36, 544, 545) publishes versions
from the Persian, Arabic, Kashmiri, Tibetan, Italian, German, French, Portuguese, and Latin.[66a] Closest parallel
to the *Pardoners Tale* is one of the Italian versions, which
is found in the 1572 edition of the *Cento Antiche Novelle*,
a collection of tales which probably dates back to the thirteenth century. The story relates that a hermit, walking one
day through a forest, came upon a cave where a great heap
of gold lay hidden. As soon as he knew it for what it was,
he fled as fast as he could; but in his flight through the
forest, he was stopped by three robbers, who asked him
why he fled. "My brothers," said he, "I flee death, who
comes behind me, pursuing me." They, seeing neither man
nor beast pursuing him, demanded to be shown this death
from which he fled. So he led them back to the cave and
showed them the gold, telling them that this was the death
which had pursued him. In great joy at sight of the treasure, they immediately allowed the hermit to go about his
business, setting him down for a very simple fellow. One

[66a] Prof. Tupper (*Sources and Analogues,* 415–36) prints three
Italian *novelle,* five Latin *exempla,* an Italian miracle-play, and Hans
Sachs' play, *Der Dot im Stock* (ca. 1555).

of the thieves was then sent to the city to sell some of the treasure and buy bread and wine; but on the way, the Devil put it into his heart to poison the food which he was to take to his companions, so that he might be lord of all the treasure and the richest man of the country. Accordingly, he ate what he needed, and all the rest he poisoned; and so he returned with it to his comrades. While he was on his errand, the other two robbers laid a plot to slay him, that they might own all the treasure between them. As soon as they saw him coming, they were upon him, with lances and with knives, and killed him. Then they ate what he had brought them, and as soon as they were filled, they fell down dead. "And thus they died, all three; for the one slew the other, as you have heard, and did not have the treasure."

Since it is quite clear that we do not possess the actual original of the *Pardoners Tale,* it is impossible to determine the extent to which Chaucer has altered his source material. It is probably significant that no known version of the tale utilizes the dark background of the Plague or the sinister figure which meets the three rioters at the stile. One naturally suspects the hand of Chaucer in these dramatic additions to the ancient story.

Some of the moral reflections in the Pardoner's sermon are taken from the second book of Pope Innocent's *De Contemptu Mundi.* We have Chaucer's own statement, in the later version of the Prologue to the *Legend of Good Women,* that he translated this work. His translation has never come to light, but echoes of the words of Pope Innocent occur here and there in the *Canterbury Tales.* In his denunciation of swearing, dicing, and gluttony, the Pardoner uses words which are almost identical with those

used by the "povre persoun of a toune" in the sermon
which brings the *Canterbury Tales* to an end. It is possible
that in these passages Chaucer is versifying the words
of his own *Persones Tale,* but it is more likely that he is
merely drawing suggestions from the Latin treatise which
was the source of the Parson's sermon.

THE WIFE OF BATH'S PROLOGUE

The character of Alice of Bath is Chaucer's own creation, and his most thoroughly original one. Nevertheless,
much that is borrowed from other writers has gone into
the composition of the lady's autobiography. Even the
short description of Dame Alice in the Prologue to the
Canterbury Tales betrays her kinship with La Vieille, one
of the allegorical figures of the *Roman de la Rose.* It is
in Jean de Meun's portion of the *Roman* that La Vieille
is permitted to express her cynical views upon her own
sex; and the long passage, in which she touches upon
her own career and exposes the wiles which she believes
that all women employ in their dealings with men, is written with a brutal frankness and biting satire, characteristic
of the author. In the Prologue to the Wife's Tale, Chaucer
has incorporated expressions, ideas, and even entire lines
taken over from this portion of Jean's work. The Wyf of
Bath, however, is so unlike La Vieille that the relationship between them can be traced only in a few isolated
features. The extent to which Chaucer has remodeled the
character of the harsh and disillusioned Duenna of the
Roman de la Rose can be appreciated only by one who
has read the entire passage dealing with La Vieille in the
French poem, but the following extracts from her auto-

biography may give the reader some conception both of the extent and of the limitation of Chaucer's debt, in this instance, to Jean de Meun: [67]

"Believe me, if, when young as you,
I'd known love's art as now I do,
And of its ways had been aware
(For I, in youth, was passing fair),
You would not hear me groan and sigh
As I consider mournfully
My outworn visage, and repine
At every pucker, seam and line,
When of my beauty lost I think,
Whereof gay lovers fain would drink
Long draughts to quench their lovesick heat:
(Good Lord! it makes my pulses beat!)
For then was I of high renown,
Alike in countryside and town,
For fairness, and of gallants proud
And rich there never lacked a crowd
Around my dwelling. Many a score
Of blows came rattling 'gainst my door,
When I disdained with answering word
To let them know their calls were heard,
Because it happed forsooth that I
Already had good company.
Hereout grew oft a wild uproar,
And monstrous wroth was I therefor.
The porch, 'neath stout and sturdy stroke,
Would yield sometimes, and then awoke
A fierce mellee, and lives and limbs
Were lost to please my wayward whims,
For sharply raged fierce contests then.

[67] Ellis's translation, II. pp. 199, ff.

If learned Algus, of all men
The wisest in his reckoning,
Should his ten wondrous figures bring
To bear thereon, I doubt if well
By multiplying he could tell
The number of the deadly fights
Wherein my gallants strove o' nights.
Right fair of face was I, and sound
Of body, and of sterlings round
Had many a thousand, glistering white,
But like a dunce my business dight.
I was, in truth, a fair young fool,
Of no experience in love's school.
Nought of love's theory I knew,
But learned in its practice grew,
And all throughout my life have I
Its battles fought unflinchingly.

.   .   .   .

"When I had wit through practice won,
A thing with no small labour done,
Full many a noble man did I
Trick and beguile most skilfully;
But also, often was deceived
Ere yet full wit had I achieved.
Unhappy wretch! 'twas all too late,
Youth failed and left me desolate.

"And now beheld I that my door,
Which on its hinges heretofore
Swung day and night, stood idly to,
From hour to hour none passed therethrough,
Until I thought: 'Alas! poor soul,
Thy life is changed to grief and dole!'
When thus I saw my dwelling left

Deserted, nigh in twain was cleft
My heart, and I betook me thence,
Shamed and abashed my every sense.
Such misery scarce could I endure,
What balsam my deep wounds could cure,
When gay-clad gallants in the street,
Who lately fawned before my feet,
And spent their breath to sing my praise,
Now passed me in the public ways
Unheedingly, with heads tossed high,
As I were struck with leprosy?
They'd pass me by with hop and skip
As one not worth an apple pip:
And some, to whom I'd favour shown,
Now voted me a wrinkled crone.
It seemed as each would put on me
Some new refined indignity.

"Upon the other hand, no man,
How fine soe'er of feeling, can,
Dear friend, believe the woes I felt,
Or how mine eyes in tears would melt,
When rose the picture in my mind
Of old good days when kisses kind
Were showered upon me 'mid delights
Of joyous days and passioned nights—
Sweet words to sweeter actions wed.
Alas! for ever all are fled,
Past over to return no more.

                        Regrets are vain;
Time flown can ne'er return again,
Nor could I, of all those who bowed
Before me ere my face was ploughed
With wrinkles, keep on one my hold,

My menace was a tale that's told,
But, by the ribalds, I thereof
Was warned erewhile with many a scoff.
Believe you, much I wept therefor,
Aye, and shall weep for evermore,
Yet, when thereon I musing think,
Long draughts of joy supreme I drink
From memory's well. Oh, dear delights!
Whereof the very thought excites
A thrill through every limb, as though
The merry life of long ago
I lived once more. My body seems
Rejuvenate, as in sweet dreams
Sometimes appears. Now, by the rood,
I swear it does me untold good
To muse on youth's sweet joys, though I
By men was cozened cruelly." [68]

Chaucer has made use of other passages in the *Roman,*
particularly that in which Jean de Meun, through the
mouth of "Ami," exposes the tortures of the jealous husband. Something more than fifty lines, out of the 828 of
Alice's "long preamble of a tale" are clearly modeled upon
lines in the *Roman,* and some others contain expressions
or ideas which may well have been suggested by Jean de
Meun.

For the discussion of celibacy in the Wife's Prologue,
Chaucer has drawn largely upon a Latin work by St.
Jerome, which defends the practice of celibacy against the
arguments of a certain Jovinian. "The holy Father," says
Tyrwhitt, "by way of recommending celibacy, has exerted

[68] Cf. D 469–73. It should be understood that these passages
have not been included here with the purpose of presenting source
material.

all his learning and eloquence (and he certainly was not deficient in either) to collect together and aggravate whatever he could find to the prejudice of the female sex." [69] This spirited treatise by St. Jerome, it will be remembered, was bound up in the volume which Alice's fifth husband was at last compelled to burn; and from its pages came the anecdote of Socrates and the examples of Pasiphaë, Clytemnestra, and Eriphyle, which Clerk Jankin read aloud to his wife, as they sat before the fire. In the same ill-fated volume were two other works which Chaucer utilized, both for the discussion of celibacy and for the anecdotes which goaded Alice to fury as Jankin read them to her from his book. One of them was a lost work by a Greek named Theophrastus, the *Liber Aureolus de Nuptiis,* a translation of which St. Jerome included in his treatise against Jovinian. The other was the *Epistola Valerii ad Rufinum de non Ducenda Uxore,* a work very similar in its sentiments to the treatise of St. Jerome, and printed among his works, but now ascribed to Walter Map. Of these various treatises, which rehearse the familiar arguments against marriage and repeat the common slanders against woman, Chaucer has made most use of the *Hieronymus contra Iovinianum,* from which he has drawn suggestions for more than thirty passages in the Wife's Prologue. The most significant passages from St. Jerome's *epistola* are printed by Professor Whiting (*Sources and Analogues,* 207–22), along with extracts from Jean de Meun's portion of the *Roman de la Rose,* from Walter Map, and from the *Miroir de Mariage* of Eustache Deschamps. [70]

[69] *Introd. Disc.,* xvii, note.

[70] Professor Lowes (*Modern Philology,* 8, 165–86, 305–34) discusses the possible influence upon the Prologue to the Wife's Tale

In the fifth chapter of his *Chaucer and the Mediaeval Sciences* (91–118), Professor Curry interprets the character of the Wife of Bath in the light of her horoscope, reaching the conclusion that she "is in some measure the living embodiment, both in form and in character, of mingled but still conflicting astral influences . . . a fair Venerean figure and character imposed upon and oppressed, distorted in some measure and warped, by the power of Mars."

THE TALE OF THE WYF OF BATHE

The story of the Knight and the Loathly Lady is doubtless a very ancient one, having its roots in some remote folk-tale. Stories upon a similar theme appear in many lands and many languages. The references to fairies at the opening of the tale, though Alice contrives to give it a satirical twist, suited to her own purposes, betrays the ancient origin of the story among folk who still believed in fairies; and the glimpse which the knight catches of "ladies foure and twenty and yet mo," dancing "under a forest-syde" is another unmistakable bit of evidence pointing in the same direction. The fact that the tale has its setting in the court of King Arthur, moreover, at once suggests a Celtic origin, and it may well be that the ultimate source of the story was some old Irish folk-tale.[71]

Any definite original of the Wife's Tale, however, whether immediate or remote, has never been discovered.

and upon the Merchant's Tale of the *Miroir de Mariage* of Deschamps. Cf. *infra,* pp. 315, 316.

[71] Cf. G. H. Maynadier: *The Wife of Bath's Tale, its Sources and Analogues,* London, 1901.

The Chaucer Society has gathered many interesting analogues, including Icelandic, Gaelic, Turkish, and Sanskrit versions, as well as two Kaffir folk-tales, which deal with a somewhat similar theme, and a travellers' tale, from Sir John Mandeville, of a fair damsel in the "Ile of Lango," transformed into a great dragon and condemned to retain her loathsome form "unto the tyme that a Knyghte come, that is so hardy, that dar come to hire and kiss hire on the Mouthe." The Icelandic legend of Helgi, King of the Danes, who was induced to share his bed with a hideous old woman, whom he found transformed, at dawn, into a beautiful maiden, and the Kaffir tale of the crocodile who shed his skin and became a strong and sturdy man when his mortal bride was induced to lick his face, are doubtless related, in some obscure and intricate way, to the Wife's Tale; but no one would suggest that they have the slightest bearing upon the problem of the actual source of Chaucer's story.[72]

It is hardly more probable that the old English ballads dealing with the theme of the Loathly Lady furnished Chaucer with his actual source; but the *Marriage of Sir Gawaine* and the *Wedding of Sir Gawain and Dame Ragnell,* printed by Whiting (*Sources and Analogues,* 235–64), offer striking parallels to the incidents of the Wife's Tale. Professor Child gives the following outline of the second of these ballads:

"Arthur, while hunting in Ingleswood, stalked and finally shot a great hart, which fell in a fern-brake. While the king, alone and far from his men, was engaged in making the assay, there appeared a groom, bearing the quaint name of Gromer Somer Joure, who grimly told him that

[72] Cf. *Originals and Analogues,* 483–524, 546–49.

he meant now to requite him for having taken away his lands. Arthur represented that it would be a shame to knighthood for an armed man to kill a man in green, and offered him any satisfaction. The only terms Gromer would grant were that Arthur should come back alone to that place that day twelvemonth, and then tell him what women love best; not bringing the right answer, he was to lose his head. The king gave his oath, and they parted. The knights, summoned by the king's bugle, found him in heavy cheer, and the reason he would at first tell no man, but after a while he took Gawain into confidence. Gawain advised that they two should ride into strange country in different directions, put the question to every man and woman they met, and write the answers in a book. This they did, and each made a large collection. Gawain thought they could not fail, but the king was anxious, and considered that it would be prudent to spend the only month that was left in prosecuting the inquiry in the region of Ingleswood. Gawain agreed that it was good to be speering, and bade the king doubt not that some of his saws should help at need.

"Arthur rode to Ingleswood, and met a lady riding on a richly-caparisoned palfrey, but herself of a hideousness which beggars words; nevertheless the items are not spared. She came up to Arthur, and told him that she knew his counsel; none of his answers would help. If he would grant her one thing, she would warrant his life; otherwise, he must lose his head. This one thing was that she should be Gawain's wife. The king said that this lay with Gawain; he would do what he could, but it were a pity to make Gawain wed so foul a lady. 'No matter,' she rejoined, 'though I be foul, choice for a mate hath an owl. When thou comest to thine answer, I shall meet thee; else art thou lost.'

"The king returned to Carlisle with a heart no lighter, and the first man he saw was Gawain, who asked him how he had sped. Never so ill; he had met a lady who had offered to save his life, but she was the foulest he had ever seen, and the condition was that Gawain should be her husband. 'Is that all?' said Gawain. 'I will wed her once and again, though she were the devil; else were I no friend.' Well might the king exclaim, 'Of all knights thou bearest the flower!'

"After five or six days more the time came for the answer. The king had hardly ridden a mile into the forest when he met the lady, by name Dame Ragnell. He told her Gawain should wed her, and demanded *her* answer. 'Some say this, and some say that, but above all things women desire to have the sovereignty; tell this to the knight; he will curse her that told thee, for his labour is lost.' Arthur, thus equipped, rode on as fast as he could go, through mire and fen. Gromer was waiting, and sternly demanded the answer. Arthur offered his two books, for Dame Ragnell had told him to save himself by any of those answers if he could. 'Nay, nay, King,' said Gromer, 'thou art but a dead man.' 'Abide, Sir Gromer, I have an answer shall make all sure. Women desire sovereignty.' 'She that told thee that was my sister, Dame Ragnell. I pray I may see her burn on a fire.' And so they parted.

"Dame Ragnell was also waiting for Arthur, and would hear of nothing but immediate fulfilment of her bargain. She followed the king to his court, and required him to produce Gawain instantly, who came and plighted his troth. The queen begged her to be married privately, and early in the morning. Dame Ragnell would consent to no such arrangement. She would not go to church till high-mass time, and she would dine in the open hall. At her wedding she was dressed more splendidly than the queen, and she sat at the head of the table at the dinner after-wards. There her appetite was all but as horrible as her person: she ate three capons, three curlews, and great bake meats—all that was set before her, less and more.

"A leaf is wanting now, but what followed is easily imagined. She chided Gawain for his offishness, and begged him to kiss her, at least. 'I will do more,' said Gawain, and, turning, beheld the fairest creature he ever saw. But the transformed lady told him that her beauty would not hold: he must choose whether she should be fair by night and foul by day, or fair by day and foul by night. Gawain said the choice was hard, and left all to her. 'Gramercy,' said the lady, 'thou shalt have me fair both day and night.' Then she told him that her step-dame had turned her into that monstrous shape by necromancy, not to recover her own till the best knight in England had wedded her and given her sovereignty in all points. A charming little scene follows, in which Arthur visits Gawain in the morning, fearing lest the fiend may have slain him."

In the other ballad, *The Marriage of Sir Gawaine,* the story follows much the same course, save that King Arthur very generously offers the hag the hand of Sir Gawaine, if she will aid him:

> "Giue thou ease me, lady," he said,
>   "Or helpe me in any thing,
> Thou shalt have gentle Gawaine, my cozen,
>   And marry him with a ring."

A ballad included by Scott in his *Minstrelsy of the Scottish Border* tells a somewhat similar story of an adventure which befell "King Henrie" in a "haunted hunt's ha." After a good day's hunting, during which King Henrie has slain the fattest buck in the herd, a terrific tempest bursts upon the hunting hall.

> And louder houled the rising wind,
>   And burst the fast'ned door;
> And in there came a griesly ghost,
>   Stood stamping on the floor.
>
> Her head touched the roof-tree of the house;
>   Her middle ye weel mot span;
> Each frighted huntsman fled the ha',
>   And left the king alone.
>
> Her teeth were a' like tether stakes,
>   Her nose like a club or mell;
> And I ken naething she appeared to be
>   But the fiend that wons in hell.

The frightful apparition demands food and drink and makes a repulsive meal off King Henrie's berry-brown steed, his "gude gray houndes" and his gay goss-hawks, washed down with a pipe of wine, which she drinks from a bag made of the horse's hide. Then she demands a bed, and when the king has pulled heather to make her one, she bids him share it with her. But when day breaks, King Henrie sees between him and the wall the fairest lady that ever was seen.

> "O weel is me!" King Henrie said,
>   "How long will this last wi' me?"

> And out and spak that ladye fair:
>   "E'en till the day ye dee.
>
> "For I was witched to a ghastly shape,
>   All by my stepdame's skill,
> Till I should meet wi' a courteous knight,
>   Wad gie me a' my will."

It is probable that the original of the Wife's Tale was some version of the story of the Loathly Lady which had been developed beyond the more primitive stage represented by the old ballads. It would be interesting to know whether the same source furnished Gower with material for his Tale of Florent, which occurs in the first book of the *Confessio Amantis*. In Gower's version, as in the Gawain ballads, the lady offers her husband the choice between beauty by day or by night; and there are other important differences between his story and the Wife's Tale, which make it appear extremely unlikely that one poet copied from the other, or that both used the same source.

THE FRERES TALE

The tale with which the Friar provokes the ire of the Summoner is merely an adroit application of a familiar story, which could be fastened upon nearly any unpopular functionary. It is safe to assume, at least, that the central incident was not original with Chaucer, for similar stories have been discovered in compilations which could hardly have been influenced by the *Freres Tale*.[72a] The

[72a] Archer Taylor: *The Devil and the Advocate,* in *Publ. Mod. Lang. Assn.,* 36. 35–59; *Sources and Analogues,* 269–74.

Libri Octo Miraculorum of Caesarius of Heisterbach, collector of folk tales in the thirteenth century, contains one of the earliest versions. Perhaps the liveliest of the analogues is that found by Wright in a fifteenth-century manuscript in the British Museum and published by him in *Archaeologia* in 1847. A translation follows:

TALE OF A CERTAIN WICKED SENESCHAL

There was once a certain man, a seneschal and lawyer, who practised trickery against the poor and despoiled them of all their goods. One day, as he was going to court, to try a case and make some money, he fell in with another man, who said to him, "Where are you going, and what is your business?" "I am going to make some money," said the seneschal. "I am your fellow at that," said the other; "let us go together." When the lawyer consented, the stranger said, "And what is the source of your income?" To which he replied, "The property of the poor— so long as they have any—which I take from them through lawsuits, extortion, and persecution, both justly and unjustly. Now I have told you whence I derive my income; prithee, tell me the source of yours." The other made answer and said, "Whatever is consigned to the Devil in a curse I reckon to my profit." The lawyer laughed and made fun of his companion; for he did not know he was the Devil.

A little later, as they were passing through a town, they heard a poor fellow cursing a calf, which he was leading to market, because it made but crooked progress. At the same time, they heard similar language from a woman, who was beating her small boy. Then said the lawyer to his companion, "Look here, you can make some profit, if you want to. Take the boy and the calf." The other replied, "I cannot do it, for they are not cursing from their hearts."

When they had gone a little farther, some poor people, who were going toward the court-house, caught sight of the seneschal, and they all began, with one accord, to heap curses upon him. Then said the Devil, "Do you hear what they are saying?" "I do," said he, "but it is nothing to me." "They are cursing you from the bottom of their hearts," said his companion, "and they are consigning you to the Devil. Therefore you shall be mine." And catching him up straightway, he vanished with him.

Another analogue, from the *Promptuarium Exemplorum* compiled in the fifteenth century by John Herolt, a Dominican friar of Basle, runs as follows:

OF THE DEVIL AND AN ADVOCATE

A certain lawyer, who practised in several villages, was a merciless, grasping fellow, who laid heavy toll upon those who were set under his power. One day, as he was hastening toward a village, in order to make an exaction, the Devil joined him on his journey, in the form of a man. He knew him to be the Devil, not only by his own horror, but also by the conversation that passed between them. He was much afraid to journey with him; but in no way—neither by entreaty nor by making the sign of the cross—could he be separated from him. While they pressed on together, a certain poor man met them, driving a pig in a noose; and when the pig turned aside, now here, now there, the man was angry and cried out, "Devil take you!" Hearing these words, the lawyer, in hopes of being rid of the Devil through such an occasion, said to him, "You hear, my friend: the pig is donated to you; go, take him." The Devil made answer. "It is by no means given me from the heart; therefore, I cannot take it." Later, as they passed through another village, where a child was crying, the mother, standing at her door, cried out angrily, "The Devil take you! Why do you fret me with your wailing?" Then the lawyer said, "Lo, you have a fine bargain of one soul! Take the child, for it is yours." But the Devil, as before, said, "It is not given me from the heart; such is the manner of speaking among mortals, when they are angry." But as they were approaching the place toward which they were journeying, the men from the village, seeing them afar and not ignorant of the cause of the lawyer's coming, cried out with one voice, saying, "The Devil take you! May you go to the Devil!" Hearing this, the Devil, nodding his head and setting up a loud laugh, said to the lawyer, "Lo, these men bestow you upon me from the depths of their hearts; and therefore you are mine!" And in that hour, the Devil snatched him away, and what he did with him no man knows. The words of their conversation and what the Devil did were made known through the lawyer's servant, who had journeyed with him.

Neither of these stories nor an older version printed by Professor Taylor from a fourteenth-century manuscript in the British Museum (*Sources and Analogues*, 269, 270) furnishes an actual source for the *Freres Tale*. Doubtless the story reached Chaucer by word of mouth.

The Somnours Tale

The tale of Old Thomas and the wheedling friar, with which the Somnour eases his wrath against Frere Hubert, appears to have been founded upon a popular anecdote. Like the story out of which the *Freres Tale* was made, and the unsavory anecdote told in the Summoner's Prologue, it probably came to Chaucer by word of mouth. No story that resembles the *Somnours Tale* at all closely has been discovered; but the central incident, of a humiliation put upon begging friars in revenge for their pestering, is to be found in a lively tale in verse written in the early fourteenth century by a certain Jacques de Baisieux and entitled *Li Dis de le vescie à prestre*. The tale may be summarized as follows:

A priest, who lived near Antwerp, being about to die of dropsy, sends for his Dean and his friends and gives them all his property to divide, when he is dead, among the people he names. Two Jacobin Friars come to the priest, ask how he is, handle him all over, and conclude that he must die. Friar Lewis says, "It is too late for us to cure him; but out of the property he has amassed, he ought to give our convent twenty pounds to mend our books." "True, by God the Father," says Friar Simon, "I will show him our necessity." So they tell the sick priest that he must think of his soul and give money for God's use. The priest replies that he has given everything for God. "But how have you ordered the matter?" say the friars; "for Scripture tells us we must be careful to whom we give alms." The priest says he has given his cattle to his poor relations and more than ten pounds' worth of corn to the poor of the town, besides legacies to the orphans and the nuns and 100 sous to the Franciscans. "These alms are right fair," declare the friars; "but have you given nothing to the friars of our house?" The priest says he has not. "What! when we are your neighbors and so worthy and live so soberly! You'll not die well if you give us nothing!" The priest swears he has nothing left to give, but they continue to solicit him, showing him that he could revoke one of his other gifts and give it to them. "We'll help your soul. An alms to us is well bestowed; we never wear shirts, and we fare hardly." The priest thinks he will be revenged and trick them. So he says he'll give them a jewel, which he holds dearer than any other thing, and which he wouldn't part with for more than 1000 silver marks. To-morrow let them fetch their Prior, and he will then tell them where the jewel is.

The Friars go back to Antwerp and tell their chapter. A great feast is ordered on the strength of the jewel which has been promised them. They toast the dying priest, rejoice, and ring their bells as for a saint's corpse, until the neighbors wonder what is up. Friar Lewis asks how they can best get the priest's promise out of him. They settle that next day the friars shall set off, Friar Lewis and Friars William, Nicholas, and Robert (with their breviary), but not the Prior. So in the morning, the friars set out for the priest's house; but before the day is over, they wish they had staid at home. They salute the priest and ask if he is better. The priest welcomes them and says he has not forgotten the gift he promised them, but they must fetch the aldermen and the mayor, and then he will tell them what the gift is to be and where it may be found. Friar Robert fetches the

aldermen and mayor. The priest says, "My friends, yes-
terday Friar Lewis and Friar Simon came to preach to
me, and asked me if I'd thought of my soul, and if
I'd given their house anything. I said No; and they told
me I should die in danger if I didn't give them something. So I've thought of a thing which I value very
much, but which I can't give away while I live, so much
do I love it. But I'll bestow it in your presence." The
five friars say, "Tell us what it is." "Well," says the
priest, "It's my bladder. If you will have it well cleaned,
you'll find it better than leather and more durable. You
can keep your pepper in it." "False priest, you've brought
us here to shame us!" "Quite true. You treated me like
a brute when you asked me to revoke my gifts when I
told you I'd nothing for you." The Jacobins go home
with sorry face, and the neighbors all laugh at them
about the cheat of the bladder that they feasted over.[73]

THE CLERKES TALE

Chaucer derived the tale told by the Clerk of Oxenford
directly from "Fraunceys Petrark, the laureat poete."
That the two poets met at Padua, when Chaucer was in
Italy in 1372–3, is now regarded as extremely improbable,
but it is certain that an acquaintance with the work of
Petrarch, as with that of Boccaccio, came to Chaucer
through his Italian journeys. Probably he brought home
manuscripts from Italy, and Petrarch's Latin version of
the story of Griselda may well have been among them.

[73] My summary is based on that of Furnivall (*Originals and Analogues,* 137–44). W. M. Hart prints the text of the story and the
three *exempla* from Seneca (*Sources and Analogues,* 275–87).

Chaucer followed his Latin original faithfully, but Prof. Severs has shown that he leaned heavily on a French redaction. A translation of Petrarch's story follows.[74]

A FABLE OF WIFELY OBEDIENCE AND DEVOTION

In the chain of the Apennines, in the west of Italy, stands Mount Viso, a very lofty mountain, whose summit towers above the clouds and rises into the bright upper air. It is a mountain notable in its own nature, but most notable as the source of the Po, which rises from a small spring upon the mountain's side, bends slightly toward the east, and presently, swollen with abundant tributaries, becomes, though its downward course has been but brief, not only one of the greatest of streams but, as Vergil called it, the king of rivers. Through Liguria its raging waters cut their way, and then, bounding Aemilia and Flaminia and Venetia, it empties at last into the Adriatic sea, through many mighty mouths. Now that part of these lands, of which I spoke first, is sunny and delightful, as much for the hills which run through it and the mountains which hem it in, as for its grateful plain. From the foot of the mountains beneath which it lies, it derives its name; and it has many famous cities and towns. Among others, at the very foot of Mount Viso, is the land of Saluzzo, thick with villages and castles. It is ruled over by noble marquises, the first and greatest of whom, according to tradition, was a certain Walter, to

[74] My translation, originally based on the text of the Basle edition, has been checked against the critical text printed by Prof. Severs (*Originals and Analogues*, 288–331), who also prints the French translation. See also Severs: *The Literary Relationships of Chaucer's Clerkes Tale*, New Haven, 1942.

whom the direction of his own estates and of all the land pertained. He was a man blooming with youth and beauty, as noble in his ways as in his birth; marked out, in short, for leadership in all things,—save that he was so contented with his present lot that he took very little care for the future. Devoted to hunting and fowling, he so applied himself to these arts that he neglected almost all else; and—what his subjects bore most ill—he shrank even from a hint of marriage. When they had borne this for some time in silence, at length they came to him in a company; and one of their number, who had authority and eloquence above the rest and was on more familiar terms with his overlord, said to him, "Noble Marquis, your kindness gives us such boldness that we come separately to talk with you, with devoted trust, as often as occasion demands, and that now my voice conveys to your ears the silent wishes of us all; not because I have any especial privilege, unless it be that you have shown by many signs that you hold me dear among the others. Although all your ways, then, justly give us pleasure and always have, so that we count ourselves happy in such an overlord, there is one thing in which we should assuredly be the happiest of all men round about, if you would consent to it and show yourself susceptible to our entreaties; and that is, that you should take thought of marriage and bow your neck, free and imperious though it be, to the lawful yoke; and that you should do this as soon as possible. For the swift days fly by, and although you are in the flower of your youth, nevertheless silent old age follows hard upon that flower, and death itself is very near to any age. To none is immunity against this tribute given, and all alike must die; and just as that is certain, so is it uncertain when it will come to pass. Give ear, therefore, we pray you, to the entreaties of those who have never refused to do your bidding. You may leave the selection of a wife to our care, for we shall procure you such an one as shall be truly worthy of you, and sprung of so high a lineage that you may have the best hope of her. Free all your subjects, we beseech you, of the grievous apprehension that if anything incident to our mortal lot should happen to you, you would go leaving no successor to yourself, and they would remain deprived of a leader such as their hearts crave."

Their loyal entreaties touched the man's heart, and he made answer: "My friends, you constrain me to that which never entered my thoughts. I have had pleasure in complete liberty, a thing which is rare in marriage. Nevertheless, I willingly submit to the wishes of my subjects, trusting in your prudence and your devotion. But I release you from the task, which you have offered to assume, of finding me a wife. That task I lay on my own shoulders. For what benefit can the distinction of one confer upon another? Right often, children are all unlike their parents. Whatever is good in a man comes not from another, but from God. As I entrust to Him all my welfare, so would I entrust to Him the outcome of my marriage, hoping for His accustomed mercy. He will find for me that which shall be expedient for my peace and safety. And so, since you are resolved that I should take a wife, so much, in all good faith, I promise you; and for my part, I will neither frustrate nor delay your wishes. One promise, in your turn, you must make and keep: that whosoever the wife may be whom

I shall choose, you will yield her the highest honor and veneration; and let there be none among you who ever shall dispute or complain of my decision. Yours it was that I, the freest of all the men you have known, have submitted to the yoke of marriage; let it be mine to choose that yoke; and whoever my wife may be, let her be your mistress, as if she were the daughter of a prince of Rome."

Like men who thought it hardly possible that they should see the wished-for day of the nuptials, they promised with one accord and gladly that they should be found in nothing wanting; and with eager alacrity they received the edict from their master, directing that the most magnificent preparations be made for a certain day.[75] So they withdrew from conference; and the marquis, on his part, laid care upon his servants for the nuptials and gave public notice of the day.

Not far from the palace, there was a village, of few and needy inhabitants, one of whom, the poorest of all, was named Janicola. But as the grace of Heaven sometimes visits the hovels of the poor, it chanced that he had an only daughter, by name Griseldis, remarkable for the beauty of her body, but of so beautiful a character and spirit that no one excelled her. Reared in a frugal way of living and always in the direst poverty, unconscious of any want, she had learned to cherish no soft, no childish thoughts; but the vigor of manhood and the

---

[75] *Promictunt unanimiter ac lete nichil defuturum, ut quibus vix possibile videretur optatum diem cernere nuptiarum, de quibus in diem certum magnificentissime apparandis domini iubentis edictum alacres suscepere.* My earlier translation, based on the substitution of *expectaverunt* for the *susceperunt* of the Basle text, has no manuscript authority.

wisdom of age lay hidden in her maiden bosom. Cherishing her father's age with ineffable love, she tended his few sheep, and as she did it, wore her fingers away on the distaff. Then, returning home, she would prepare the little herbs and victuals suited to their fortune and make ready the rude bedchamber. In her narrow station, in fine, she discharged all the offices of filial obedience and affection. Walter, passing often by that way, had sometimes cast his eyes upon this little maid, not with the lust of youth, but with the sober thoughts of an older man; and his swift intuition had perceived in her a virtue, beyond her sex and age, which the obscurity of her condition concealed from the eyes of the common throng. Hence it came about that he decided, at one and the same time, to take a wife—which he had never before wished to do—and to have this woman and no other.

The day of the nuptials drew on, but no one knew whence the bride should come, and there was no one who did not wonder. Walter himself, in the meanwhile, was buying golden rings and coronets and girdles, and was having rich garments and shoes and all necessities of this kind made to the measure of another girl, who was very like Griseldis in stature. The longed-for day had come, and since not a word about the bride was to be heard, the universal bewilderment had risen very high. The hour of the feast arrived; and already, the whole house was in a great ferment of preparation. Then Walter came out of the castle, as if he were setting out to meet his approaching bride, and a throng of noble men and matrons followed in his train.

Griseldis, ignorant of all the preparations which were being made on her account, had performed what was to be done about her home; and now, with water from the distant well, she was crossing the threshold of her father's house, in order that, free from other duties, she might hasten, with the girls who were her comrades, to see her master's bride. Then Walter, absorbed in his own thoughts, drew near and, calling her by name, asked her where her father was; and when she had replied, reverently and humbly, that he was within, "Bid him," he said, "come hither."

When the old man was come, Walter took him by the hand and drew him a little aside; and lowering his voice, he said, "Janicola, I know that I am dear to you. I have known you for my faithful liegeman, and I believe you wish whatever suits my pleasure. One thing in particular, however, I should like to know: whether you would take me, whom you have as your master, for a son-in-law, giving me your daughter as a wife?"

Stupefied at this unlooked-for matter, the old man went rigid. At length, hardly able to stammer out a few words, he replied, "It is my duty to wish or to deny nothing, save as it pleases you, who are my master." "Let us, then, go in alone," said the marquis, "that I may put certain questions to the girl herself in your presence." They entered the house, therefore, while the populace stood expectant and wondering, and found the maiden busying herself about her father's service and abashed by the unexpected advent of so great a throng of strangers. Walter, approaching her, addressed her in these words: "It is your father's pleasure and mine that you shall be my wife. I believe that this will please you, too. But I have one thing to ask you: when that is done which shortly shall take place, will you be prepared, with consenting mind, to agree with me in all things; so that you dispute my wish in nothing, and permit me, with mind consenting, and without remonstrance of word or look, to do whatever I will with you?"

Trembling at this marvelous thing, the girl made answer: "I know myself unworthy, my lord, of so great an honor; but if it be your will, and if it be my destiny, I will never consciously cherish a thought, much less do anything, which might be contrary to your desires; nor will you do anything, even though you bid me die, which I shall bear ill."

"It is enough," said he; and so, leading her out before the throng, he showed her to the people, and said, "This is my wife, this is your lady; cherish her and love her; and if you hold me dear, hold her most dear of all." Then, lest she carry into her new home any relic of her former fortune, he commanded her to be stripped, and clad from head to heel with new garments; and this was done, reverently and swiftly, by matrons who stood around her and who embraced her each in turn. So this simple peasant girl, new clad, with her dishevelled tresses collected and made smooth, adorned with gems and coronet, was as it were suddenly transformed, so that the people hardly knew her. And Walter solemnly plighted her his troth with a precious ring, which he had brought with him for that purpose; and having placed her on a snow-white horse, he had her conducted to the palace, the populace accompanying her and rejoicing. In this way, the nuptials were celebrated, and that most happy day was passed.

Shortly thereafter, so much did God's favor shine upon the lowly bride, it seemed she was reared and bred, not in a shepherd's cottage, but in the imperial court; and to all she became dear and venerable beyond belief. Even those who had known her from her birth could hardly be persuaded she was Janicola's daughter; such was the graciousness of her life and of her ways, the gravity and sweetness of her speech, by which she had bound the hearts of all the people to her with the bond of a great love. And already her name, heralded by frequent rumor, had spread abroad, not only within the confines of her fatherland, but through every neighboring province; so that many men and matrons, with eager desire, came flocking to see her. So, graced [76] by a marriage, which, however humble, was distinguished and prosperous, Walter lived in the highest peace and honor at home; and abroad he was held in the highest esteem; and because he had so shrewdly discovered the remarkable virtue hidden under so much poverty, he was commonly held to be a very prudent man. Not only did his wife attend adroitly to those domestic matters which pertain to women; but when occasion demanded, in her husband's absence, she undertook state affairs, settling and composing the country's law-suits and disputes among the nobles, with such weighty opinions and so great a maturity and fairness of judgment, that all declared this woman had been sent down from heaven for the public weal.

Not long time had passed ere she became pregnant; and after she had held her subjects for a time in anxious expectation, at length she bore the fairest of daughters. Though they had preferred a son, nevertheless she made both her husband and her country happy by this proof of the fertility they longed for. In the meanwhile,

[76] For *honestatis* read *honestatus.*

it so happened, when his little daughter had been weaned, that Walter was seized with a desire more strange than laudable—so the more experienced may decide [77]—to try more deeply the fidelity of his dear wife, which had been sufficiently made known by experience, and to test it again and again. Therefore, he called her alone into his chamber and addressed her thus, with troubled brow: "You know, Griseldis—for I do not think that amid your present good fortune you have forgotten your former state—you know, I say, in what manner you came into this house. To me, indeed, you are dear enough and well beloved; but to my nobles, not so; especially since you have begun to bear children. For they take it most ill that they should submit to a low-born mistress. Since, therefore, I desire peace with them, I must follow another's judgment, not my own, in the case of your daughter, and do that which is most grievous to me. But I would never do it without letting you know, and I wish you to accommodate your will to mine and to show that obedience which you promised at the outset of our married life."

She listened without a protesting word or glance. "You are our master," she said, "and both this little girl and I are yours. Do, therefore, as you will with your own; for nothing can please you which would displease me. There is absolutely nothing which I wish to have or fear to lose, save you. This is fixed in the very center of my heart, and never, either by lapse of years or by death,

---

[77] *mirabilis quaedam quam laudabilis (doctiores judicent) cupiditas.* Three manuscripts read *magis quam laudabilis,* which seems more satisfactory. Chaucer's manuscript may have read *laudabilem.* Cf. Severs: *The Literary Relationships of Chaucer's Clerkes Tale,* 116, 268.

will it be torn away. Anything can happen ere I shall change my mind."

Happy in her reply, but feigning sadness in his looks, he left her; and a little later, he sent to her one of his underlings, a most faithful man, whose services he was wont to use in his most weighty affairs, and whom he instructed in the task before him. The fellow, coming to Griseldis by night, said to her, "Spare me, my lady, and do not lay to my blame what I am forced to do. You are right knowing, and you understand what it is to be subject to a master; nor is the harsh necessity of obedience unknown to one endowed with so much sense, though inexperienced. I am bidden to take this little baby girl, and—" Here, breaking off his speech,[78] he ceased, as if he would indicate his cruel business by his silence. Suspect was the reputation of the man, suspect his face, suspect the hour, suspect his words. By these tokens, she clearly knew her sweet daughter was to be killed; yet she shed no tear, she breathed no sigh,—a thing most hard, even for a nurse, much more so for a mother. But taking up the little girl, with tranquil brow, she looked at her a little, and kissing her, blessed her and made the sign of the Holy Cross upon her. Then she gave the child to the fellow, and said, "Go; and whatever our lord hath laid upon you, see that you perform it. One thing I beg of you: take care lest beasts or birds tear her little body; and this, only if no contrary orders have been laid upon you."

The fellow returned to his master and told him what

[78] The pointing in the text given by the Chaucer Society is misleading. It seems evident that Petrarch wrote: *atque eam—hic sermone abrupto.* I do not translate *eam,* since the English order hardly permits a direct object at the beginning of a clause.

he had said and how Griseldis had replied; and when he had given him his daughter, paternal pity touched the marquis to the heart. Nevertheless, he did not relax the rigor of his purpose. He ordered his slave to wrap the child in cloths, to place it in a wickerwork basket upon a beast of burden, and carry it, secretly and with all the diligence he could command, to Bologna, to Walter's sister, who had married the Count of Panago. He should hand the child over to her, to be cherished with maternal care, to be reared in gentle ways. and to be concealed, moreover, with so much care that no one could know whose daughter she was. The slave journeyed thither and fulfilled with care what had been laid upon him.

Walter, in the meanwhile, though he often studied his wife's face and words, never detected any sign of a change of feeling: equal alacrity and diligence, her accustomed complaisance, the same love, no sadness, no mention of her daughter! Never did the girl's name fall from her mother's lips, either by design or by chance. In this way, four years went by; and being again with child, behold she brought forth a most excellent son, a great delight to his father and all their friends. But when, after two years, this child had been weaned,[79] the father fell back into his former caprice. And again he said to his wife, "Once before you have heard that my people bear our marriage ill, especially since they knew you capable of bearing children; but it has never been so bad as since you gave birth to a son. For they say—and the murmur of it comes often to my ears, 'So, when Walter

[79] *quo nutricis ab ubere post biennium subducto.* The Basle text, corrupt at this point, reads: *Quo nutrici ab urbe, etc.* The text which Chaucer used obviously had the correct reading.

dies,[80] Janicola's grandson shall rule over us, and so noble a land will be subject to such a master.' Each day many things of this tenor are current among my people; and I, eager for peace and—to say sooth—fearing for myself, am therefore moved to dispose of this infant as I disposed of his sister. I tell you this beforehand, lest the unexpected and sudden grief disturb you."

To which she made answer: "I have said, and I say again, that I can have no wishes save yours. In these children, indeed, I have no share, beyond the pangs of labor. You are my master and theirs: use your power over your own. Nor seek my consent; for when I entered your house, as I put off my clothes, so I put off my wishes and desires, and put on yours. Whatever you wish to do, therefore, about anything whatsoever, that is what I wish, too. Nay, if I could foresee your future wishes, I should begin beforehand, whatever it might be, to wish and desire what you wish. Now I gladly follow your desire, which I cannot anticipate. Suppose it pleased you that I should die, I would die gladly; nor is there any other thing—not death itself—to equal our love."

Marvelling at the steadfastness of the woman, he took his departure, his face agitated with emotion; and straightway he sent to her the servant whom he had sent before. The latter, with many a plea of the necessity of obedience, and with many an entreaty for forgiveness, if he had done or was doing her a wrong, demanded her child, as one who is about to commit a monstrous crime. But she, with unchanged mien, whatever might be passing

---

[80] *Obeunte igitur Valterio,* not *obeunte . . . altero* as in the text printed by the Chaucer Society. The manuscript Chaucer was using seems to have had the correct reading.

in her mind, took up in her arms the son who was so
well beloved, not only by his mother but by everyone,
for the beauty of his body and his disposition; and she
made upon him the sign of the Cross, blessing him, as
she had blessed her daughter, clinging to him just a
little while with her eyes, and bending down to kiss him;
but she gave absolutely no other sign of her grief. Then
she gave him to the fellow who had come to seek him, and
she said, "Take him, too, and do what you are bidden.
But one thing I beg of you: that if it can be done, you
will protect the tender limbs of my beautiful baby against
the ravages of birds and beasts."

The man, returning to his master with these words
of hers, drove him to yet greater wonder, so that if he
had not known her for the most loving of mothers, he
might have had some faint suspicion that the strength
of the woman came from a certain hardness of heart;
but while she was strongly attached to all that were hers,
she loved no one better than her husband.[81] The servant
was then bidden to set out for Bologna and to take the
boy where he had taken his sister.

These trials of conjugal affection and fidelity would
have been sufficient for the most rigorous of husbands;
but there are those who, when once they have begun anything, do not cease; nay, rather, they press on and cling
to their purpose. Keeping his eyes upon his wife, therefore, Walter watched continually for any change in her
behavior toward him, and he was not able to find any

---

[81] The Latin is decidedly elliptical at this point and the text printed
by the Chaucer Society contains one obvious misreading (*nullus* for
nullius). The ellipsis might be expanded as follows: *sed cum suorum
omnium valde erat amans, tum nullius erat amantior quam viri.*

at all, save that she became each day more devoted and more obedient to his wishes; so that it seemed there was but one mind between them, and that not common to them both, but, to say truth, the husband's alone; for the wife had declared, as has been said, that she had no wishes of her own.

Little by little, an ugly rumor about Walter had begun to spread abroad; namely, that with savage and inhuman cruelty, out of regret and shame for his humble marriage, he had ordered his children slain; for neither did his children appear, nor had anyone heard where in the world they were. Wherefore, he who had once been a man of spotless reputation, dear to his people, had become in the eyes of many men infamous and hateful. Not on that account, however, was his stern purpose altered, but he persevered in the severity which he had assumed [82] and in his harsh caprice of testing his wife. And so, when twelve years had passed since the birth of his daughter, he sent envoys to Rome to bring back thence documents bearing the appearance of a papal bull, which should cause the rumor to circulate among the people that license had been granted him by the Roman pontiff, with a view to his own peace and that of his people, to annul his first marriage and to take another wife; nor was it difficult, in fact, to convince those untutored Alpine folk of anything you pleased. When this rumor reached Griseldis, she was sad, I think; but as one who had made her decision, once and for all, about herself and her destiny, she stood unshaken, awaiting what should be decreed for her by him to whom she had submitted herself and all that was hers.

[82] For *suspecta* of the Basle edition, read *suscepta*.

Walter had already sent to Bologna and had asked his kinsman to send him his children, spreading the story in every quarter that this maiden was to be Walter's bride. His kinsman faithfully performed [83] these orders and set out upon his journey on the appointed day, bringing with him, amid a brilliant throng of noblemen, the young maiden, who was now of marriageable age, of excellent beauty, and adorned with magnificent attire; and with her he brought her brother, who was now in his seventh year.

Walter, in the meanwhile, with his accustomed inclination to try his wife, even to the heights of grief and shame, led her forth before the multitude and said, "I have been wont to take ample delight in our marriage, having regard for your character, not your lineage; [84] but now, since I perceive that great place is always great servitude, it is not permitted me to do what any peasant may. My people compel me—and the Pope consents—to take another wife. Already my wife is on her way, and presently she will be here. Therefore, be of stout heart, and yielding your place to another, take back your dowry and return to your former home with equal mind. No good fortune lasts forever."

She made answer: "My lord, I have always known that there was no proportion between your greatness and my lowly station. I have never considered myself worthy to be—I will not say, your wife, but your servant; and in this house, in which you have made me mistress, I call God to witness that I have remained in spirit as a hand-

[83] *Quod ille fideliter executurus.*
[84] Read: *mores tuos non originem respiciens.* The reading *origine* is due to failure to expand a contracted form.

maid. For these years, therefore, that I have dwelt with you in honor far beyond my deserts, I give thanks to God and you. For the rest, I am ready, with good heart and peaceful mind, to return to my father's house, to pass my age and to die where I have passed my youth, always happy in the honorable estate of widowhood, since I have been the wife of such a man. I readily yield place to your new bride—and may her coming bring you joy! —and I will not take away any ill feeling from this place, where I was wont to live most happily, while it so pleased you. But as for my dowry, which you bid me take back with me, I see of what sort it is, and it has not been lost; for as I came to you long since, stripped at my father's threshold of all my clothes and clad in yours, I had no other dowry but nakedness and devotion. Lo, therefore, I strip off this dress and restore this ring, with which you wed me. And the other rings and finery, with which your gifts have enriched me to the point of envy, are in your chamber. Naked I came from my father's house, and naked shall I return again,—save that I think it unseemly that this belly, in which the children you begot were shaped, should appear naked before the people. Wherefore, if it please you—but not otherwise—I pray and beseech you, as the price of the maidenhood which I brought hither and do not take hence, bid me keep one shift, out of those I have been wont to wear, that I may cover therewith the belly of her who was once your wife."

The tears welled into her husband's eyes, so that they could no longer be restrained; and so, turning his face aside, "Take your one shift," he said, and his voice trembled so that he could scarcely say it. So, weeping, he took his departure. Before them all, she stripped off her clothes, keeping upon her only her shift; and covered with that alone, she went forth before them with feet and head quite bare. Followed by many, who wept and railed at fortune, she alone dry-eyed and to be honored for her noble silence, returned to her father's house. The good man, who had always held his daughter's marriage in suspicion and had never allowed himself high hopes, ever expecting it to turn out that so high-born a husband, proud after the fashion of noblemen, would one day be sated with so lowly a bride and send her home, had kept her coarse and well-worn gown hidden away in some corner of his narrow dwelling. Hearing the uproar, not of his daughter, who returned in silence, but of the accompanying throng, he ran to meet her at the threshold and covered her, half naked as she was, with the old gown. She remained with her father a few days, showing marvelous equanimity and kindness; for she gave no sign of the sadness of her heart and showed no trace of her more favorable lot, since, forsooth, she had always dwelt amid riches with lowly and humble spirit.

Now the Count of Panago was drawing near; and, on every hand, rumors of the new nuptials were rife. Sending forward one of his train, he announced the day on which he would arrive at Saluzzo. The day before, therefore, Walter sent for Griseldis, and when she had come with all fidelity, he said to her, "It is my desire that the maiden who is coming on the morrow to dine with us should be received sumptuously, as well as the men and matrons who come with her and such of our own people as are present at the feast, so that honor of place and welcome may be preserved unspotted, according to the dignity of each and all. But I have no women in the house who are suited to cope with this task; therefore, though your garments are but poor, you may best assume the duty of receiving and placing my guests, for you know my ways."

"I will do this," said she, "and whatever else I see will please you, not only willingly, but eagerly. Nor shall I grow weary or sluggish in this labor, so long as the least remnant [85] of my spirit shall last." And when she had said this, straightway she caught up the implements of servant's toil and set to work, sweeping the house, setting the tables, making the beds, and urging on the others, like the best of handmaids.

At the third hour of the next day, the count arrived; and all the people vied in commending the manners and the beauty of the maiden and her youthful brother. There were those who said that Walter had been fortunate and prudent in the change he made, since this bride was more delicate and of nobler breeding, and had so fine a kinsman into the bargain. So, while the preparations for the feast went feverishly on, Griseldis, who had been present everywhere and solicitous of all—not cast down by so grievous a lot nor confused with shame for her old-fashioned clothing, but serene of countenance—came to meet the maiden as she entered. Bending the knee before her, after the manner of servants, with eyes cast reverently and humbly down, she said, "Welcome, my lady." Then she greeted others of the guests with cheerful face and marvelous sweetness in her words, and she managed the vast household with great skill; so that everyone greatly

[85] *reliquie ulle*. The printed editions of the sixteenth century have the incorrect reading *velle* for *ulle*.

wondered—especially the newcomers—whence came that dignity of manner and that discretion beneath such a dress. She, in her turn, could not grow weary of praising the maiden and the boy: now she extolled the maiden's beauty, now the boy's.

Just as they were to sit down at the tables, Walter turned toward her and said before them all, as if he were making game of her, "What think you, Griseldis, of this bride of mine? Is she pretty and worthy enough?"

"Surely," said she, "no prettier or worthier could be found. Either with her or with no one, can you lead a life of tranquillity and happiness; and that you may find happiness is my desire and my hope. One thing, in all good faith, I beg of you, one warning I give you: not to drive her with those goads with which you have driven another woman. For since she is younger and more delicately nurtured, I predict she would not be strong enough to bear so much."

Walter, seeing the cheerfulness with which she spoke, and turning over in his mind the steadfastness of the woman, who had been so often and so bitterly injured, took pity on the unworthy fate that had befallen her so unjustly. Able to bear it no longer, he cried out, "It is enough, my Griseldis! Your fidelity to me is made known [86] and proved; nor do I think that under heaven there is another woman who has undergone such trials of her conjugal love." And saying this, with eager arms he embraced his dear wife, who stood all overcome with stupor and as if waking from a troubled sleep. "And you," he said, "are my only wife. I have no other, nor ever shall have. This maiden, whom you think to be

[86] For *cogitata* read *cognita*.

my bride, is your daughter; and he, who is thought to be my kinsman, is your son. They whom you believed you had lost, each in turn, you get back both together. Let all know, who thought the contrary, that I am curious and given to experiments, but am not impious: I have tested my wife, not condemned her; I have hidden my children, not destroyed them."

Almost out of her wits for joy and beside herself with maternal love, on hearing these words, Griseldis rushed into her children's arms, shedding the most joyous tears. She wearied them with kisses and bedewed them with her loving tears. And straightway the ladies gathered about her with alacrity and affection; and when her vile apparel had been stripped off her, they clothed her in her accustomed garments and adorned her. The most joyous plaudits and auspicious words from all the throng resounded all about; and the day was the most renowned that ever was for its great joy and sorrow,—more renowned, even, than the day of her nuptials had been.

Many years thereafter they lived in great peace and concord; and Walter, who had appeared to neglect his father-in-law, lest he should stand in the way of the experiment he had conceived, had the old man moved into his palace and held him in honor. His own daughter he gave in noble and honorable marriage, and his son he left behind him as his heir, happy in his wife and in his offspring.

This story it has seemed good to me to weave anew, in another [87] tongue, not so much that it might stir the matrons of our times to imitate the patience of this wife—who

[87] The text which Chaucer used evidently read *stylo nunc alto* for *stylo nunc alio*. Cf. Hendrickson, *Modern Philology*, 4. 179–92.

seems to me scarcely imitable—as that it might stir all those
who read it to imitate the woman's steadfastness, at least;
so that they may have the resolution to perform for God
what this woman performed for her husband. For He
cannot be tempted with evil, as saith James the Apostle,
and He himself tempts no man. Nevertheless, He often
proves us and suffers us to be vexed with many a grievous
scourge; not that He may know our spirit, for that He
knew ere we were made, but that our own frailty may
be made known to us through notable private signs. Therefore I would assuredly enter on the list of steadfast men
the name of anyone who endured for his God, without a
murmur, what this obscure peasant woman endured for
her mortal husband.

Petrarch's attention was drawn to the story of Griselda
by the *Decameron,* which had come into his hands, apparently for the first time, only a few years before his
death. Boccaccio's great work does not seem to have commanded quite the attention that it merited from a man
who had, for many years, professed himself the author's
friend. The *Decameron* had been in circulation since 1353,
but it was not until 1373 that Petrarch looked into it; and
even then he had to confess, in a letter to Boccaccio, that
he had not found time to do more than run through it
"like a hurried traveller, glancing about, here and there,
and nowhere tarrying long." [88] The last tale in the collection, however, he had not only read but had committed to
memory, that he might repeat it for his own pleasure, from
time to time, and might, on occasion, tell it to his friends.

[88] *Epistolae Seniles,* xvii. 3. The material for this paragraph is
all drawn from this letter.

Finally, he had translated it into Latin, that "so sweet a tale" might bring delight to those who knew no Italian. "It always pleased me when I heard it years ago," he wrote to Boccaccio, "and I should judge that it pleased you to such an extent that you deemed it not unworthy of your Italian prose, and of the end of your book, where the teaching of the rhetoricians requires that matter of greater import should be placed."

The tale which held this place of honor was the story of Griselda. That Petrarch had heard it "years ago" is evidence that it had been in existence before the *Decameron* was written; but its origins are shrouded in uncertainty, through which scholars are at present tracing it back into the doubtful region of folk-lore.[89] In its theme, quite apart from the artistic treatment which it has been given by the poets, the story belongs in the class of the *exempla,* and as such it may very well have been a favorite with many a prosy moralist of the Middle Ages, along with stories of other women (like the saintly Constance of the *Tale of the Man of Lawe*), who were not so much women as personifications of the virtues. It remained for the great writers who told the tale to lift it out of this humble category and to give it a place in literature, as a glowing tribute to feminine ideals in the great feudal age. To Petrarch, who memorized it that he might repeat it over to himself, and to his friend, who, as he wrote Boccaccio, was so moved by it that he could not read it for his tears, the story carried a wealth of meaning, much of

[89] D. D. Griffith: *The Origin of the Griselda Story,* Seattle, 1931 (*University of Washington Publications in Language and Literature,* VIII). See also, W. A. Cate: *The Problem of the Origin of the Griselda Story in Studies in Philology,* 29. 389–405 and the bibliography printed by Severs (*Sources and Analogues,* 294, 295).

which has been taken from it by the despoiling years. Unless the modern reader, by the alchemy of his imagination, can recreate at least a part of the riches that the story held for the fourteenth-century idealist, he is not likely to understand why Petrarch thought that it was worth re-telling, nor why Chaucer assigned it to his young undergraduate, lately come down from Oxford, the "home of lost causes, and forsaken beliefs, and unpopular names, and impossible loyalties."

THE MARCHANTES TALE

The first line of the Merchant's Prologue, echoing the last line of the Envoy to the *Clerkes Tale,* emphasizes the connection between the two stories and suggests a growing determination, on the part of the poet, to give a separate unity to the portion of the *Canterbury Tales* which has been called the Marriage Group. Further evidence of such an intention is to be found in the cancellation of the following stanza, which is inserted, in some of the manuscripts, after the Clerk's envoy:

> This worthy Clerk, whan ended was his tale,
> Our hoste seyde, and swoor by goddes bones,
> 'Me were lever than a barel ale
> My wyf at hoom had herd this legende ones;
> This is a gentil tale for the nones,
> As to my purpos, wiste ye my wille;
> But thing that wol nat be, lat it be stille.'

The use of a portion of this passage at another point in the *Canterbury Tales* (B 3081, ff.) is evidence both for the authenticity of the stanza and for its cancellation as a link between the stories of the Clerk and the Merchant. That Chaucer's plans for the framework of his Tales underwent revision as the collection grew under his hand is beyond question; in the cancellation of this particular passage, we have an unusually interesting glimpse into the processes of that revision.

The unity of the Marriage Group is yet further emphasized by the reference to the Wyf of Bath in the *Marchantes Tale* (E 1685). This reference, which the Merchant most curiously puts in the mouth of Justinus,[90] seems to have been inspired by the same considerations which led the poet to alter his plans for connecting the Merchant's tale and the Clerk's, and, perhaps, to append the ironic envoy to the story of Griselda. Like the Clerk, the Merchant finds it difficult to rid his mind of the disquieting ideas presented by Alice of Bath.

The reference to Alice's views on marriage also makes it evident that the *Marchantes Tale* was written later than the Prologue to the *Tale of the Wyf of Bathe*. There is every reason to accept Skeat's opinion that it was "among the latest written of the *Canterbury Tales*." In point of time, as well as in its spirit, the first part of it, at least, seems to belong with "the counseil of Chaucer touching mariage, which was sent to Bukton" (1393–6). That poem, too, contains a reference to "the Wyf of Bathe" as an authority upon the discomforts of marriage.

The long discussion of matrimony in the first part of the tale and the dialogue between Pluto and Proserpine toward the close are Chaucer's additions to an old and familiar story. For these parts of the poem, he has drawn material from several sources. Most singularly, he has used

[90] I do not accept Skeat's punctuation of the passage.

for a second time, and in a very different setting, the *Liber Consolationis* of Albertano of Brescia, the work which formed the ultimate source of his own tale of Melibeus. The allusions to Rebecca, Judith, Abigail, and Esther (E 1362–74) were derived from this source, and several shorter passages can be traced to the same original. Another work by Albertano, the *Liber de amore et dilectione Dei,* has also contributed several lines, notably the passage on the creation of Eve (E 1323–36). Other authorities, including Boethius, Claudian, Ovid, and Theophrastus, have been laid under contribution for an occasional allusion or a bit of proverbial wisdom.

In two articles published in *Modern Philology* (8. 165–86; 305–34), Professor Lowes argues for a connection between the *Marchantes Tale* and the *Miroir de Mariage,* a lengthy poem by Deschamps, in which a certain Franc Vouloir seeks counsel on the subject of matrimony. Arguments in favor of marriage are presented by Desir, Folie, Servitute, and Faintise; and then a very prosy fellow, named Repertoire de Science, refutes their arguments in an epistle of some 7000 lines. The similarity in theme and treatment between this work of Deschamps and the first part of Chaucer's poem is striking enough to suggest the possibility of borrowing; and Professor Lowes has found enough passages in the *Miroir de Mariage* which bear a resemblance to lines in the *Marchantes Tale* to bring him to the conclusion that the poem "was the chief source of the specific and characteristic setting which Chaucer gave to the *fabliau*-like story which formed the gist of the Merchant's Tale." [90a] The parallels, however, may well derive

[90a] Mrs. Dempster (*Sources and Analogues,* 333, ff.) prints the most relevant passages from the *Miroir de Mariage.*

rather from identity of theme or common sources than from direct borrowing, and it seems hardly safe to accept the French poem as a source of the *Marchantes Tale*. The argument upon marriage at the opening of the poem, like the dialogue between Pluto and Proserpine at its close, appears to have been an original conception of Chaucer's.

The incident which furnishes the plot of the Tale was certainly not original with Chaucer. The pear-tree, which bears such sorry fruit, appears with lamentable frequency in earlier fiction; and the Chaucer Society has been able to discover five analogous stories, in European compilations, besides nine oriental tales dealing with a similar theme. They are printed in the Society's volume of *Originals and Analogues* (177–88, 341–64, 544), where they may be consulted by those who are curious in such matters. Many of these tales, particularly several from the Orient, will be found to bear only the faintest resemblance to the *Marchantes Tale;* and Mrs. Dempster, in her admirable presentation of the analogous material (*Sources and Analogues,* 341–56), wisely limits her selection to those versions of the fruit-tree story that represent the wronged husband as a blind man who recovers his sight through the intervention of supernatural bystanders or in answer to his own prayers.

Pope's retelling of the *Marchantes Tale,* entitled *January and May,* was published in Tonson's *Poetical Miscellanies* in 1709, when the poet was but twenty-one years old.

THE SQUIERES TALE

In the early editions of Chaucer, the Squire's Tale, which was usually placed after the Lawyer's and before

the Merchant's, was invariably introduced by the passage
which appears in Skeat's edition as prologue to the *Shipmannes Tale*. The '*Epilogue to the Marchantes Tale* and
the Squire's prologue were first printed by Tyrwhitt, in
his edition of the *Canterbury Tales* (1775–8). "I have
chosen," he says, "rather to follow the Mss. of the best
authority in placing *the Squier's Tale* after *the Marchant's,*
and in connecting them together by this Prologue, agree-
ably, as I am persuaded, to Chaucer's intention. The lines
which have usually been printed by way of Prologue to
the Squier's Tale, as I believe them to have been really
composed by Chaucer, though not intended for *the Squier's*
Prologue, I have prefixed to *the Shipman's Tale*." [91] Modern editors follow Tyrwhitt in placing the Squire's Tale
after the Merchant's, but the reader should observe that
there is no certain evidence that this arrangement was
what Chaucer intended.

The *Squieres Tale* breaks off before the poet has given
any real indication of the story he intended to develop.
It is, therefore, impossible to determine whether he was
building the tale upon some familiar plot or inventing
a romance of his own. Scholarship is no better able to
resolve this puzzling problem than it was a hundred and
fifty years ago, when Tyrwhitt wrote: "I have never been
able to discover the probable original of this tale, and yet
I should be very hardly brought to believe that the whole,
or even any considerable part of it, was Chaucer's invention." [92]

It can be shown, of course, that the magic elements
introduced into the tale are the stock-in-trade of many

[91] *Introd. Disc.,* xxiii.
[92] *Introd. Disc.,* xxiv.

writers, particularly in the Orient. Magic horses, mirrors, swords, and rings abound in the tales of the East, and they found their way quite naturally into many of the romances of mediæval Europe. An interesting study of these elements in the *Squieres Tale* is to be found in an essay by W. A. Clouston, appended to the Chaucer Society's volume containing the continuation of the Tale, written in the seventeenth century by John Lane.

Professor H. S. V. Jones (*Sources and Analogues,* 357–76) presents material more directly relevant to Chaucer's Tale: selections from the *Epistola Presbyterii Johannis* (ca. 1165) ; passages from a fourteenth-century poem in which a German writer, Osswalt, makes liberal use of this celebrated "letter" from the fabulous Prester John; and extracts from *Li Roumans de Cléomadès* of Adenès li Rois and from an Arabic story of the same cycle. These selections from works that illustrate possible influences upon Chaucer contain accounts of magic mirrors, rings, or horses. Professor Jones also prints a Hindu story and one from the *Arabian Nights* which relate love affairs of birds to the general theme of infidelity.

The "Tartre Cambinskan" himself is undoubtedly Jenghiz (or Chinghiz) Khan, the great Mongol emperor, who died in 1277, after a career of conquest that has seldom been equalled. Skeat endeavors to show that Chaucer's knowledge of Jenghiz Khan came to him from the Travels of Marco Polo, and that many descriptive details in the early part of the poem were derived from the account given, in that famous work, of Kublai Khan, the grandson of Jenghiz; but Professor Manly has shown that the theory is untenable.[93]

[93] *Publ. Mod. Lang. Assn.,* 11. 349–62.

Perhaps, as Professor Root has shrewdly argued, the *Squieres Tale* exercises a greater fascination over the imaginative mind, because it was left incomplete, than if it had been brought to a conclusion.[94] Certainly the two continuations which have been attempted are disappointing, although one of them is from the pen of a great poet. Spenser's treatment of the story, in the fourth book of the *Faerie Queene* (Cantos 2 and 3), neglects the very features which most excite our curiosity in Chaucer's fragmentary tale. John Lane's heavy-footed continuation of the story has been justly characterized by Skeat, as "bad almost beyond belief." John Lane was a friend of Milton's father, and if this family connection made it necessary for the young poet to listen to an author's reading of Lane's continuation of the *Squieres Tale,* it is not difficult to conjecture why Il Penseroso yearned to

> call up him that left half-told
> The story of Cambuscan bold,
> Of Camball, and of Algarsife,
> And who had Canace to wife,
> That owned the virtuous ring and glass,
> And of the wondrous horse of brass
> On which the Tartar king did ride.

THE FRANKELEYNS TALE

In the black-letter editions of the *Canterbury Tales,* the Squire's Tale is followed by the Merchant's, and the "wordes of the Frankelin to the Squier" are attributed to the Merchant, although this alteration involves the absurdity of ascribing a full-grown heir to the man who

[94] *The Poetry of Chaucer,* 267–69.

presently declares that he has been married but two
months. In the same editions, the Franklin's Tale is
placed immediately after the Clerk's. The arrangement
in Skeat's edition has the authority of the most reliable
manuscripts and may be accepted as Chaucerian. It seems
certain that the poet intended to connect the Franklin's
Tale with the Squire's by the "wordes" which stand in
Skeat's text at F 673–708.

There would seem to be every reason for accepting as
genuine the Franklin's statement that his story is based
upon a Breton lay. The scene is laid in Brittany, "nat fer
fro Penmark," i. e., Penmarch Point, a headland near
Quimper; and the sinister aspects of the rocky Breton
coast are presented with a sincerity and a simple melancholy which certainly suggest a native source.[95] The names
of the principal actors in the story, moreover, are undoubtedly of Celtic origin. Very much about the *Frankeleyns Tale,* including some features of its narrative structure, lends support to the narrator's statement that he is
retelling one of the lays made by "thise olde gentil Britons
in hir dayes."

Nevertheless, scholarship now regards this statement
with a certain scepticism; for investigation has failed to
disclose any evidence, other than the words of the Franklin himself, for the existence of a Breton lay which might
have been the source of Chaucer's story. To argue with
Skeat that the whole character of the story agrees well
with that of the Breton lays versified by Marie de France,
is hardly convincing; and Professor Schofield's elaborate
attempt to prove that the story originated in Wales, and

[95] Cf. J. S. P. Tatlock: *The Scene of the Franklin's Tale
Visited,* Chaucer Society, 1914.

was thence carried over into Brittany, rests almost entirely on conjecture.[96] In the absence of more convincing evidence, and in view of the fact that Chaucer's own statements about his sources are frequently misleading, it is certainly unsafe to accept the Franklin's words as proof that the poet had read the story of Dorigen and Arveragus in a Breton lay.

The one thing which has been thoroughly demonstrated by investigations into the problem of the sources of the Tale is the oriental origin of the three principal features of the plot. The rash vow of the lady who seeks to rid herself of an importunate suitor by promising to comply with his wishes in certain remote circumstances, the dilemma in which she finds herself when the conditions are unexpectedly fulfilled, and the subsequent contest in generosity are all to be found in certain ancient tales of the East. The earliest known story to utilize this plot material is found in a famous Sanskrit collection of fiction, the *Kathá Sarit Ságara*, "Ocean of the Rivers of Story." The story relates that the daughter of a wealthy merchant, fearing that an importunate lover may attempt to win her by force, promises to visit him upon her marriage night before she goes to her husband. When the time comes to fulfill her promise, she gains the consent of her husband and takes her way sorrowfully to the woods, where she has promised to meet her lover. On the way, she is captured by a robber; but she induces him to let her go, by telling him her story and promising to return as soon as she has kept her word to the other man. The lover, impressed by her faithfulness to her promise, dismisses her inviolate; and the robber, having heard that her lover has

[96] *Publ. Mod. Lang. Assn.,* 16. 405-49.

spared her, is not to be outdone in generosity, but sends
her back, with all her ornaments upon her, to her husband.
King Trivikramasena, to whom the story is related, gives
it as his opinion that the really generous man of the three
was the robber.

The full story may be found in the Chaucer Society's
volume of *Originals and Analogues* (291, ff.), together
with versions of the tale from the Persian, the Burmese,
the Hebrew, the Siberian, and the Turkish. A curious
feature of the history of the tale is the fact that a Gaelic
variant has been discovered in the West Highlands of
Scotland.

None of these versions, of course, was available to
Chaucer. The story must have reached him through some
European source, and it has been argued that he found
it in Boccaccio. A version which appears as the fifth tale
told on the tenth day in the *Decameron* may be epitomized
as follows:

Dianora, the wife of a very agreeable and wealthy man,
named Gilberto, has captured the fancy of a great and
noble lord called Ansaldo. Wearied with his importunities,
she at length promises to be at his service if he will provide her with a garden in the month of January "as full
of green herbs, flowers, and trees laden with fruit, as
though it were the month of May." Through the aid of a
magician, Ansaldo performs her commands. When
Dianora tells her husband of her predicament, he urges her
to fulfill her promise to Ansaldo, lest the latter bring
some mischief upon them through the art of the necro-
mancer. Ansaldo, however, perceiving her generosity and
her husband's, releases her from her promise. The magician likewise, "having observed Gilberto's generosity

to Ansaldo, and that of Ansaldo to the lady," refuses to accept pay for his services.

We cannot be sure that Chaucer knew the *Decameron* or that this version was in his mind as he wrote the *Frankeleyns Tale;* but an earlier telling of the story by the same author may have been known to him. In his long prose romance, the *Filocolo,* Boccaccio has presented the same story, more fully and with a few variations.[97] Scholars who are convinced that Chaucer was acquainted with the *Filocolo* naturally believe that this Italian version of the story had a profound influence upon the *Frankeleyns Tale,* if it was not the actual source.[98] The fact that both writers modify this ancient tale in much the same way may be taken to support the view that Chaucer was acquainted with the *Filocolo,* and one need not argue, as some scholars have, that they were both following some lost European version of the story. If the hypothesis of a lost original be once adopted, moreover, we are back where we started, and there is no valid objection to believing that the *Frankeleyns Tale* was derived, as its narrator says it was, from a Breton lay.

Chaucer's treatment of the ancient story is more elaborate than any other version that has been preserved. Although he agrees with Boccaccio in introducing a magician into the tale, he chooses a very different method of presenting the apparatus of the feat of magic upon which the plot is made to turn, and he surrounds the magician himself with an atmosphere of charlatanism which is prob-

[97] *Il Filocolo,* ed. Battaglia. Bari, 1938. Cf. *Sources and Analogues,* 377–83.
[98] Cf. Pio Rajna: *Le origini della novella narrata dal Frankeleyn, Romania,* 32. 204–67. Rajna's article is reviewed by Professor Lowes in *Modern Philology,* 15. 689–728.

ably his own peculiar contribution to the story.[99] Another addition of his own, in all probability, is the complaint of Dorigen (F 1342–1456). The virtuous women, whose examples she holds before herself in her sad plight, are all mentioned by St. Jerome in his *Contra Iovinianum*, the work which furnished so many suggestions for passages in the Prologue to the *Tale of the Wyf of Bathe*. Some lines in the discussion of "maistrie" in love, at the opening of the poem, are based upon lines in the *Roman de la Rose*.

The Seconde Nonnes Tale

A reference to the "Lyf of seynt Cecyle," in the earlier version of the Prologue to the *Legend of Good Women* (B-text, 426), puts it beyond question that the tale assigned to the Second Nun was in existence as early as 1385 or 1386, before the *Canterbury Tales* had been begun. It is usually dated shortly after 1373. The legend is inserted among the *Canterbury Tales* without any introduction from the Host or any indication of the narrator's identity, other than the rubric. The expression "unworthy sone of Eve," which the Nun most inappropriately applies to herself, has sometimes been cited as evidence that Chaucer did not originally intend the story for the person to whom it is assigned in the rubric; but the words occur in a passage which is obviously based, in part, upon the Marian antiphon, *Salve regina,* and they simply reflect the "filii Hevae" of the following lines:

[99] In the *Filocolo,* the magician is transported through the midnight air in a chariot drawn by dragons, and gathers the magic properties which he requires from many quarters of the globe.

Salve regina, mater misericordiae
Vita, dulcedo et spes nostra, salve.
Ad te clamamus exules filii Hevae,
Ad te suspiramus gementes et flentes in hac lacrimarum valle.

It is clear, however, that Chaucer did not give much care to the revision of this earlier work when he incorporated it in the *Canterbury Tales;* for he has allowed the line

Yet preye I yow that reden that I wryte

to stand unaltered, although the story, in its new setting, is supposed to be delivered orally.

There is every reason to believe, in fact, that the "Lyf of seynt Cecyle" was practically identical with the *Seconde Nonnes Tale.* The "Inuocacio ad Mariam" may very well be a later addition. Professor Carleton Brown has shown that it is woven together from material taken from widely scattered sources, and the skill with which this work has been done is certainly superior to anything to be found elsewhere in the poem.[100] It is to be said, however, that this superiority may be due simply to the fact that much of this invocation was derived from a nobler source than the rest of the poem. With the opening lines of the last canto of the *Divine Comedy* before him as a model, Chaucer could hardly have failed to write in nobler strain.

No such inspiration animated his labors upon the legend itself. The Saints' Lives, so popular in the Middle Ages, were written with great piety, to be sure, but they were seldom the work of men of genuine literary power. It is certain that Chaucer was following a Latin model as he wrote his life of St. Cecilia, and following it so closely

[100] *Modern Philology,* 9. 1–16.

that the poem may fairly be called a mere translation. It is unlikely that the actual text upon which his translation was based will ever be discovered, but it is clear that the first part of his Latin original closely resembled the corresponding portion of the story of St. Cecilia in the *Legenda Aurea*, a famous collection of saints' legends written by Jacobus Januensis, who was consecrated Archbishop of Genoa in 1292.[101] Beyond Line 358, or thereabouts, there is unmistakable evidence that Chaucer's original did not present the text of the Golden Legend as we now know it but much more closely resembled other Latin versions of the story which eventually found their way into print. The fifteenth-century scholar Mombritius, whose *Sanctuarium* was first printed about 1480, offers a text of the Legend of Saint Cecilia which probably approximates this portion of Chaucer's original more closely than any other we yet know.

Assuming that Mombritius gives us a fairly accurate representation of the text which Chaucer had before him, we may gain some idea of his treatment of his source-material by comparing Lines 468–528 of the *Seconde Nonnes Tale* with the passage from the *Sanctuarium* which is given in the appendix (cf. pp. 369, 370, below).

It is clear that Chaucer's translation represents a considerable abridgment of his original. In the passage under consideration, for example, he has dropped out one of St.

---

[101] Cf. the rubric before Line 85.

[102] Cf. F. Holthausen: *Zu Chancer's Cäcilien Legende*, in Herrig's *Archiv*, 87. 265–73. Professor Kölbing's article in *Englische Studien*, 1. 215–48, although important, is somewhat misleading. Translations from Simeon Metaphrastes, who was himself translating from earlier Latin versions, are sure to be far removed from the original which we are seeking.

Cecilia's speeches, with the result that Almachius takes her to task for evil spoken against his gods, although she has not yet mentioned them. It is possible, of course, that Chaucer's original also was defective at this point; but it seems more likely that the inconsistency was the result of a process of condensation which the poet followed throughout his translation.

It is to be noted that the position which St. Cecilia was to occupy, at a later era, as the patron saint of music, is faintly suggested by Lines 134–37. Professor Lowes has pointed out that the lilies and roses of the "corones two," which are brought by the angel to Cecilia and her husband, were commonly used in mediæval literature to symbolize virginity and martyrdom.[103]

The Chanouns Yemannes Tale

The connection between the Second Nun's Tale and the *Chanouns Yemannes Tale* is thoroughly established by the reference, in the opening line of the Yeoman's Prologue, to the "lyf of seint Cecyle." The lines which follow, moreover, make it clear that both stories belong toward the end of the collection, for they contain an allusion to "Boghton under Blee," now Boughton-under-Blean, which is but five miles from Canterbury. The Canon and his yeoman, having seen the pilgrims ride forth from their "hostelrye" at Ospringe, where the company passed its third night upon the journey, have ridden after them for a distance of five miles, while the Squire, the Franklin, and the Nun have been telling their tales.

"The introduction of *the Chanones Yeman* to tell a

[103] *Publ. Mod. Lang. Assn.*, 26. 315–23.

Tale," says Tyrwhitt, "at a time when so many of the original characters remain to be called upon, appears a little extraordinary. It should seem, that some sudden resentment had determined Chaucer to interrupt the regular course of his work, in order to insert a Satire against the Alchemists." TenBrink, going a step farther, speculated upon the possibility that Chaucer, toward the close of his life, was victimized by some alchemical swindler. Scholars have not generally accepted this rather alluring hypothesis; but it has recently been revived by Professor Manly, who suggests, rather as an amusing speculation than as a theory which he actually accepts, that Chaucer's borrowings from the exchequer and from Gilbert Maghfeld, during the last eight years of his life, may have been due to unsuccessful experiments with the "science" which he denounces so vehemently through the mouth of the Canon's Yeoman.[104]

The violence of this denunciation makes it hard to believe that Chaucer did not have some particular impostor in mind, even though he himself may not have been a victim. The fact that the alchemist in the second part of the *Chanouns Yemannes Tale*, as well as the pitiable swindler who actually appears among the Canterbury pilgrims, is a canon may be merely a dramatic device, by which the poet seeks to emphasize the bitterness of the yeoman's disillusionment with his master and his craft; but it certainly seems to indicate that the satire was directed against some particular

> chanoun of religioun
> Amonges us, wolde infecte al a toun.

[104] Cf. *Some New Light on Chaucer*, 235–52.

The elaborate apology to canons in general, for the slanderous remarks which the Yeoman passes upon one of their number, also suggests, as Professor Manly argues, that the poet had a particular black sheep in mind. Although it is hardly necessary to follow Professor Manly in his conjecture that the *Chanouns Yemannes Tale* "was originally composed, not for inclusion in the Canterbury series but to be read or recited to an audience which included some canons of the church," it seems highly probable that the story was inspired by the activities of some swindler in holy orders, and that Chaucer wrote with full consciousness that some of his readers would apply his satire to this specific case.

That there were alchemists conducting their experiments, during Chaucer's lifetime, in the neighborhood of the court, if not actually under royal sanction, has long been known. A recent discovery, published by H. G. Richardson in the *Transactions of the Royal Historical Society* for 1922 (38–40), has brought one of these alchemists to light. In the forty-seventh year of Edward III, one William de Brumley, "chaplain, lately dwelling with the Prior of Harmandsworth," arrested with four counterfeit pieces of gold upon him, confessed that he had made the metal alchemically, according to the teaching (*per doctrinam*) of William Shuchirch, canon of the King's Chapel at Windsor.

Unfortunately, we know nothing further, as yet, about this interesting canon. Whether he was still alive and still pursuing his studies in the "science" in 1390, when Geoffrey Chaucer, as clerk of the king's works, was charged with repairing the royal chapel at Windsor, it is impossible to say. If he was still conducting his experiments there at that time, it is more than likely that he was the original of Chaucer's canon, and that the satire of the *Chanouns Yemannes Tale* was directed against him. His "doctrina" was not without its dangers to his disciples in 1374, when William de Brumley got himself into difficulties by offering to sell his manufactured gold to the keeper of the king's money at the Tower; and it is possible that at a later date the alchemical experiments at the royal chapel at Windsor had grown to be something of a scandal. Giving rein to the imagination, one may picture Canon William Shuchirch slipping gradually away from respectability, led by the delusive promises of his science, until he came to be, at last, a lurker

> in hernes and in lanes blinde
> Wher-as thise robbours and thise theves by kinde
> Holden hir privee fereful residence,
> As they that dar nat shewen hir presence.

One may even amuse oneself, like Professor Manly, by guessing that Chaucer coöperated with the canon in the pursuit of Elixir and that bitter personal experience inspired the denunciation of the science in the *Chanouns Yemannes Tale*. Before entering too far upon these speculations, however, it were well to reflect upon the extraordinary power of dramatic characterization with which Chaucer was endowed. Such reflections, it seems to me, are far more likely to lead to a proper understanding of the poet's aims and purposes in writing the *Chanouns Yemannes Tale* than any attempt to trace a connection between Canon William Shuchirch and the loans which Chaucer negotiated at the exchequer and with Gilbert Maghfeld in his old age. Professor Manly himself comments upon the consummate art with which "names of the materials and implements of alchemy, technical terms for some of the processes, glimpses of unfortunate experiences in actual experiments, are all jumbled together . . . in order to produce a picture of an ignorant helper who has no clear understanding of the mysterious undertakings in which he has borne a part, and an impression of the wild irrationality of this pursuit of the impossible." The vividness and consistency of this portrait of the ignorant helper betoken the inspired artist rather than the disillusioned dupe, and the peculiar tartness of the satire against the alchemists finds its natural explanation in the desire of the poet to represent the emotions of the poor, bedevilled Yeoman, who pours out, before these sympathetic listeners in the Forest of Blean, the anger and bewilderment which have grown to intolerable dimensions within him during his years of service with the canon. Like the cynical confession of the Pardoner, the *Chanouns Yemannes Tale* may best be understood, not by indulging in conjectures about Chaucer's possible experiences with swindlers in holy orders, but by regarding it simply as a work of the creative imagination.

It is quite possible, on the other hand, that the poet's attention was drawn to the subject of alchemy by actual contact with some practitioner of the art or with some disillusioned victim. If it could be shown that Canon William Shuchirch was still pursuing his studies in alchemy in 1390, when Chaucer was superintending the repairs of the King's Chapel at Windsor, or that his researches had recently been interrupted by some scandalous exposure of his operations, we should hardly need to search farther for the "source" of the *Chanouns Yemannes Tale*. The poet must have been thrown into intimate contact with some of the canons of the Chapel Royal, and if one of the chapter had been conducting experiments in alchemy, the fact would certainly have reached his ears. A man of Chaucer's intellectual curiosity, endowed as he was with a rather unusual taste for science, could hardly have failed to take an interest in these pseudo-scientific researches going on in his immediate vicinity. Some hours spent with Canon Shuchirch would have supplied much of the knowledge which the poet displays of the technical processes of the alchemists and of the curious astrological lore which threw an atmosphere of mystical philosophy about their experiments. Although we cannot be sure, in the absence of further data about this interesting canon, that we have traced Chaucer's interest in alchemy to its source, the discovery of William Shuchirch may be said to lend greater probability to the assumption, which has long been made by scholars, that the *Chanouns Yemannes Tale* was founded upon personal knowledge rather than upon any written original.

Professor J. W. Spargo (*Sources and Analogues,* 685–98) discusses the present state of studies in fourteenth-century alchemy and offers material to illustrate mediaeval warnings against alchemy, tricks of alchemists, and sources and analogues of passages on the science.

Skeat is probably correct in his assertion (III. 492, 493), that the Yeoman's Prologue and Tale belong to the very latest period of Chaucer's work. "This is clear at once," he says, "from its originality, as well as from the metre, and the careless ease of the rhythm, which sometimes almost degenerates into slovenliness, as though our author had written some of it in hot haste, with the intention of revising it more carefully afterwards."

THE MAUNCIPLES TALE

Research has failed to discover the

> litel toun
> Which that y-cleped is Bob-up-and-doun,
> Under the Blee, in Caunterbury weye.

Possibly it survives as Harbledown, a village which stands a mile and a half to the west of Canterbury; or it may be that "Up-and-down Field," in the parish of Thannington, derives its name from Chaucer's "litel toun." In any case, it is clear that the pilgrims are drawing very close to Canterbury when the Host begins to "Iape and pleye" at the expense of the drunken cook. That Harry Bailly should call for a story from one who has already made his contribution is further evidence of the unsettled condition of Chaucer's plans for the *Canterbury Tales*. It may be, as Professor Root suggests, that the poet had not yet abandoned his original scheme, which called for more than one tale from each of the pilgrims.[105] It is possible, on the other hand, that he intended to cancel the Cook's Prologue and Tale of the first day's journey; or it may be that the Prologue to the Manciple's Tale had already been written when the idea of following the Reeve's Tale by one from the Cook occurred to him. The fragmentary condition of the *Cokes Tale* might be used as evidence to support any one of these three conjectures. TenBrink's sug-

[105] *The Poetry of Chaucer*, 283.

gestion that the Manciple's Prologue and Tale were intended for the return journey has not been accepted.

The tale presented by the Manciple, as a substitute for the incapacitated Cook, must certainly have reached Chaucer through Ovid. The story is to be found in the *Metamorphose*s, II. 534–632. The many interesting analogues included by W. A. Clouston in his essay on the Tale, in the Chaucer Society's volume of *Originals and Analogues* (437–80, 545, 546), show that the story of the tell-tale bird, originating in the Orient, enjoyed great popularity in the East and in Europe; but they cannot be regarded as having exercised any influence upon Chaucer's version.

Professor Work (*Sources and Analogues,* 699–722) prints the text of Ovid's story, together with other versions from poems of Chaucer's century: Gower's *Confessio Amantis* (III. 765–835), Guillaume de Machaut's *Le livre, du Voir dire,* the *Ovide Moralisé,* and *The Seven Sages of Rome.* He adds material analogous to the sententious passages in Chaucer's tale.

THE PERSONES TALE

The opening lines of the Parson's Prologue, as they stand in modern editions, would lead us to believe that the Manciple had taken an unconscionably long time to tell his brief fable of the tell-tale bird. If we may believe the statement of the Host (H 16), it was morning when the Cook was aroused from his drunken slumber and the Manciple volunteered to tell a tale in his stead; yet it is now four o'clock in the afternoon, and the tale is but just concluded. This inconsistency in the time-scheme lends support to Furnivall's theory that the word "maunciple," in the first line of the Parson's Prologue, was inserted by the scribes in a space left blank by the author. It is certain that the *Persones Tale* was intended to be the last in the collection,

> To knitte up al this feeste, and make an ende;

but it is by no means certain that the tale was intended to follow directly after the Manciple's. It is to be said, however, that Chaucer must have been aware that he was running short of material, and it is quite possible that he meant to spin out his last two stories as far as they would go. He was very, very far from the hopeful ambitions with which he began his account of the pilgrimage, crowding nearly 4000 lines of poetry into the first two hours or so of the morning, because he was still planning for some sixty tales upon the outward journey.

The immediate source of the *Persones Tale* has not been discovered; but it has been made clear that the ultimate source of the main body of the work was a Latin tract by St. Raymund of Pennaforte, a thirteenth-century Dominican, who became general of the order in 1238 and was penitentiary to Pope Gregory IX.[106] His *Summa Casuum Poenitentiae* was probably written as a manual for the guidance of priests, whose power over the consciences of their people had been increased when the fourth Lateran Council (1215–16) made auricular confession obligatory. A work of this sort, written by the Pope's own penitentiary

[106] Kate Petersen: *The Sources of the Parson's Tale*, Boston, 2001.

and supported by the prestige of an author whose *De-cretals* of Gregory IX had been prescribed by the Pope as the standard text-book in canon law at the universities of Bologna and Paris, must have enjoyed a wide circulation; and there is abundant evidence that it was well known in fourteenth-century England. In what form it reached Chaucer we have no means of knowing, but it is evident that some work based upon Raymund's *De Poenitentia* was before him as he wrote the *Persones Tale*. With the exception of the passage on the Seven Deadly Sins, the Tale follows very closely a tract from the third book of Raymund's work. The correspondence between the two texts begins, as Miss Petersen remarks, "with the first paragraph of the Parson's Tale and runs on pretty consecutively, with the exception of the break at the digression on sin . . . almost to the end of the Tale."

For this digression on sin, Miss Petersen has discovered an ultimate, though remote, source in the *Summa de Vitiis,* a work by another thirteenth-century Dominican, Guilielmus Peraldus. It is her conjecture that "Chaucer's original was a single treatise, consisting of a worked-over copy of the *De Poenitentia* into which had been fitted a similarly worked-over copy of the *Summa de Vitiis*." It is possible, of course, that it was Chaucer himself who fitted the two tracts together, but it seems more likely that the inartistic combination had already been made by some other hand. Mrs. Dempster (*Sources and Analogues,* 723–60) discusses the problem and presents extracts from St. Raymund, Peraldus, and other penitential manuals.

Miss Petersen's investigations have thoroughly disposed of Simon's Theory that the *Persones Tale* is filled with interpolations, made by some unscrupulous person, in the interests of orthodoxy.[107] This theory, which rested on the assumption that Chaucer was a Wycliffite, had already been undermined by the researches of Köppel, who showed that a number of passages from the *Persones Tale* appear in slightly modified form in other parts of the *Canterbury Tales*.[108] It is sufficiently clear that Chaucer could have had no quarrel with the orthodox piety of the thirteenth-century Dominicans, whose works represent the ultimate sources of the *Persones Tale*. Doubtless some Latin treatise, based upon their manuals for the confessor, had been in his possession for many years; and he seems to have been so familiar with its contents that he frequently drew pious sentiments from its pages, for use in sundry places in the Tales. It is possible that his own rendering of the treatise into English was in existence when the Tales were begun, but it seems more probable that the translation was made with the "povre persoun of a toun" particularly in view. Chaucer could hardly have found, in the whole field of mediæval writing, a work better suited to the character of the narrator, the conscientious parish priest, to whom the spiritual welfare of his people was a sacred trust. It was for just such churchmen as this that the manuals of Raymund and Peraldus were prepared.

While the shadows lengthen, along the road that leads down into Canterbury, Chaucer's pilgrims ride on in silence, while the honest Parson does his best to fill their minds with a consciousness of their own sin and with thoughts of divine mercy. Not all the members of that

[107] H. Simon: *Chaucer a Wicliffite,* in *Essays on Chaucer* (Chaucer Society), 227–92.
[108] Herrig's *Archiv,* 87. 33–54.

diverse company come to the shrine of the martyr "with ful devout corages"; but the poet who has travelled with them, as they have crossed the hills and valleys of human life, reaches the end of his journey with a sober spirit, very far removed from the boisterous mirth of the first morning of the pilgrimage, when the choleric Reeve took umbrage at the Miller's Tale, as the company passed within sight of the spires of Greenwich and Deptford. Surely, it is not strange that this mediæval poet, probably neither more nor less devout than most of his contemporaries, should have seen fit to conclude his great collection of tales with such a work as the Parson's sermon. Neither is it very strange, it seems to me, that the last words appended to the *Canterbury Tales* should be a penitential prayer for forgiveness for the "translacions and endytinges of worldly vanitees." The famous "retractation," with which the maker of the book takes leave of the reader, has frequently been attacked as a spurious addition to the text; but it has always had for me the look of a genuine expression of the poet's own feelings, as he drew near the end of his life and knew that he would write but little more, whether of "worldly vanitees" or of "moralitee and devocioun." To conclude his last great work in such a fashion was the natural act of the devout Catholic. A more fanatic piety, hardly content to "revoke" the offending works, would have committed the mad sin of consigning them to the flames; but Geoffrey Chaucer, who was better instructed in "what is bihovely and necessarie to verray parfit Penitence," let his account stand as he had written it, very sure that "the benigne grace of him that is king of kinges and preest over alle preestes" could strike a just balance between the evil and the good.

CHAPTER VI

CHAUCER'S LANGUAGE AND VERSIFICATION

TWO foreign languages were in common use in England, both for speech and for writing, during the lifetime of Geoffrey Chaucer. Latin was the language of the Church and of the learned, and as the recognized universal tongue, it was used in every variety of writing. The chronicles of the times, the controversial tracts of the theologians, and all manner of scientific treatises were written in Latin; and the works of the poets, as well as of the scholars, afford evidence that Latin was still a living language in Chaucer's England. A knowledge of French, which was the language of the court, utilized in all the intricate processes of government, from the procedure of the law-courts to the keeping of the king's household accounts, was a part of the education of a gentleman, up to so late a date as 1385; and French was as natural a vehicle for poetry, if it was written for the educated classes, as English itself. Chaucer's contemporary, John Gower, wrote his first long work, the *Mirour de l'omme,* in French; and he followed that by the *Vox Clamantis,* which was written in Latin. It is only surprising that Chaucer himself left behind him no works written in either of these languages.

It is to be said, however, that in using English as the vehicle of his poetry, Chaucer was following the tendency

339

of his age. Latin was losing ground in fourteenth-century England, its hold weakened by the Wycliffite translation of the Bible, and its vitality not yet renewed by the humanistic studies of the Renaissance. French, too, was on the decline. The Anglo-French of the Normans had already yielded place to "Frensh of Paris" as the language of those who wished to do better than counterfeit the "chere of court"; and by the end of the century, a knowledge of French was no longer a distinguishing mark of the gentleman. Trevisa records, "now, the yere of oure Lorde a thowsand thre hundred and foure score and fyve . . . in alle the gramere scoles of Engelond, children leveth Frensche and construeth and lerneth an Englische."[1] It is clear that conditions had materially altered since 1363, when Higden complained that "Children in scole, ayenst the vsage and manere of alle othere naciouns beeth compelled for to leue hire owne langage, and for to construe hir lessouns and here thynges in Frensche, and so they haueth seth the Normans come first into Engelond. Also gentil men children beeth i-taught to speke Frensche from the tyme that they beeth i-rokked in here cradel, and kunneth speke and playe with a childes broche. And vplondisshe men wil likne hym self to gentil men, and fondeth with greet besynesse for to speke Frensce, for to be i-tolde of."[2] That Gower, after writing his first two monumental works in French and Latin, should have thought it safe to entrust the fame of his third, the *Confessio Amantis,* to the language of his native land, is an indication that the vernacular had become the accepted

[1] Higden: *Polychronicon,* ed. Babington (Rolls Series) II. 161, Trevisa's note, 1385.

[2] *Polychronicon,* II. 158–60, Trevisa's translation.

literary language of England by the last decade of the fourteenth century.

English might not have been without this honor in its own country for so long a period if it had been a unified language, held within the fixed laws of grammar, pronunciation, and spelling which give it stability in all quarters of the world to-day. The native language of fourteenth-century England, derived from four dialects of Old English, was spoken and written very diversely in different parts of the land. In general, we recognize five distinct dialects in Middle English, as follows:

Southern {South-Western derived from O. E. West Saxon / South-Eastern derived from O. E. Kentish

Midland {East Midland / West Midland} derived from O. E. Mercian

Northern   derived from O. E. Northumbrian

No certain boundaries can be fixed, to define precisely what is meant by "Southern" or "Northern"; but in general, we may regard the Thames as the boundary between Southern and Midland, and the Humber as that between Midland and Northern.

The dialects of Middle English differed from one another in vocabulary, pronunciation, inflectional forms, and spelling; although in this last respect, tradition sometimes stepped in to make the written dialect less individualistic than the spoken. So divergent were the forms of English used in different sections of Chaucer's England, that it is safe to say that the poet would have had some difficulty in reading the work of certain of his contemporaries.

Only the East Midland dialect, which was the English of Chaucer, need concern us here. It should be said at once that this dialect, partly because it came to be the language of the metropolis, and partly because Chaucer, Gower, and Wycliffe employed it, gradually gained the supremacy. No one should suppose, however, that this was the standard English of the day, or that the use of other dialects betokened the illiterate. Educated and cultivated persons used the English that was being spoken or written about them, and each of the dialects of Middle English produced literary work of a very high order.

The English language of the fourteenth century, in short, was a vigorous and growing thing, as yet unconfined by artificial standardization. It follows that no authoritative word can be spoken on many matters connected with the language of Chaucer's England. For each author, something like a distinctive grammar must be written. A multitude of chances, connected with his birthplace, education, contact with men from other sections of England or from foreign lands, contributed to shape the language that he wrote; and when his work was done, it passed into the hands of scribes, whose personal habits in the use of language were sure to be reflected in the copies of the work which they prepared. Since many of the manuscripts of fourteenth-century works, which have come down to us, were written after the authors had died, and in a time when the language was undergoing yet further changes, it is not surprising that inconsistencies abound in the documents from which scholars must draw their data, and that conjecture must still play a part in much that is said, even about the usage of a poet whose works have been as thoroughly scrutinized as Chaucer's.

It is the object of this chapter to give the elementary student, in as brief a space as may be, the most essential facts about the pronunciation, spelling, inflections, and syntax of Chaucer's English, together with some brief comments upon his versification. The matter of his vocabulary is not included in this discussion, since no summary can give the student much assistance in mastering the wealth of Chaucer's language in this respect.

PRONUNCIATION

VOWELS [3]

Short *a* pronounced as in German *Mann* or French *patte*

Short *e* as in Modern English *fell*
Short *i* as in Modern English *fill*
Short *o* as in Modern English *folly*
Short *u* as in Modern English *full*

Long *a* as in Modern English *father*
Long *i* as in Modern English *machine*
Long *u* as in Modern English *crude*
Long open *o* as *oa* in Modern English *broad*
Long close *o* as *eau* in French *beau*
Long open *e* as *a* in Modern English *Mary*
Long close *e* as *é* in French *été*
Final unstressed *e* as *a* in Modern English *China*

[3] It should be understood that the sounds given as the equivalents of Chaucer's vowels and diphthongs are, in some cases, only approximate equivalents. Cf. Moore: *Historical Outlines of English Phonology and Morphology* (1925), 86, ff.

The quantity of the vowels in Chaucer's English can hardly be discussed, with any pretense at fullness or accuracy, without reference to the phonology of Old English and Old French. The following simple rules are stated, for the benefit of the novice, with the reservation that they are subject to many exceptions:

1. Middle English vowels are short when unstressed.

2. Middle English vowels are short before two consonants, except *-ld, -nd, -rd, -rth, -mb*.

3. Middle English vowels are long (except *i* and *u*) before a single consonant directly followed by a vowel.

4. Middle English short vowels, in monosyllables, are lengthened when a vowel is added in inflection or otherwise, unless the consonant is doubled at the same time.

The distinction between open *o* and close *o*, open *e* and close *e* was scrupulously observed by Chaucer in his rimes. The modern reader of his verse can most easily master the distinction by observing that:

1. Open *o* (pronounced as *oa* in *broad*) usually results in the modern spelling *oa, o,* or *oe*. E. g., *open, goon* (go), *so, holy, spoken, anon, brood* (broad), *foo* (foe).

2. Close *o* (pronounced as *eau* in French *beau*) usually results in the modern spelling *oo*. E. g., *rote* (root), *good, tooth, bokes* (books), *cook, dom* (doom). But observe: *sote, to, fredom, bord* (board).

3. Open *e* (pronounced as *a* in *Mary*) usually results in the modern spelling *e* or *ea*. E. g., *were, rede* (red), *breeth* (breath), *heeth* (heath), *speke* (speak), *bete* (beat), *mete* (meat), *teche* (teach), *del* (deal), *deef* (deaf).

4. Close *e* (pronounced as in French *été*) usually results in the modern spelling *ee,* or *ie*. E. g., *swete* (sweet), *sleepe* (sleep), *seeke* (seek), *meke* (meek), *grene* (green),

wepe (weep), *leue* (believe), *thef* (thief). Also *seke* (sick), which like *thef,* derives from Old English *eo.*

DIPHTHONGS

ai (*ay*), *ei* (*ey*) as *ay* in Modern English *way* (prolonged)
au (*aw*) as *ow* in Modern English *now*
oi (*oy*) as *oi* in Modern English *boil*
eu (*ew*) usually, as *u* in Modern English *mute.* In a few words (*dew, dronkelewe, fewe, hewen, lewed, rewe, shewen, shrewe, thewe*), as *e* in *met* plus *u* in *crude.*

CONSONANTS

Most of the consonants were pronounced in Chaucer's day much as at present; but the modern student will do well to pronounce them more distinctly, as he reads Chaucer aloud, than he is wont to do in this era of haste, when there is scarcely time to enunciate our words. The following matters, however, should be particularly borne in mind:

1. Every written consonant should be sounded distinctly. E. g., *gnawe, knight, wright, folk, palmers.*

2. Double consonants should be distinguished from single consonants in pronunciation (cf. *penknife* and *penny* in Modern English). E. g., *sonne* (sun) is pronounced *sun-ne; sone* (son) is pronounced *su-ne.*

3. The letter *r* is slightly trilled.

4. The letter *c* is pronounced as in *cat* except before *e* or *i,* where it is pronounced as in *city.*

5. The letter *g* is pronounced as in *go* except before *e* or *i,* where it is pronounced as in *age.*

6. *gh* has somewhat the sound of *ch* in Scotch *loch*.

7. *g* is silent before *n* after a long vowel.

8. *ng* is pronounced as in modern *linger*.

9. *ch* is pronounced as in modern *church;* *cch,* as *tch* in modern *catch*.

10. Initial *h* is frequently silent in French words and English pronouns.

11. Final *s* is always pronounced as *s* not *z*; final *f* is always pronounced as *f* not *v*. Initial *th* is pronounced as in Modern English *thin*.

SPELLING

The spelling of the Middle English poet was probably not so irrational as sometimes appears. The hands of a multitude of scribes, each incorporating his own orthographical peculiarities in the work which he undertook to copy, have frequently confused the spellings of the original, and it is not likely that even the author himself was entirely consistent; but the modern reader's difficulties are as likely to be caused by his ignorance of certain accepted mediæval practices as by the inconsistency either of the author or of the copyist. Some misunderstanding, at least, can be avoided by observing the following matters of orthography:

1. *i* and *y* as vowels are interchangeable. N.B. Skeat usually prints *i* when the vowel is short.

2. *u* and *v* are interchangeable.

3. Long *a, e,* and *o* are often spelled *aa, ee,* and *oo. This does not alter the pronunciation.*

4. *o* is the spelling for short *u* (pronounced as in Modern English *full*) when the letter precedes or follows *m*, *n*, or *u* (*v*). E. g., *sonne, y-ronne, sondry, come, companye, love*. (This usage was adopted to avoid confusion between letters which looked much alike as written by the mediæval scribe.)

5. *ou* (*ow*) is the regular spelling of long *u;* but in some French words the spelling *o* is sometimes found instead. E. g., *seson* for *sesoun.*

6. Final -*n* is often dropped in inflectional forms of the verb.

Inflection

Old English, in all its dialects, was an inflected language, though its system of inflection was very imperfect, if compared with that of Latin or of Greek. Throughout its early history, the language preserved its inflectional system without essential change; but from the twelfth century onward, simplification of declension and conjugation went on very rapidly all over England. The Danish and Norman conquests were not without their influence upon this process of simplification; but scholars now recognize the fact that the principal factors in the changes wrought were internal agencies, working to eliminate practical inconveniencies inherent in the very imperfect inflectional systems of the various Old English dialects. Inflection plays a part in the language which Chaucer wrote, but not a much more important part than in Modern English. His declension of substantives, for example, is as simple as our own.

NOUNS

The regular declension of nouns is as follows:

	Singular	Plural
Nom., Dat., Acc.	*knight*	*knightes*
Genitive	*knightes*	*knightes*

The ending *-es* is usually pronounced as a separate syllable; but in words of three or more syllables, the *e* may be silent. Monosyllabic nouns in *-s* usually remain unchanged in the plural; and proper nouns in *-s* do not take the genitive ending. Nouns of French origin often form their plurals in *-s* only. A few nouns show vowel-change in the plural; e. g., *goos, gees*.

A few survivals of Old English usage should be noted:

1. Nouns in *-er* denoting relationship sometimes remain uninflected in the genitive singular. E. g., *my fader soule; kynges brother sone*.

2. Nouns which belonged to the Old English weak declension appear sometimes without ending. E. g., *his lcdy grace; at the sonne up-riste*.

3. In certain phrases, consisting of a preposition immediately followed by a noun, the old dative ending *-e* is preserved. E. g., *of towne; on lyve; in lande; by kinde*.

4. Old English neuter nouns with long stems were not inflected in the plural. E. g., *his hors were gode; twenty yeer of age; sheep, neet, swyn*, etc.

5. Plurals in *-en* represent Old English forms which were gradually passing out of usage. E. g., *eyen, asshen*,

been (also *bees*), *foon* (also *foos*), *toon* (also *toos, toes*), *shoon* (also *shoos*).

ADJECTIVES

The forms of the two declensions of the adjective, the strong and the weak, are as follows:

	Strong Declension	Weak Declension
Singular	*good*	*goode*
Plural	*goode*	*goode*

The weak declension is used when the adjective is preceded by the definite article, by a demonstrative, by a possessive pronoun, or by a noun in the genitive case; when in agreement with a noun in the vocative; or when used before proper nouns (including the name of the Deity). E. g., *the yonge sonne; this ilke monk; hir gretteste ooth; Epicurus owne sone; now, dere lady; goode Arcite.*

The following exceptions should be noted:

1. Adjectives of two or more syllables, ending in a consonant are not usually inflected. E. g., *at mortal batailles.*

2. When the plural form of the adjective is used predicatively, it may remain uninflected. In such cases, the final *-e* may be written, though it is not pronounced. E. g., *Nat fully quike, ne fully dede they were; Of which thise ladyes were nat right glad.*

3. In the singular strong form, some relics of an Old English dative remain in certain phrases. E. g., *of evene lengthe.*

4. An Old English strong genitive plural survives in *aller, alder*. E. g., *hir aller cappe; our aller cost; alderbest*.

Adjectives are compared, as in Modern English, by adding *-er* and *-est* to the stem. Some adjectives also show vowel-change in comparison; e. g., *old, elder, eldest; long, lenger, lengest; strong, strenger, strengest*.

The following are irregular:

god	*bet*	*beste*
yvel	*wers*	*werste*
muchel	*mo (more)*	*moste*
litel (lite)	*lesse*	*leeste*
(far)	*fer*	*ferreste*
(neigh)	*neer*	*nexte*

The superlative, but not the comparative, of an adjective is inflected.

Adverbs are formed from adjective stems by the addition of *-ly* (as in Modern English) *-lich (liche)* or *-e*. E.g., *trewely, softe, roialliche*.

PERSONAL PRONOUNS

		First Person	Second Person
Sing.	Nom.	*I, ich, ik*	*thou*
	Gen.	*my, myn*	*thy, thyn*
	Dat.	*me*	*thee*
	Acc.	*me*	*thee*
Plur.	Nom.	*we*	*ye*
	Gen.	*oure*	*youre*
	Dat.	*us*	*you*
	Acc.	*us*	*you*

Third Person

		Masculine	Feminine	Neuter
Sing.	Nom.	*he*	*she*	*hit, it*
	Gen.	*his*	*hire*	*his*
	Dat.	*him*	*hire, hir*	
	Acc.	*him*	*hire, hir*	*hit, it*

All genders

Plur.	Nom.	*they*
	Gen.	*here, hir*
	Dat.	*hem*
	Acc.	*hem*

The possessives are the genitive forms of the personal pronouns. *Myn* and *thyn* drop the *-n* when they precede a substantive beginning with a consonant (except *h*).

The personal pronouns, usually augmented by the addition of *-self* (*-selven, -selve*), are used as reflexives.

INDEFINITE PRONOUNS

The indefinite *men*, "one," "some one," takes a singular verb. E. g., *Or if men smoot it with a yerde smerte.*

DEMONSTRATIVE PRONOUNS

1. *That;* plur. *tho.*
2. *This;* plur. *thise, these, thes* (all monosyllabic).
3. The definite article is often joined to its noun if the latter begins with a vowel. E. g., *thestat, tharray* (for *the estat, the array*). Cf. *thilke* (for *the ilke*).

4. The Old English neuter of the article is preserved in the expressions *that oon, that other*.

5. *At the* frequently becomes *atte*. E. g., *And wel we weren esed atte beste*.

INTERROGATIVE PRONOUNS

1. *Who, what;* gen. *whoos, whos;* dat. *whom;* acc. *whom, what*.

2. *Which;* plur. *whiche, which*.

3. *Whether, wher,* "which of the two?"

RELATIVE PRONOUNS

1. *That* is the usual relative pronoun. It is both singular and plural and is used for persons as well as for things.

2. *Which;* plur. *whiche, which*. Frequently preceded by *the* or followed by *that*.

3. *Whos,* used for the genitive; *whom,* used for the dative. The nominative form *who* does not occur as a relative.

STRONG VERBS

Past participle in *-en, -e*

	Indicative	Subjunctive
Pres. Sing. 1.	*find-e*	*find-e*
2.	*find-est*	*find-e*
3.	*find-eth, fint* (*fynt*)	*find-e*
Plur.	*find-e(n)*	*find-e(n)*

Pret. Sing.	1. *fond*	*found-e*
	2. *found-e, fond*	*found-e*
	3. *fond*	*found-e*

| Plur. | *found-e(n), fond(-e)* | *found-e(n)* |

Infinitive　　　*find-e(n)*

Imperative Sing.　　*find*
　　　　Plur.　　*find-eth find(-e)*

Present Participle　　*find-yng(e)*
Past Participle　　　*(y)found-e(n)*

1. The vowel is often dropped in the endings -*est*, -*eth*. E. g., *cometh, comth*.

2. -*t* is the contracted form of -(*d*)*deth*, -(*t*)*teth*. E. g., *slideth, slit; biddeth, bit; findeth, fint; meteth, met*.

3. -*st* is the contracted form of -*seth*. E. g., *riseth, rist*.

A distinguishing feature of the strong verb (as in Old or Modern English) is the vowel-change which takes place in the root in conjugation. It should be observed, however, that some weak verbs also show vowel-change (see below). There are seven classes of strong verbs, as follows:

Class I

Infin.	Pret. Sing.	Pret. Plur.	Past Part.
ryde	*rood*	*riden*	*riden*
wryte	*wroot*	*writen*	*writen*

Similarly: *abyde, agryse, byde, byte, dryve, glyde, ryve, ryse, shyne, shryve, slyde, smyte, stryke, stryve, thryve*.

Class II

Infin.   Pret. Sing.   Pret. Plur.   Past Part.

chese	*chees*	*chosen*	*chosen*
flee (flye)	*fleigh, fley*	*flowen*	*flowen*
shouve	*shoof*		*shoven*

Similarly: *flee* (to flee); *flete; lese* (past part. *loren, lorn*); *lye* (to tell lies); *shete* (past part. *shoten*); *brouke.* The tendency of strong verbs to assume forms of the weak conjugation appears in the preterit forms of: *cleve* (*clefte*); *lese* (*loste*); *crepe* (*crepte*); *flee* (*fledde*).

Class III

Infin.   Pret. Sing.   Pret. Plur.   Past Part.

helpe	*halp*	*holpen*	*holpen*
sterve	*starf*	*storven*	*storven*
fighte	*faught*	*foughten*	*foughten*

Similarly: *breste, delve, kerve, melte, swelle, thresshe, yelde, yelpe.*

winne	*wan*	*wonnen*	*wonnen*
(bi)ginne	*(bi)gan*	*(bi)gonnen*	*(bi)gonnen*

Similarly: *drinke, renne, shrinke, sinke, spinne, stinke, swimme, swinke.*

climbe	*clomb*	*clomben*	*clomben*
binde	*bond*	*bounden*	*bounden*
finde	*fond*	*founden*	*founden*
ringe	*rong*	*rongen*	*rongen*

Similarly: *grinde, winde, singe, springe, stinge, thringe, wringe*. To this class belongs *abreyde; pret. abrayd (abreyd)*.

Class IV

Infin.   Pret. Sing.   Pret. Plur.   Past Part.

bere	*bar (ber, beer)*	*beren*	*boren (born)*
come	*cam (coom)*	*camen*	*comen*
(neme)	*nam (nom)*		*nomen*
to-tere	*to-tar*		*to-toren (to-torn)*

Similarly: *breke, shere, speke, stele, trede, weve, wreke*.

Class V

Infin.   Pret. Sing.   Pret. Plur.   Past Part.

bidde	*bad*		*beden*
ete	*eet*	*eeten*	*eten*
lye	*lay*	*leyen*	*leyen (layen)*
yeve	*yaf*	*yeven (yaven)*	*yeven (yiven)*
(quethe)	*quoth (quod)*		

Similarly: *forgete; gete; steke* (pret. sing. *stak*); *weve* (pret. sing. *waf;* past part. *woven*); *sitte* (pret. sing. *sat, seet;* pret. plur. *seten*); *see* (pret. sing. *seigh, sey, say, sy, saugh, saw;* past part. *seyen, seyn*).

Class VI

Infin. Pret. Sing. Pret. Plur. Past Part.

Infin.	Pret. Sing.	Pret. Plur.	Past Part.
shake	*shook*	*shooken*	*shaken*
drawe	*drow*		*drawen*
stonde	*stood*	*stooden*	*stonden*
laughe	*lough*	*lowen (loughen)*	*laughen*
sle	*slow (slough)*		*slawen (slayn)*
waxe	*wex*	*wexen*	*woxen*

Similarly: *awake* (pret. sing. also *awaked*); *bake; fare* (has weak pret. sing. *ferde*); *forsake; gnawe* (pret. sing. *gnow*); *grave; shape; shave; take; wake; wasshe* (pret. sing. *wessh*); *heve* (pret. sing. *heef, haf*); *swere* (pret. sing. *swoor;* past part. *sworen, sworn*).

Class VII

The verbs of this class originally had reduplicated preterit tense-stems. Many of them, which had assumed weak forms during the Old English or Middle English period show both strong and weak forms in Chaucer.

Infin. Pret. Sing. Pret. Plur. Past Part.

Infin.	Pret. Sing.	Pret. Plur.	Past Part.
lete	*let*		*leten*
slepe	*sleep*	*slepen*	*slepen (slept)*
wepe	*weep (wepte)*		*wepen (wept)*

Similarly: *lepe, bete.*

knowe	*knew*		*knowen*

Similarly: *blowe, crowe, growe, sowe, throwe.*

falle	fel (fil)	fellen (fillen)	fallen
holde	heeld	helden	holden
honge	heng		wk. honged
hote	het (hight)		hoten

WEAK VERBS

Past Participle in -ed, -d

The weak verb is conjugated in two ways: Class I with the preterit in -de or -te; Class II with the preterit in -ede or -ed. Some grammarians reverse this classification.

Class I

	Indicative		Subjunctive
Pres. Sing.	1.	her-e	her-e
	2.	her-est	her-e
	3.	her-eth	her-e
Plur.		her-e(n)	her-e(n)
Pret. Sing.	1.	her-de	her-de
	2.	her-dest	her-de
	3.	her-de	her-de
Plur.		her-de(n)	her-de(n)
Infinitive:		her-e(n)	
Imper. Sing.		her (-e)	
Plur.		her-eth, her-e	
Pres. Part.		her-ynge	
Past Part.		(y)her-d	

1. The -d becomes -t in the preterit and past participle after *f, p, s, t.* E. g., *grete, grette; kepe, kepte; kisse, kiste; leven, lafte.*

2. *-de, -d* becomes *-te, -t* after *l, n.* E. g., *fele, felte; dwelle, dwelte; mene, mente; brenne, brente.*

3. In the past participle, *-tt* is written *-t;* and *-ldd, -ndd, -rdd* become *-lt, -nt, -rt.* E. g., *girde, girt(e); bilde, bilt(e); wende, went(e).*

Vowel-change occurs in the conjugation of some verbs of this class. Some change *e* to *a* in the preterit and past participle. E. g., *drede, dradde; lede, ladde; leve, lafte; rede* (to advise), *radde; reve, rafte; sprede, spradde. Clothe* has both *clothed* and *cladde, clad.*

Some verbs of this class show consonantal irregularities as well as vowel-change. E. g., *begge (bye), boghte (boughte); bringe, broghte (broughte); cacche, caughte; drenche, dreynte; fecche, fette* (also *fetched); leye* (to lay), *leyde; recche* (to care), *roghte; reche* (to reach), *raughte; seke, soghte (soughte); selle, solde; seye, seyde; shryke, shrighte; strecche, straughte; teche, taughte; telle, tolde; thenke* (to think), *thoghte (thoughte); thinke* (to seem), *thoughte; werche, wroghte (wroughte).*

Class II

		Indicative	Subjunctive
Pres. Sing.	1.	*lov-e*	*lov-e*
	2.	*lov-est*	*lov-e*
	3.	*lov-eth*	*lov-e*
Plur.		*lov-e(n)*	*lov-e(n)*

Pret. Sing.	1. *lov-ede*	*lov-ede*
	2. *lov-edest*	*lov-ede*
	3. *lov-ede*	*lov-ede*
Plur.	*lov-ed(en)*	*lov-ed(en)*

Infinitive: *lov-e(n)*

| Imper. Sing. | *lov-e* | Pres. Part. *lov-ynge* |
| Plur. | *lov-eth, lov-e* | Past Part. *(y)lov-ed* |

Past tenses in which the full form *-ede* is used are rare. E. g., *axed, folwed, loked,* etc., omitting the second *e;* *answerde, made, pleyde,* etc., omitting the first *e.*

Nearly all verbs of French origin belong to this class. E. g., *passe, passed (paste), passed (past)* ; *rome, romed; conveye, conveyed; graunte, graunted; suffise, suffised; honoure, honoured; punysshe, punysshed.*

Preteritive-Present and Irregular Verbs [4]

1. *am, art, is;* plur. *ben (be, beth, aren, are, arn).* Pret. sing. *was, were, was;* plur. *weren (were, wer).* Pres. subj. *be;* plur. *been (be).* Pret. subj. *were;* plur. *were(n).* Imper. *be;* plur. *beeth (be).* Infin. *been (ben, be).* Part. *beynge; ben (be).*

2. *can, canst, can;* plur. *conne (connen, can).* Pret. *couthe, coude.* Pres. subj. *conne;* plur. *conne(n).* Infin. *conne.* Past Part. *coud, couth.*

3. *dar, darst, dar;* plur. *dar (dorren).* Pret. *dorste (durste).*

[4] The preteritive-present verbs (*can, dar, may, moot, ow, shal, thar, wot*) have forms for the present indicative which show no ending in the first and third person singular, because they were originally preterit forms of strong verbs.

4. *may, mayst, may;* plur. *mowe(n).* Pret. *mighte.* Pres. subj. *mow(e).* Infin. *mowen.*

5. *moot (mot), most, moot (mot);* plur. *mote(n).* Pret. *moste.* Pres. subj. *mote (moot, mot).*

6. *ow(?), owest, oweth;* plur. *owen.* Pret. *oghte (oughte).*

7. *shal, shalt shal;* plur. *shullen (shuln, shul, shal).* Pret. *sholde (shulde).*

8. *thar* (impersonal). Pret. *thurfte* (impersonal).

9. *wol (wil), wolt (wilt), wol (wole, wil);* plur. *wollen (woln, wole, wol, willen).* Pret. *wolde.* Subj. *wile (wolle).* Past Part. *wold.*

10. *wot, wost, wot;* plur. *wite(n).* Pret. *wiste.* Pres. subj. *wite.* Infin. *witen (wite, weten).* Past Part. *wist.*

11. *have, hast, hath;* plur. *haven (have, han).* Pret. *hadde (hade).* Infin. *haven (have, han).* Past Part. *had.*

12. *do, doost, dooth (doth);* plur. *doon (don).* Pret. *dide* (weak). Pres. subj. *do;* plur. *doon (don).* Imper. *do;* plur. *dooth (doth).* Infin. *doon (don).* Part. *doynge; doon (don).*

13. *go, goost, goth;* plur. *goon (gon, go).* Imper. *go;* plur. *gooth.* Infin. *goon (gon, go).* Part. *goinge; goon (gon, go).* Preterit tense supplied by *yede* or *wente.*

NEGATIVE FORMS

nam for *ne am; nart* for *ne art; nis* for *ne is; nas* for *ne was; nere* for *ne were; nadde* for *ne hadde; nadstow* for *ne haddest thou; nath* for *ne hath; nil* for *ne wil; niltow* for *ne wilt thou; nolde* for *ne wolde; noot* for *ne woot; niste* for *ne wiste.*

SYNTAX

Since the syntax of Chaucer's English was for the most part that of the language as we use it to-day, it will be necessary to comment only upon a few matters in which the poet's usage differs from our own.

1. The subject of a verb is frequently omitted, particularly with the impersonal construction. E. g., *Bifel that in that seson,* etc.

2. A pronoun is frequently used to repeat the subject. E. g.,

> *That* fro the tyme that he first bigan
> To ryden out, *he* loved chivalrye.

3. The partitive genitive should be recognized in such an expression as, *Of smale houndes* had she.

4. The dative is often used with the impersonal verb. E. g., *Me* thinketh it acordaunt to resoun.

5. The adjective is used as a substantive without the article. E. g., But al with *riche* and sellers of vitaille.

6. The article is omitted in stating a general idea. E. g., But she was som-del deef, and *that was scathe.* Cf. *swifte as fowel* in flight.

7. The personal pronoun is used reflexively. E. g., he shoop *him* for to swinke.

8. The demonstrative is very frequently used with a proper noun. E. g., *This Nicholas* sat gaping ever up-righte.

9. *That* is used as a double relative, meaning *that which.* E. g., He kepte *that* he wan in pestilence.

10. The verb agrees with the predicate, not the subject, in such a phrase as "It *am* nat I."

11. *Ther* is frequently used as if it were a relative and should then be translated *where*.

12. More than one negative may be used. E. g.,

> He *never* yet *no* vileinye *ne* sayde
> In al his lyf, un-to *no* maner wight.

13. The student should observe that the subjunctive is used very freely in Chaucer's poetry and should not fail to appreciate the fact that it usually implies condition, hypothesis, or concession. Occasionally, the subjunctive is used merely to denote a temporal relation. E. g.,

> And shame it is, if a preest *take* keep
> Ful looth *were* him to cursen for his tythes
> And though that he *were* worthy, he was wys.

VERSIFICATION

Long before the age of Chaucer, English poetry had outlived the day when the old alliterative line, without definite measure and without rime, was its only metrical vehicle. To be sure, two of the most important poems produced during the fourteenth century, *Piers the Plowman* and *Gawayne and the Grene Knight,* were written in alliterative verse; but the use of the ancient meter in these poems was a part of a revival of poetry in the West-Midland, where the native form of an earlier day had probably survived, through oral tradition, if not in writing, while the poets of southern England had been developing new forms and experimenting with new ornaments. Rime, which originated with the monastic writers of Latin religious verse, had passed over into French; and from French poetry, written at a time when every educated Englishman was bilingual, it had naturally found its way into England. In English poetry, as in French and Latin, the art of riming was developed rapidly and with an elaboration which was to be expected in the golden age of craftsmanship. The poets of the later Middle Ages not only employed rime, both final and internal, but they showed the greatest ingenuity in devising complex stanza-forms, which laid their rimes down in the most complicated patterns. Even the mystery plays, written for popular production in the guild cycles, were frequently cast in elaborate stanza-forms.

Chaucer himself delighted to play with rime, if not with rhythm. A dozen different metrical patterns, not to be found in English poetry before his day, are utilized in the poems which have come down to us;[5] and it is probable that some of the lost works of his youth represented experiments with other forms which he did not use again. Of the verse forms most commonly utilized by his contemporaries, he made comparatively little use. We have no work of his written in the alliterative verse, and the "ballad-meter" of the rimed romance he used only for purposes of burlesque, in the *Rime of Sir Thopas*. The octosyllabics, which had been in use in England for more than a century and which Gower employed in his *Confessio Amantis,* Chaucer utilized only for the *Book of the Duchesse,* the *Hous of Fame,* and his translation of the *Roman de la Rose.* His other metrical forms, if not actually his own invention, were certainly molded to the perfection which he gave them without much assistance from native models.

[5] The metrical forms used by Chaucer in his shorter poems are described in Chapter III, above.

His most significant contributions to English prosody are the seven-line stanza of the *Troilus* and the so-called Heroic Couplet. Both are written in decasyllabic verse, with the stress falling normally on the second, fourth, sixth, eighth, and tenth syllables:

> Of which' vertu' engen'dred is' the flour'.

As in modern poetry, the line is varied by the shifting of the accent, to break the monotony of a succession of lines of equal length all stressed exactly alike. The student will find no great difficulty in determining where the stress should fall; but the following matters should be noted:

1. The unaccented first syllable is frequently omitted. E. g.,

> Twen'ty bo'kes, clad' in blak' or reed'.

2. In a number of words, the accent is variable and sometimes falls on a later syllable than in the corresponding word in Modern English. E. g., *answérde, forhéed, gladnésse,* etc.;

> But si'kerly' she hadd'(e) a fair' forheed'.

3. In words of French origin, the accent is usually on a syllable nearer the end than in the corresponding word in Modern English. E. g., *vertú, natúre, honóur, pitée, manére, contrárie, acceptáble, advócat,* etc.;

> So prik'eth hem' natur'(e) in hir' corag'es
> Trouth'(e) and honour', fre'dom and cur'teisy'e

Sometimes, however, the accent is thrown farther back, as in Modern English. E. g.,

In hon'our dett'(e)lees, but' he wer'e wood'.

4. The ending *-i-oun* (Modern English *-ion*) is dis-syllabic, with a secondary accent upon *-oun*. E. g.,

> To tel'le yow' al' the condi'cioun'.

In Chaucer's verse, there is always a slight pause (cæsura) in the middle of the line, naturally indicated by the sense of the passage. This divides the line into two parts, each of which contains at least one stressed syllable. In a great majority of Chaucer's verses, there are either two or three stressed syllables before the cæsura.

An unstressed final *-e, -es, -ed, -en, -er* at the end of a line adds an eleventh syllable to the ten-syllable line and makes a "feminine ending." *The extra syllable should always be pronounced.* E. g.,

> Hath' in the Ram' his hal'fe cours' yron'ne
> To ri'den out' he lov'ed chi'valry'e.

An extra syllable is also frequently to be found before the cæsura. It should usually be pronounced, but a final unstressed *-e* before the cæsura was elided according to the rules for elision given below. Some authorities hold that *all* unstressed syllables before the cæsura should be sounded clearly. They should certainly be given full syllabic value when the pause is decidedly marked. E. g.,

> Whan they' wer(e) won'ne; and in' the Gret'e See'.

ELISION

1. Except at the end of a line or before the cæsura, final unstressed *-e* is usually elided (a) before a vowel;

(b) before French words beginning with silent *h*; (c) before pronouns with unemphatic *h* (*he, his, him, her, hir*); (d) before *heer* and *how*. The *-e* is frequently elided in a number of words in common use, such as *were, hadde, sholde. Thise* is always monosyllabic. E. g.,

> The droght'(e) of Mar'ch(e) hath per'ced to' the rot'e
> Of smal' coral' about'(e) hir arm' she bar'
> That hem' hath hol'pen whan' that they' wer(e) sek'e.

2. If an unstressed *e* occurs in two consecutive syllables, one of them will invariably lose its syllabic value (syncope). E. g., fether; plur. feth(e)res. Accordingly, *evere, nevere, owene, everich* are pronounced *evre, nevre, owne, evrich*. Note that in these words a final unstressed *-e* will be elided, as above, and that a three-syllable word may thus be reduced to a monosyllable.

3. A medial *-e-* is usually elided in weak syllables, such as *er, el, en, ed,* etc., if these syllables are followed by a vowel. E. g.,

> And ov'(e)r-al, ther' as prof'it shold'(e) arys'e.

4. Final vowels, other than unstressed *-e,* are sometimes elided before a word beginning with a vowel. E. g.,

> S(o) estat'ly was' he of' his gov'ernaun'ce.

The *e* of the definite article is frequently elided according to this rule.

5. The vowel *i* (*y*) is frequently blended with a following vowel. Thus *specially* has but three syllables in the line

> And spe'cially' from ev'(e)ry shir'es end'e.

6. Final *e* is sometimes lost before words beginning with a consonant (apocope). E. g.,

> Ther as' he wist'(e) to han' a good' pitaun'ce.

7. The following unusual contractions should be noticed:

(a) *This is* should usually be pronounced as one word.

(b) *Whether* is usually monosyllabic; i.e., *whe'r*.

(c) *Benedicite* sometimes has its full five syllables but is usually pronounced *ben'cite* (three syllables).

(d) *Caunterbury* is sometimes contracted into three syllables, by elision of the second *u*.

(e) The -*e* in *ne* is sometimes elided before a consonant at the beginning of a line. E. g.,

> I n(e) saugh' this yeer' so mer'y a com'pany'e

It should be understood that what has here been said about elision and accentuation in the decasyllabic line applies also to the shorter lines in Chaucer's poetry. Any remarks upon Chaucer's versification, moreover, should conclude with a reminder that every great poet is a law unto himself.

APPENDIX

The Life of Saint Cecilia

The following passage is taken from the *Sanctuarium* of Boninus Mombritius (Paris, 1910, I. 340, lines 38, ff.) It should be compared with the *Seconde Nonnes Tale,* Lines 468–528.

Almachius dixit: Infelix ignoras quoniam interficiendi et uiuificandi mihi ab inuictissimis principibus potestas data est? Et quid cum tanta superbia loqueris? Caecilia respondit: Aliud est esse superbum; aliud est esse constantem. Ego constanter locuta sum non superbe, quia superbiam et nos fortiter execramur. Tu autem, si uerum audire non times, iterum docebo te falsissime nunc locutum. Almachius dixit: Quae sum falsissime prosecutus? Caecilia respondit: Hoc quod principes tuos uiuificandi et interficiendi tibi tradidisse asseris potestatem. Almachius dixit: Ergo mentitus sum? Caecilia respondit: Contra ueritatem publicam, si iubes, probo te esse mentitum. Almachius dixit: Doce. Caecilia respondit: Dixisti principes tuos uiuificandi et interficiendi tibi copiam tribuisse, cum solam mortificandi scias tibi traditam potestatem; uitam enim uiuentibus tollere potes mortuis autem dare non potes. Dic ergo: quia Imperatores tui mortis te ministrum esse uoluerunt. Nam si quid plus dixeris, uideberis frustra mentitus. Almachius dixit: Depone iam audaciam tuam; et sacrifica diis. Caecilia respondit: Nescio ubi tu oculos amiseris. Nam quos tu deos dicis, ego et omnes qui oculos sanos habent saxa uidemus esse et aerementum et plumbum. Almachius dixit: Meas iniurias phylosophando comtempsi, sed deorum ferre non possum. Caecilia respondit: Ex quo os aperuisti, non fuit sermo quem non probauerim iniustum stultum et uanum. Sed nequit deesse: etiam exterioribus oculis te cecatum ostendi. Cum quod omnes lapides uidemus esse et saxum inutile, hoc tu deum esse testaris. Do, si iubes, consilium: mitte manum tuam et tangendo disce hoc saxum esse, si uidendo non nosti. Nefas est enim, ut totus populus de te risum habeat. Omnes enim sciunt deum esse in caelis. Istas autem figuras saxeas per ignem melius in calcem posse conuerti, quae modo sui otio pereunt, ut neque tibi pereunti neque sibi ne in ignem mittantur poterunt subuenire. Tunc iratus uaehementer Almachius iussit eam domum suam reduci et in sua domo flammis balnearibus concremari. Cumque fuisset in calore balnei sui inclusa, subter incendia nimia lignorum pabula ministrarent, die integro et tota nocte quasi in loco frigido illibata perstitit sanitate; ita ut nec una pars membrorum eius saltem sudoris signo labasset. Quod cum audisset Almachius, misit qui eam ibidem in ipsis balneis decollaret. Quam spiculator tertio percussit, et caput eius amputare non potuit.

Professor Gerould, in his judicious study of the Second Nun's Prologue and Tale (*Sources and Analogues,* 664–84), prints the text of the *De Sancta Cecilia* from the *Legenda Aurea,* as well as the full text of the *Passio S. Caeciliae* from Mombritius. He conjectures that Chaucer may have used "a text of the *Legenda aurea* much fuller in its later course than the one we know."

BIBLIOGRAPHY

EDITIONS

The Canterbury Tales of Chaucer. Edited by Thomas Tyrwhitt. London 1775–78; five volumes. Of great historical importance, as the first serious attempt to restore Chaucer's text.

The Complete Works of Geoffrey Chaucer. Edited by W. W. Skeat. Oxford, 1894; six volumes. The *Oxford Chaucer.* A seventh volume, published in 1897, contains many of the works formerly attributed to Chaucer. The fullest edition of the Works extant, but not a definitive edition.

The Student's Chaucer. Edited by W. W. Skeat. New York and London, 1895; one volume. The text of the *Oxford Chaucer,* with glossary and brief introduction.

The Works of Geoffrey Chaucer. Edited by A. W. Pollard, H. F. Heath, M. H. Liddell, and W. S. McCormick, London, 1898; one volume. The *Globe Chaucer.* Not to be preferred to the one-volume edition by Skeat.

The Complete Works of Geoffrey Chaucer. Edited by F. N. Robinson. Cambridge, Mass., 1933; one volume. *The Cambridge Chaucer.* An invaluable work of scholarship, with very full notes and complete glossary.

The Kelmscott Chaucer. "Edited by F. S. Ellis, ornamented with pictures designed by Sir Edward Burne-Jones, and engraved on wood by W. H. Hooper. Printed by me William Morris at the Kelmscott Press, Upper Mall, Hammersmith, in the County of Middlesex. Finished on the 8th day of May, 1896." The most celebrated modern edition of the poet.

The Book of Troilus and Criseyde by Geoffrey Chaucer. Edited by R. K. Root, Princeton, 1926. The definitive text, edited from all the known manuscripts.

The Text of the Canterbury Tales. Studied on the basis of all known manuscripts. By J. M. Manly and Edith Rickert, with a chapter on illuminations by Margaret Rickert. Chicago, 1940; eight volumes. A magnificent monument of scholarship.

Canterbury Tales. Edited by J. M. Manly. New York, 1928. Valuable introduction and notes. Expurgated text.

BOOKS OF REFERENCE

Chaucer, A Bibliographical Manual. By E. P. Hammond. New York, 1908. Indispensable.

A Bibliography of Chaucer, 1908–1924. By D. D. Griffith. Seattle, 1926. A necessary supplement to Miss Hammond's Manual.

A Chaucer Bibliography, 1925–1933. By W. E. Martin, Jr. Durham, N. C., 1935. Continues Mr. Griffith's work.

Publications of the Chaucer Society. London, 1868, ff. Listed in Hammond, *op. cit.,* 523–41, and in Griffith, *op. cit.,* passim. Of particular importance are the society's publications of manuscript texts.

A Manual of Writings in Middle English, 1050–1400. By J. E. Wells. New Haven, 1916. This work, with the eight supplements issued, 1918–1941, is the authoritative bibliography of mediaeval English literature.

The Year's Work in English Studies, edited for the English Association and published by the Oxford University Press, 1921, ff., contains critical reviews, from year to year, of books and articles on Chaucer. See also the *Annual Bibliography of English Language and Literature* of the Modern Humanities Research Association, 1920, ff., and the "American Bibliography" published annually in the *Publications of the Modern Language Association.*

A Concordance to the Complete Works of Geoffrey Chaucer

and to the Romaunt of the Rose. By J. S. P. Tatlock and H. G. Kennedy. Washington, 1927.

Chaucers Sprache und Verskunst. By B. Ten Brink. Third edition, revised by Eckhardt. Leipzig, 1920. Translation of the second edition entitled *The Language and Metre of Chaucer,* by M. Bentinck Smith. London, 1901. Still a standard work.

Index of Proper Names and Subjects to Chaucer's Canterbury Tales. By H. Corson. New York, 1911. Also indexes comparisons and similes, metaphors, proverbs, maxims, etc., in the *Canterbury Tales.*

Five Hundred Years of Chaucer Criticism and Allusion, 1357–1900. By C. F. E. Spurgeon. Issued in seven parts by the Chaucer Society, 1914–18. Cambridge, 1925.

Chaucer devant la Critique en Angleterre et en France. By C. F. E. Spurgeon. Paris, 1911. A study based on the material gathered by the author for the work cited above.

Historical Outlines of English Phonology and Morphology. By S. Moore. Ann Arbor, 1919. Revised edition, 1925. Designed for use in courses in Chaucer, Middle English, and the history of the language.

BIOGRAPHICAL

Life-Records of Chaucer. Issued in four parts by the Chaucer Society, 1875–1900. The documents relating to Chaucer, with "Forewords" in Part IV by R. E. G. Kirk, summarizing the evidence. These records form the only adequate basis for a study of the life of Chaucer. Material which has come to light since 1900 is noted in the bibliographical manuals listed above.

Index to the Life-Records. By E. P. Kuhl. *Modern Philology,* 10. 527–52 (1913).

The Ancestry of Chaucer. By A. A. Kern. Baltimore, 1906. An authoritative study, based on the documents.

Chaucer's Official Life. By J. R. Hulbert. Menasha, Wisc.,

1912. Indispensable for an understanding of Chaucer's career at court.

The Life of Chaucer. By Sir Nicholas Harris Nicolas. Prefixed to the *Aldine Chaucer,* London, 1845. Of historical importance, as the earliest biography of Chaucer drawn up on sound scholarly principles.

Chaucer. By A. W. Ward. In the English Men of Letters Series. London and New York, 1909. A conservative study.

Geoffroy Chaucer. By E. Legouis. Paris, 1910. The best French study of Chaucer and his poetry. Translation by L. Lailavoix. London, 1913.

Geoffrey Chaucer of England. By Marchette Chute. New York, 1946. A study of Chaucer, primarily biographical, which presents a great deal of learning in highly readable fashion.

The Portraits of Chaucer. By M. H. Spielman. Chaucer Society, 1900.

The article on Chaucer in the *Dictionary of National Biography* by J. W. Hales, and that in the *Encyclopedia Brittanica* (11th edition) by A. W. Pollard, are somewhat disappointing.

FAMOUS CHAUCER STUDIES

F. J. Child: *Observations on the Language of Chaucer.* Published in the *Memoirs of the American Academy,* 1863. This paper may be said to mark the beginning of modern Chaucerian scholarship.

James Russell Lowell: *My Study Windows.* Boston, 1871. Includes an essay on Chaucer first published in the *North American Review,* July 1870.

Bernhard Ten Brink: *Chaucer: Studien zur Geschichte seiner Entwicklung und zur Chronologie seiner Schriften.* Münster, 1870. An epoch-making work, in which the poetry of Chaucer was for the first time brought into definite relation to the influences at work upon the poet.

F. J. Furnivall: *Temporary Preface to the Chaucer Society's*

Six-Text Edition of Chaucer's Canterbury Tales. London, 1868. *Trial Forewords to my Parallel-Text Edition of Chaucer's Minor Poems.* London, 1871. The very titles of these two works reflect the scientific spirit and the modesty of this great scholar, for many years the guiding spirit of the Chaucer Society.

T. R. Lounsbury: *Studies in Chaucer.* New York, 1892. A book rich with the vitality of a vigorous mind. The chapter on the "Learning of Chaucer" is still of the first importance.

Chaucer and his Poetry. By G. L. Kittredge. Harvard University Press, 1915. As important as it is interesting.

Some New Light on Chaucer. By J. M. Manly. New York, 1926. A stimulating adventure in Chaucerian scholarship.

GENERAL STUDIES

English Writers. By Henry Morley. London, 1887, ff. Vol. V contains a discussion of Chaucer, with summaries of his works.

Chaucer. By G. Saintsbury. In the Cambridge History of English Literature, Vol. II. New York, 1908.

The Poetry of Chaucer. By R. K. Root. Boston, 1906. Revised Edition, 1922.

Untersuchungen zu Chaucer. By V. Langhans. Halle, 1919. Individualistic.

A Commentary on the Poetry of Chaucer and Spenser. By A. A. Jack, Glasgow, 1920.

The Chaucer Tradition. By A. Brusendorff. London, 1925. Not a book for the beginner.

Chaucer. By John Masefield. New York, 1931. Another laureate pays his tribute to Chaucer in a lecture delivered at Cambridge, March 2, 1931.

The Art of Geoffrey Chaucer. By J. L. Lowes. London, 1931.

Chaucer. By G. K. Chesterton. London, 1932. An illuminating and provocative study by a Catholic layman.

Geoffrey Chaucer and the Development of his Genius. By J. L.

Lowes. Boston, 1934. Lectures delivered at Swarthmore College in 1932.

On Rereading Chaucer. By H. R. Patch. Cambridge, Mass., 1939. Contains, among other thoughtful studies, a valuable essay on Troilus and Determinism.

The Living Chaucer. By P. V. D. Shelly. Philadelphia, 1940.

The Chaucer Canon. By W. W. Skeat. Oxford, 1900.

The Chronology of Chaucer's Writings. By J. Koch. Chaucer Society, 1890.

The Development and Chronology of Chaucer's Works. By J. S. P. Tatlock. Chaucer Society, 1907. A very valuable work, although some of Professor Tatlock's conclusions have not been accepted.

Étude sur G. Chaucer considéré comme Imitateur des Trouvères. By E. C. Sandras. Paris, 1859. A pioneer work, which overemphasizes the influence of French literature upon Chaucer.

Chaucer and the Roman de la Rose. By D. S. Fansler. New York, 1914.

The Indebtedness of Chaucer's Works to the Italian Works of Boccaccio. By H. M. Cummings. Menasha, 1916.

Chaucer and the Liturgy. By Karl Young. *Modern Language Notes*, 30. 97–99 (1915).

Chaucer and the Hours of the Blessed Virgin. By Carleton Brown. *Modern Language Notes*, 30. 231–32 (1915).

Chaucer and Dante. By J. L. Lowes. *Modern Philology*, 14. 705–35 (1917).

Chaucer and the Consolation of Philosophy of Boethius. By B. L. Jefferson. Princeton, 1917.

Chaucer and the Rhetoricians. By J. M. Manly. Warton Lecture on English Poetry. *Proceedings of the British Academy*. London, 1926.

Chaucer and the Roman Poets. By E. F. Shannon. Cambridge, Mass., 1929.

Chaucer, ses modèles, ses sources, sa religion. By C. Looten. Lille, 1931.

Dramatic Irony in Chaucer. By Germaine Dempster. Stanford University Press, 1932.

The Education of Chaucer. By G. A. Plimpton. London, 1935. Manuscript material, presented photographically to illustrate the poet's reading from his earliest days.

Courtly Love in Chaucer and Gower. By W. G. Dodd. Boston, 1913.

Chaucer and the Mediaeval Sciences. By W. C. Curry. London and New York, 1926.

Chaucer's Use of Proverbs. By B. J. Whiting. Cambridge, Mass., 1934.

Chaucer and the Custom of Oral Delivery. By Ruth Crosby. *Speculum,* 13. 413–32 (1938).

Chaucer's Romance Vocabulary. By Joseph Mersand. New York, 1939.

Chaucer's Art in Relation to his Audience. By B. H. Bronson. *University of California Publications in English.* 8. 1–53 (1940).

Chaucer and Music of the Fourteenth Century. By C. C. Olson. *Speculum,* 16. 64–91 (1941).

ON THE LESSER WORKS

Mediaeval Rhetoric in the Book of the Duchesse. By B. S. Harrison. *Publications of the Modern Language Association,* 49. 428–42 (1934).

Chaucer's Book of the Duchess and Two of Granson's Complaints. By H. Braddy. *Modern Language Notes,* 52. 487–91 (1937).

The Sources of Chaucer's Parlement of Foules. By W. E. Farnham. *Publications of the Modern Language Association,* 32. 492–518 (1917).

The Contending Lovers. By W. E. Farnham. *Publications of the Modern Language Association,* 35. 247–323 (1920).

The Parlement of Foules in Its Relation to Contemporary Events. By H. Braddy. In *Three Chaucer Studies.* New York, 1932.

In Appreciation of Chaucer's Parlement of Foules. By B. H. Bronson. *University of California Publications in English,* 3. 193–224 (1935).

A Note on Chaucer's Adam. By E. P. Kuhl. *Modern Language Notes,* 29. 263–64 (1914).

Publication before Printing. By R. K. Root. *Publications of the Modern Language Association,* 28. 417–31 (1913).

Chaucer's 'Lac of Stedfastnesse.' By L. H. Holt. *Journal of English and Germanic Philology,* 6. 419–31 (1907).

The Date of Chaucer's Lak of Stedfastnesse. By H. Braddy. *Journal of English and Germanic Philology,* 36. 481–90 (1937).

Henry Scogan. By G. L. Kittredge. *Harvard Studies,* 1. 109–17 (1892).

John (Henry) Scogan. By W. E. Farnham. *Modern Language Review,* 16. 120–28 (1921).

Chaucer's Envoy to Bukton. By G. L. Kittredge. *Modern Language Notes,* 24. 14–15 (1909).

Oton de Granson et ses Poesies. By A. Piaget. *Romania,* 19. 237–59, 403–48 (1890).

Chaucers Boethiusübersetzung: Ein Beitrag zur Bestimmung der Chronologie seiner Werke. By J. Koch. *Anglia,* 46. 1–51 (1922).

Chaucer's Boethius and Jean de Meun. By J. L. Lowes. *Romanic Review,* 8. 383–400 (1917).

Studies in Chaucer's Hous of Fame. By W. O. Sypherd. Chaucer Society, 1907.

The Hous of Fame and the Corbaccio. By M. L. Brown. *Modern Language Notes,* 32. 411–15 (1917).

Chaucer's Hous of Fame: Another Hypothesis. By Bertrand

H. Bronson. *University of California Publications in English*, 3. 171–92 (1934).

Chaucer's "The House of Fame." By P. F. Baum. *Journal of English Literary History*, 8. 248–56 (1941).

The Problem of the Two Prologues of Chaucer's Legend of Good Women. By J. C. French. Baltimore, 1905.

The Prologue to the Legend of Good Women. By J. L. Lowes. *Publications of the Modern Language Association*, 19. 593–683; 20. 749–864 (1904–05).

The Prologue to Chaucer's Legend of Good Women in Relation to Queen Anne and Richard. By S. Moore. *Modern Language Review*, 7. 488–93 (1912).

The Two Prologues to the Legend of Good Women: A New Test. By J. L. Lowes. Kittredge Anniversary Papers. Boston, 1913.

The Text of Chaucer's Legend of Good Women. By E. F. Amy. Princeton, 1918.

Vincent of Beauvais and Chaucer's Cleopatra and Croesus. By W. K. Wimsatt. *Speculum*, 12. 375–81 (1937).

Chaucer's Legend of Cleopatra and the Speculum Historiale. By Pauline Aiken. *Speculum*, 13. 232–36 (1938).

On the Date of Chaucer's Astrolabe. By S. Moore. *Modern Philology*, 10. 203–5 (1912).

ON THE TROILUS AND CRISEYDE

Observations on the Language of Chaucer's Troilus. By G. L. Kittredge. Chaucer Society, 1891.

The Indebtedness of Chaucer's Troilus to Benoit's Roman. By J. W. Broatch. *Journal of English and Germanic Philology*, 2. 14–28 (1898).

The Indebtedness of Chaucer's Troilus and Criseyde to Guido delle Colonne's Historia Trojana. By G. L. Hamilton. New York, 1903.

The Origin and Development of the Story of Troilus and Criseyde. By Karl Young. Chaucer Society, 1908.

The Date of Chaucer's Troilus and Criseyde. By J. L. Lowes. *Publications of the Modern Language Association*, 23. 285–306 (1908).

The Date of Chaucer's Troilus and other Chaucer Matters. By G. L. Kittredge. Chaucer Society, 1909.

The Textual Tradition of Chaucer's Troilus. By R. K. Root. Chaucer Society, 1916.

Chaucer's Lollius. By G. L. Kittredge. *Harvard Studies in Classical Philology*, 28. 47–134 (1917).

The Troilus-Cressida Story from Chaucer to Shakespeare. By H. E. Rollins. *Publications of the Modern Language Association*, 32. 383–429 (1917).

The Epilog of Chaucer's Troilus. By J. S. P. Tatlock. *Modern Philology*, 18. 625–59 (1921).

Chaucer's Renunciation of Love in Troilus. By Karl Young. *Modern Language Notes*, 40. 270–76 (1925).

Defense of Criseyde. By J. S. Graydon. *Publications of the Modern Language Association*, 44. 141–77 (1929).

The Story of Troilus as Told by Benoit de Sainte-Maure, Giovanni Boccaccio, Geoffrey Chaucer, and Robert Henryson. Translations and introduction by R. K. Gordon. London, 1934.

Character and Action in the Case of Criseyde. By A. Mizener. *Publications of the Modern Language Association*, 54. 65–81 (1939).

Chaucer's Troilus: A Study in Courtly Love. By W. A. Kirby. University, La., 1940.

The Troilus and Christian Love. By J. L. Shanley. *Journal of English Literary History*, 6. 271–81 (1939).

Chaucer's Troilus and Criseyde as Romance. By Karl Young. *Publications of the Modern Language Association*, 53. 38–63 (1938).

The People in Chaucer's Troilus. By J. S. P. Tatlock. *Publi-*

cations of the Modern Language Association, 56. 85–104 (1941).

The Dual Time-Scheme in Chaucer's Troilus. By H. W. Sams. *Modern Language Notes,* 56. 94–100 (1941).

On the Canterbury Tales

The Manuscripts of Chaucer's Canterbury Tales. By Sir William McCormick. Oxford, 1933.

The Sources and Analogues of Chaucer's Canterbury Tales. General editors, W. F. Bryan and G. Dempster. Chicago, 1941. Source material, so far as it can be identified, for all the Tales and the Prologue, presented in the original language with marginal summaries in English. Supersedes the Chaucer Society's *Originals and Analogues.* Indispensable.

The Plan of the Canterbury Tales. By Karl Young. *Kittredge Anniversary Papers.* Boston, 1913.

Boccaccio and the Plan of Chaucer's Canterbury Tales. By J. S. P. Tatlock. *Anglia,* 37. 69–117 (1913).

Observations on the Shifting Positions of Groups G and DE in the Manuscripts of the Canterbury Tales. By C. R. Kase. In *Three Chaucer Studies.* New York. 1932.

The Canterbury Tales in 1400. By J. S. P. Tatlock in *Publications of the Modern Language Association,* 50. 100–39 (1935).

Author's Revision in the Canterbury Tales. By Carleton Brown. *Publications of the Modern Language Association,* 57. 29–50 (1942).

Manly's Conception of the Early History of the Canterbury Tales. By G. Dempster. *Publications of the Modern Language Association,* 61. 379–415 (1946).

The Duration of the Canterbury Pilgrimage. By J. S. P. Tatlock. *Publications of the Modern Language Association,* 21. 478–85 (1906).

The Historical Background of Chaucer's Knight. By A. S. Cook. *Transactions of the Connecticut Academy,* 20. 166–238 (1916).

Beginning the Board in Prussia. By A. S. Cook. *Journal of English and Germanic Philology.* 14. 375–88 (1915).

Chaucer's Nuns and Other Essays. By Sister Mary Madaleva. New York, 1925.

Roger de Ware, Cook. By E. D. Lyon. *Modern Language Notes,* 52. 491–94 (1937).

Chaucer's Shipman in Real Life. By Margaret Galway in *Modern Language Review,* 34. 497–514 (1939).

Chaucer's Plowman and the Contemporary English Peasant. By G. Stillwell. *Journal of English Literary History,* 6. 285–90 (1939).

The Summoner's Malady. By Pauline Aiken. *Studies in Philology,* 33. 40–44 (1936).

The Apparitor and Chaucer's Summoner. By L. A. Haselmayer. *Speculum,* 12. 43–57 (1937).

Elements of Realism in the Knight's Tale. By S. Robertson. *Journal of English and Germanic Philology.* 14. 226–55 (1915).

Active Arcite, Contemplative Palamon. By H. N. Fairchild. *Journal of English and Germanic Philology,* 26. 285–93 (1927).

Old English Verse in Chaucer. By S. Robertson. *Modern Language Notes,* 42. 234–36 (1928). Knight's Tale, 2602, ff.

What Was Chaucer's Aim in the Knight's Tale? By J. R. Hulbert. *Studies in Philology,* 26. 375–85 (1929).

Arcite's Illness and Vincent of Beauvais. By Pauline Aiken. *Publications of the Modern Language Association,* 51. 361–69 (1936).

The Date and Revision of Chaucer's Knight's Tale. By J. Parr. *Publications of the Modern Language Association,* 60. 307–24 (1945).

Chaucer and the Decameron. By R. K. Root. *Englische Studien,* 44. 1–7 (1911). Concerning Chaucer's apology for the Miller's Tale.

Chaucer's Miller's Tale. By A. J. Barnouw. *Modern Language Review,* 7. 145–48 (1912).

The Portraits of Chaucer's Fabliaux. By L. A. Haselmayer. *Review of English Studies,* 14. 310–14 (1938).

The Reeve's Tale. A Comparative Study of Chaucer's Narrative Art. By W. M. Hart. *Publications of the Modern Language Association,* 23. 1–44 (1908).

On the Source of the Reeve's Tale. By Germaine Dempster. *Journal of English and Germanic Philology,* 29. 473–88 (1930).

The Man of Law's Head-Link and the Prologue of the Canterbury Tales. By Carleton Brown. *Studies in Philology,* 34. 8–35 (1937).

The Bearings of the Shipman's Prologue. By F. Tupper. *Journal of English and Germanic Philology,* 33. 352–71 (1934).

Chaucer's Shipman's Tale and Sercambi. By R. A. Pratt. *Modern Language Notes,* 55. 142–45 (1940).

A Study of the Miracle of Our Lady Told by Chaucer's Prioress. By Carleton Brown. Chaucer Society, 1910.

Miracles of Our Lady in Middle English Poetry. By R. W. Tryon. *Publications of the Modern Language Association,* 38. 308–88 (1923).

Chaucer's Prioress' Tale: An Early Analogue. By A. C. Friend. *Publications of the Modern Language Association,* 51. 621–25 (1936).

Stanza-Forms of Sir Thopas. By J. M. Manly. *Modern Philology,* 8. 141–44 (1910).

The Arming of Sir Thopas. By I. Linn. *Modern Language Notes,* 51. 300–11 (1936).

Satire in Sir Thopas. By W. W. Lawrence. *Publications of the Modern Language Association,* 50. 81–91 (1935).

The Tale of Melibeus. By W. W. Lawrence. *Essays and Studies in Honor of Carleton Brown,* 100–110 (1940).

The Source of Chaucer's Melibeus. By J. P. Severs. *Publications of the Modern Language Association,* 50. 92–99 (1935).

Chaucer's Metrical Prose. By P. F. Baum, *Journal of English and Germanic Philology,* 45. 38–42 (1946).

Chaucer's Monk. By J. S. P. Tatlock. *Modern Language Notes,* 55. 350–54 (1940).

Vincent of Beauvais and Chaucer's Monk's Tale. By P. Aiken. *Speculum,* 17. 56–68 (1942).

The Story of Ugolino in Dante and Chaucer. By T. Spencer. *Speculum,* 9. 295–301 (1934).

Chaucer's Monk and Nun's Priest. By S. B. Hemingway. *Modern Language Notes,* 31. 479–83 (1916).

Vincent of Beauvais and Dame Pertelote's Knowledge of Medicine. By Pauline Aiken. *Speculum,* 10. 281-87 (1935).

The Position of Group C in the Canterbury Tales. By S. Moore. *Publications of the Modern Language Association,* 30. 116–23 (1915).

Death and Old Age in the Pardoner's Tale. By M. P. Hamilton. *Studies in Philology,* 36. 571–76 (1939).

The Credentials of Chaucer's Pardoner. By M. P. Hamilton. *Journal of English and Germanic Philology,* 40. 48–72 (1941).

Chaucer's Discussion of Marriage. By G. L. Kittredge. *Modern Philology,* 9. 435–67 (1912).

Further Notes on the Marriage Group in the Canterbury Tales. By J. S. Kenyon. *Journal of English and Germanic Philology,* 15. 282–88 (1916).

The Evolution of the Canterbury "Marriage Group." By Carleton Brown. *Publications of the Modern Language Association,* 48. 1041–59 (1933).

The Marriage Debate in the Canterbury Tales. By C. P. Lyons. *English Literary History,* 2. 252–62 (1935).

A Conjecture on the Wife of Bath's Prologue. By R. F. Jones. *Journal of English and Germanic Philology,* 24. 512–47 (1925).

The Prologue of the Wife of Bath's Tale. By W. E. Mead. *Publications of the Modern Language Association,* 16. 388–404 (1901).

The Marital Dilemma in the Wife of Bath's Tale. By M.

Schlauck. *Publications of the Modern Language Association,* 61. 416–30 (1946).

The Devil and the Advocate. By A. Taylor. *Publications of the Modern Language Association,* 36. 35–59 (1921).

Chaucer's Clerk's Tale and a French Version of the Original. By A. S. Cook. *Romanic Review,* 8. 210–26 (1917).

Chaucer's Clerk's Tale. By W. E. Farnham. *Modern Language Notes,* 33. 193–203 (1918). An argument for Chaucer's use of Boccaccio as well as of Petrarch.

The Clerk of Oxenford. By H. S. V. Jones. *Publications of the Modern Language Association.* 27. 106–15 (1912).

Chaucer's Merchant's Tale. By J. S. P. Tatlock. *Modern Philology,* 33. 367–81 (1936).

The Squire's Tale and the Land of Prester John. By J. L. Lowes. *Washington University Studies,* I. Part II. 1–18 (1913).

Some Observations upon the Squire's Tale. By H. S. V. Jones. *Publications of the Modern Language Association,* 20. 346–59 (1905). A source study.

The Oriental Origin of Chaucer's Canacee-Falcon Episode. By H. Braddy. *Modern Language Review,* 31. 11–19 (1936).

Chaucer's Franklin's Tale. By W. H. Schofield. *Publications of the Modern Language Association,* 16. 405–49 (1901). An argument for a Celtic source of the Tale.

The Franklin's Tale, the Teseide, and the Filocolo. By J. L. Lowes. *Modern Philology,* 15. 689–728 (1918).

Chaucer's Second Nun. By N. E. Eliason. *Modern Language Quarterly,* 3. 9–16 (1942).

The Canon's Yeoman's Prologue and Tale. By G. L. Kittredge. *Transactions of the Royal Society of Literature,* 30. 87–95 (1910).

Chaucer's Retractions. By J. S. P. Tatlock. *Publications of the Modern Language Association,* 28. 521–29 (1913).

Some Mediaeval Manuals of Religious Instruction in England

and Observations on Chaucer's Parson's Tale. By H. G. Pfander. *Journal of English and Germanic Philology,* 35. 243–58 (1936).

Chaucer's Sermon and Retractions. By J. A. Work. *Modern Language Notes,* 47. 257–59 (1932).

MEDIAEVAL LIFE AND THOUGHT

Adams, G. B. *Civilization During the Middle Ages.* Revised edition, New York, 1922.

Adams, H. *Mont Saint Michel and Chartres.* Boston and New York, 1913.

Baldwin, C. S. *Medieval Rhetoric and Poetic.* New York, 1928.

Bennett, H. S. *Life on the English Manor.* Cambridge, 1938.

Boissonnade, P. *Life and Work in Medieval Europe.* Translated by Eileen Power. New York, 1927.

Capes, W. W. *The English Church in the Fourteenth and Fifteenth Centuries.* London, 1920.

Chadwick, D. *Social Life in the Days of Piers Plowman.* Cambridge, 1922.

Chambers, E. K. *The Mediaeval Stage.* Oxford, 1903.

Coulton, G. G. *Chaucer and his England.* Fifth edition, London, 1930.

Coulton, G. G. *The Medieval Village.* Cambridge, 1925.

Coulton, G. G. *Medieval Panorama.* Cambridge, 1938.

Cutts, E. L. *Parish Priests and Their People in the Middle Ages in England.* London, 1898.

Cutts, E. L. *Scenes and Characters of the Middle Ages.* Seventh edition. London, 1930.

Davis, H. W. C. *Mediaeval England.* Oxford, 1924. A new edition of Barnard's Companion to English History, which deals with nearly every phase of mediaeval life.

Faral, E. *Les Arts Poetiques du XIIIe Siecle.* Paris, 1924.

Funk-Brentano, Frantz. *The Middle Ages*. Translated from the French by E. O'Neill. New York, 1923.

Gasquet, Cardinal F. A. *The Black Death of 1348 and 1349*. London, 1908.

Gasquet, Cardinal F. A. *Monastic Life in the Middle Ages*. London, 1922.

Gerould, G. H. *Saints' Legends*. Boston and New York, 1916.

Gilson, E. *The Spirit of Mediaeval Philosophy*. New York, 1940.

Hartley, D. *Mediaeval Costume and Life*. With introduction and notes by F. M. Kelly. London, 1931.

Haskins, C. H. *The Rise of the Universities*. New York, 1923.

Haskins, C. H. *Studies in the History of Mediaeval Science*. Cambridge, Mass., 1924. Second edition, 1927.

Hearnshaw, F. J. C. *Mediaeval Contributions to Modern Civilization*. Lectures delivered at King's College, University of London, edited by Hearnshaw. London, 1921.

Heath, S. H. *Pilgrim Life in the Middle Ages*. London, 1911

Hepple, R. G. *Medieval Education in England*. London, 1932

Hibbard, L. A. *Mediaeval Romance in England*. Oxford, 1924.

Hopkins, A. J. *Alchemy, Child of Greek Philosophy*. New York, 1934.

Hughes, D. *Illustrations of Chaucer's England*. London, 1918. An historical source-book.

Huizinga, J. *The Waning of the Middle Ages*. London, 1937.

Jessopp, A. *The Coming of the Friars and Other Historic Essays*. London, 1922.

Jusserand, J. J. *English Wayfaring Life in the Middle Ages*. Translated by L. Toulmin Smith. Third edition, London, 1925.

Ker, W. P. *Essays on Mediaeval Literature*. London, 1905.

Ker, W. P. *Form and Style in Poetry*. London, 1928.

Leach, A. F. *The Schools of Medieval England*. New York, 1915.

Lewis, C. S. *The Allegory of Love: A Study In Medieval Tradition.* Oxford, 1936. Of the first importance.

Neilson, W. A. *Origins and Sources of the Court of Love.* Harvard Studies, Vol. VI.

Owst, G. R. *Literature and Pulpit in Medieval England.* Cambridge, 1933.

Painter, S. *French Chivalry.* Baltimore, 1940.

Pendrill, C. *London Life in the Fourteenth Century.* London, 1925.

Pendrill, C. *Wanderings in Medieval London.* New York, 1928.

Pirenne, H. *Economic and Social History of Medieval Europe.* Translated from the French by I. E. Clegg. New York, 1937.

Porter, A. Kingsley. *Mediaeval Architecture.* New Haven, 1912.

Power, E. *Medieval English Nunneries.* Cambridge, 1922.

Power, E. *Medieval People.* London, Fifth edition, 1932.

Power, E. *The Wool Trade in English Medieval History.* London, 1941.

Salzman, L. F. *English Industries of the Middle Ages.* Oxford, 1923.

Salzman, L. F. *English Trade in the Middle Ages.* Oxford, 1931.

Stuart, D. M. *Men and Women of Plantagenet England.* New York, 1932.

Taylor, H. O. *The Mediaeval Mind.* London, 1927.

Thompson, J. W. *The Medieval Library.* Chicago, 1939.

Thompson, J. W. *Reference Studies in Mediaeval History.* Chicago, 1923. Bibliographical.

Thorndike, L. *A History of Magic and Experimental Science During the First Thirteen Centuries of Our Era.* New York, 1923–41.

Trevelyan, G. M. *England in the Age of Wycliffe*. Fourth edition, London, 1929. First published in 1899.

Tupper, F. *Types of Society in Medieval Literature*. New York, 1926.

Vickers, K. H. *England in the Later Middle Ages*. London, 1926.

Ward, H. S. *The Canterbury Pilgrimages*. London, 1927. First published in 1904.

Watt, F. *Canterbury Pilgrims and Their Ways*. London, 1917.

Wedel, T. O. *The Mediaeval Attitude Toward Astrology*. New Haven, 1920.

Whitmore, Sister M. Ernestine. *Mediaeval English Domestic Life and Amusements in the Works of Chaucer*. Washington, 1937.

CHRONOLOGICAL TABLES

Life of Chaucer

1340? Born.

1357 In the service of the Countess of Ulster.

1359–60 Military service in France.

        Captured by the French and subsequently ransomed.

ca 1366 Married Philippa (Roet?).

1367 Yeoman in the king's household.

        Granted an annuity by Edward III.

1369 Second campaign in France (?).

1370 First diplomatic service abroad.

1372–73 First journey to Italy (Genoa and Florence).

1374 Pension from John of Gaunt.

        Daily pitcher of wine from Edward III.

        Appointed controller of custom and subsidy of wools, etc.

        Leases house over Aldgate.

1375 Appointed guardian of Edmund Staplegate and of the heir of John Solys.

1377 On diplomatic service in France.

        Annuities and appointments confirmed by Richard II.

1378 On diplomatic service in France.

        Second journey to Italy (Milan).

1382 Appointed controller of petty custom.

1385 Allowed to appoint permanent deputy in his office as controller.

        Takes up a residence in Kent (Greenwich?).

        Justice of the Peace for the county of Kent.

1386 Knight of the Shire for Kent in the parliament of 1386.
   Surrenders lease on house over Aldgate.
   Surrenders positions in the customs.
1387 Death of Philippa Chaucer.
1388 Transfers annuity.
1389 Appointed clerk of the king's works at Westminster,
   etc.
1390 On a commission to survey the banks of the Thames.
   Directed to repair St. George's Chapel, Windsor.
   Robbed by highwaymen.
1390–91 Appointed sub-forester of North Petherton Park.
1391 Surrenders clerkship of the works.
1394 Awarded a new annuity by Richard II.
1398 Action of debt against Chaucer.
   Granted a butt of wine yearly by Richard II.
1399 Annuity and gift of wine confirmed by Henry IV and a
   further annuity granted him.
   Leases dwelling in Westminster.
1400 Dies.

CHRONOLOGY OF CHAUCER'S MORE IMPORTANT WORKS

Note: Only the works marked with an asterisk can be
dated with any approach to certainty. The chronology of the
lesser works is considered in Chapter III.

Before 1370   *Romaunt of the Rose*
1369–70   * *Book of the Duchesse*
1374–80   *Hous of Fame*
   Lyf of Seynt Cecyle (Second Nonnes Tale)
1382   * *Parlement of Foules*
1382–85   * *Troilus and Criseyde*
   Translation of Boethius
   Palamon and Arcite (Knightes Tale)

1385–86   *Legend of Good Women* (Prologue, B text)
1387–1400   *Canterbury Tales*
1394–95   Revised version of the Prologue to the *Legend of Good Women*

A CONJECTURAL CHRONOLOGY OF THE CANTERBURY TALES

FIRST PERIOD: BEFORE 1387

Written, in whole or in part, before the scheme of the *Canterbury Tales* was conceived:

Knightes Tales (*Palamon and Arcite*)
Second Nonnes Tale (*Lyf of Seynt Cecyle*)
Monkes Tale

SECOND PERIOD: 1387–88

Written under the impulse of the first inspiration for the *Tales*:

Prologue
Milleres Tale
Reves Tale
Shipmannes Tale (originally written for the Wyf of Bath?)
Prioresses Tale

THIRD PERIOD: 1389–91

Written while the poet was clerk of the king's works and had little leisure for genuinely creative work:

Melibeus (originally written for the Man of Law?)
Tale of the Man of Lawe (originally written for the Merchant?)
Phisiciens Tale
Maunciples Tale
Persones Tale

Written with the return of leisure and with a reawakened interest in the dramatic possibilities of the pilgrimage:

Pardoners Prologue and Tale
Freres Tale
Somnours Tale
Prologue and Tale of the Wyf of Bathe
Clerkes Tale
Marchantes Tale
Squieres Tale
Frankeleyns Tale

Written with unusual independence of borrowed material, and animated, in some measure, by purposes remote from the intentions of the poet at the time when he projected the series:

The Rime of Sir Thopas
Nonne Preestes Tale
Cokes Tale
Chanouns Yemannes Tale

To the last two periods belongs the composition of the Links and Prologues, with the exception of those in Group A.

Actual evidence for the dating of any of the *Canterbury Tales* is of the slightest. It should be understood, therefore, that the chronology proposed above rests almost entirely upon conjecture. So far as I am aware, it is not inconsistent with any of the known facts, or with any theory generally accepted by Chaucerian scholars.

INDEX

A. B. C., An, discussed, 82 ff.
method of translation in, 83,
112; metrical form of, 82,
84, 256

Adam, Wordes unto, 102, 121

Against Women Unconstant,
115

Alanus de Insulis, Chaucer's
use of his *De Planctu Na-*
turae, 97, 188

Albertano of Brescia, Chaucer's
use of his *De arte loquendi,*
334; of his *Liber de amore*
Dei, 315; of his *Liber Con-*
solationis, 246, 315

Alchemist, The, 332

Alchemy, Chaucer's interest in,
328-32

Amorous Compleint, An, 115-
16

Anelida and Arcite, 98-101

Anne of Bohemia, 93, 125, 127,
190

Apocrypha, The, Chaucer's use
of, 255, 256

Arabian Nights, The, 318

Augustine, St., 264

Balade of Compleynt, A, 116

Benoit de Sainte-Maure, his
Roman de Troie, 135-39;
Chaucer's use of, 185-186

Bevis of Hampton, 243

Bible, The, Chaucer's use of,
188, 249-50, 263

Black Death, The, 10 ff.

Black Prince, The, 5, 7

Boccaccio, his *Decameron,* 193,
217-18, 233, 311-12, 316, 322;
summary of his *Filostrato,*
141-78; Chaucer's use of his
Filostrato, 141, 178-83; of his
Filocolo, 183-85, 323; of his
Teseide, 95-97, 98-100, 185,
210-14; of his *De Casibus*
Virorum, 249 ff.; of his *De*
Claris Mulieribus, 129, 250;
of his *De Genealogia De-*
orum, 131

Boethius, his life and works,
118-20; Chaucer's translation
of his *De Consolatione Phil-*
osophiae, 102, 117-22; his influence upon Chaucer, 102,
103, 107, 109, 122, 186-87, 214,
256, 315

Book of the Duchesse, The, 54,
221; discussed, 86 ff.; date
of, 86; sources of, 87-89;
metrical form of, 90, 363

Bradshaw, Henry, 78, 100, 103,
133

Bradwardine, Bishop, 264

Bretigny, Peace of, 7, 49

Brown, Carleton, 234 ff., 325

Brusendorff, A., 80, 107

Bukton, Peter de, 111

Bukton, Robert, 111

Camden, William, his *Remains*

395